Pets
and the
Family

The *Marriage & Family Review* series:

Pets
and the
Family

Marvin B. Sussman, Editor

The Haworth Press
New York

Pets and the Family has also been published as *Marriage & Family Review*, Volume 8, Numbers 3/4, Summer 1985.

The Haworth Press, Inc., 28 East 22 Street, New York, NY 10010

Library of Congress Cataloging in Publication Data
Main entry under title:

Pets and the family.

"Has also been published as Marriage & family review, volume 8, numbers 3/4, summer 1985"—T.p. verso.
Includes bibliographies.
1. Pet owners—Psychology—Addresses, essays, lectures. 2. Pets—Psychological aspects—Addresses, essays, lectures. 3. Pets—Social aspects—Addresses, essays, lectures. 4. Pets—Therapeutic use—Addresses, essays, lectures. 5. Family—Addresses, essays, lectures. I. Sussman, Marvin B.
SF411.47.P485   1985   306.8'5   85-8410
ISBN 0-86656-358-X
ISBN 0-86656-360-1 (pbk.)

Pets and the Family

Marriage & Family Review
Volume 8, Numbers 3/4

CONTENTS

Pet/Human Bonding:
Applications, Conceptual
and Research Issues

Marvin B. Sussman

In April, 1984, *Psychology Today* conducted a national survey probing for the relationship between humans and pets. Approximately 13,000 persons responded to the survey. The major results substantiate the findings of a large number of investigators working in the empirical vineyard, some who are represented in this volume. It is reported that pet, more than non-pet, owners have humanistic orientations expressed in compassion for others; are more satisfied and happy with their lives. Pets are well integrated into the majority of families in the United States. Eighty percent of pet owners report that they receive more companionship from their animals than from friends and neighbors, and view pets equal to family members and relatives in importance. Respondents, almost 100%, indicate that pets are important in the development and socialization of children and families should make effort to have a pet while a child is growing up (Ryan, 1984).

This landmark survey indicates the pervasiveness of the animal/human bond and the extremely high prevalence of pets in U.S. households. Survey respondents express positive feelings about pets and their roles in families. The data from this survey, important, positive and supportive of the animal/human connection, provide a base for probing the meaning and significance of pets for family members and families and what the human bond means to companion and domestic animals.

The papers in this volume do such probing. There are a few empirical reports with the majority being analytic papers covering ideological, theoretical, research and methodological issues. These "state of the art" reports indicate that the issues and problems of the animal/human bond are complex and deep. The work in this area has received sufficient media attention to attract competent researchers and funds to work on significant conceptual issues and empirical problems. To encourage the development of sound theoretical postures and research which will deepen our knowledge of the animal/ human bond and the applications of this information, the following recommendations are made.

1. Clinical studies and researches conducted without controls report that there is a reduction in mortality and morbidity as a consequence of a pet being a companion to an individual. Two types of studies are indicated to establish the viability of this conclusion. The first is a long scale longitudinal health study. Because such studies are so costly, a protocol containing questions on pet ownership can be piggybacked on one or more longitudinal studies in progress or in genesis. The second type of study to determine mortality and morbidity over a short time period requires a research design with a non-pet control group and further control of such variables as type of pet, previous experience with pets, marital and family status, health status, and social support networks.

2. The perception that pets affect the well-being of humans positively requires study regarding its universality, depth of affectiveness, and persistence. To explain any variability and to improve the predictability of outcomes when pets are introduced in therapy or home situations, specifying animal and human attributes is required. Initial studies would control for characteristics of an animal species and breeds, e.g., dogs: dalmation, poodle, bulldog, fox terrier, and examine the fit of the species with particular personality characteristics of the pet owner. Subsequent studies can examine the "fit" of the species and breeds with demographic, sociologic, and life cycle characteristics of family members and families. The probe is whether personality types, particular demographic, life cycle or sociologic variables affect the well-being of the individual or the characteristics of the animal species and breeds.

3. Observing or attending to pets is reported to have relaxing effects on those involved. Studies are required to specify what are these effects; the species and characteristics which optimize the relaxation of the attender and the optimal match of the type of pet with the personality characteristics, health, economic, and social status and life conditions.

4. One enduring problem in intervention studies is to determine

the power of the (s) variable. The stimulus variable in animal/ human bonding studies is the presence or introduction of a pet to an individual or family. The question is whether outcomes such as improved self worth, interpersonal competence, life satisfaction, happiness, or marital health are a consequence of pet/human interaction or interaction between family members. The pet may be a facilitator or a cause of such interaction. The issue of cause may be unimportant if the desired consequence is obtained, e.g., improved family functioning. On the other hand similar effects may be obtained using other stimuli and may be a more desirable option. Controlled family studies using observational techniques, self-reports, interviewing and testing procedures can determine the complementary effects of pet/human and human/human interaction on selected outcomes.

5. The death of pet has been described as having stressful consequences similar to those who have experienced the loss of family member, relative, or a close friend. Comparison human and animal death studies with systematic mapping of the grieving process is suggested. Measures of stress using standardized instruments should be made. Attention should be given to such variables as family structure, stage of life cycle, age, cause of death, intensity of the relationship and availability and use of social supports.

6. Pets are increasingly used in therapeutic situations involving persons with physical or mental deficits or with special problems. Their introduction into such settings has been viewed as having some desirable impact. The pet is used as a conjunctive therapist, a facilitator of the therapeutic process. In some total care institutions pets are allowed and it is reported that incarcerated patients or prisoners are more relaxed, easily handled, and satisfied. The assignment of such animals or pet visitation programs are done by chance. There is a need for investigative and controlled studies on the appropriate match of domestic and companion animals, species and breed and other life forms, e.g., fish, with particular settings, age, sex and the physical and mental status of individuals.

7. Theoretical studies on why pets have more beneficial than negative effects on humans are recommended. In doing such scholarly work consider the pet in the role of playmate, trustworthy companion, friend, and the developmental period of the indi-

vidual; changes in the individual's perception of the situation and self; satisfying and profitable exchanges between pet and human; and the conditions of dependency and responsibility.

8. Given the high incidence and prevalence of pet ownership; the significance of pets in the lives of individuals, family members, and families; and employment of pets in various custodial and therapeutic settings, there is a need for diagnostic and treatment models and new service options. Human service personnel during intake interviews should have as an integral component of their diagnostic checklist a history of current and past pet ownership. The Human Service System should provide counselling and group therapy options for the individual whose pet is ill, disabled, or has died. Procedures for caring for the pet of a disabled or terminally hospitalized patient should be in place and evoked when required. Foster care and adoption, procedures used with dependent children may be useful in managing the care of dependent pets.

9. Reports suggest that cases of family violence, and child and elder abuse are increasing in incidence. Prevalence of abuse has always been high. Today there are fewer taboos and fewer cultural constraints about reporting such cases. One basic issue is whether a domestic or companion pet exacerbates or reduces violence and abuse in the family. Since pets serve as developmental resources, being dependent friends and thus encouraging human responsibility, demonstration projects with abusing and dysfunctional families need to be designed. Pets can be introduced to encourage loving and caring responses. Controlled demonstrations with appropriate evaluation can establish the efficacy of this intervention.

REFERENCE

Ellen Ryan, letter, July 12, 1984.

Pets as Family Members

Ann Ottney Cain

The study of pets in the family is intriguing! One does not have to observe or to talk to family members for long before it is clear that pets have a very special role in the family.

The author, a family therapist whose practice is based on the theoretical orientation of Dr. Murray Bowen, has conducted two research studies, one in 1977 (Cain, 1983) and one in 1982, to explore the pet's position in the family system. Dr. Bowen, in his work with families, has conceptualized the family as a system; i.e., family members are all interrelated and comprise, by their relationships as well as by their individual existences, a system or a longer whole. In 1965, he wrote that the family emotional system "at times . . . may include members of the extended family network and even nonrelatives and pets" (Bowen, 1978, p. 123). It is important that family therapists have knowledge of the significant role of pets as family members in order to conceptualize the family as a whole.

Pet ownership is widespread in the United States; approximately 60% of American families share their homes with one or more companion animals. There is no single explanation for the wide extent of pet ownership in families, but companionship ranks very high. This is especially true in childhood, with the elderly, and when family members are vulnerable to loneliness following an extensive life change such as the death of a family member, divorce, or departure of children from the home during the "empty nest" phase of the life cycle. Pets serve other positive purposes in the family such as a means for pleasure, fun, and exercise, as a source of physical security and protection, as a means of teaching children responsibility and a respect for life, and as a catalyst for establishing human contact and interaction. Pets can provide a "dress rehearsal" for children and help them prepare for later life experiences that relate to sexual

Ann Ottney Cain is Professor, Graduate Program in Psychiatric Nursing, University of Maryland at Baltimore.

5

behavior, giving and receiving of love, parenting, birth, and death. Pets can also satisfy the need for physical contact without the fear of involvement with other human beings. When people find the give and take of normal human interaction more than they want to handle, having an emotional investment with a pet may offer them a positive experience.

It is only recently that researchers have recognized the importance of pets to families and to physical and emotional health. This relatively new field of study of the relationships between people and pets is known as the Human/Companion Animal Bond. Research has exploded in this area in the past few years, but there is much yet to be learned and explored.

The research study reported here was entitled, "A Study of the Human/Companion Animal Bond in Military Communities in the United States." This was a collaborative study conducted with Dr. Thomas Catanzaro of the U.S. Army Veterinary Corps. It was a national survey of military families with pets. The study had several purposes: (1) to survey a cross section of American families, (2) to survey mobile military families, (3) to survey the pet's role in the quality of life of service families, and (4) to survey the pet's role in Community Health.

A 32 item questionnaire based on the concepts of The Bowen Theory was used. Eight hundred ninety-six surveys were tabulated and this represented a 64% return rate. This high rate of return, in itself, reflected that families considered their pets to be very important—a useful rate of return on a questionnaire is approximately 35–40%. Thirty-eight percent of the 896 families were families of officers, 3% were families of warrant officers, and 59% were families of enlisted men.

Some of the more interesting findings were:

—93% had pets while growing up.
—99% thought that children should have pets.
—68% said that their pet was a full family member and 30% said that their pet was a close friend, i.e., 98% of the sample of 896 families considered the pet a family member or a close friend.
—72% said their pet usually to always had "people status" in the family, with 39% saying always.
—50% said their pets were extremely important to the family and 46% said that they were very important to important to the family. This accounted for 96% of the sample of 896 families.

When asked if there were changes in family interaction after they got their pet:

—70% said there was an increase in family happiness and fun after getting a pet,
—60% said there was an increased expression of affection around the pet, and
—52% said that there was increased family together time.

When asked what special characteristics their pet displayed within the family:

—77% believed that the pet understood when they talked or confided in them (one respondent described her pet as a "live-in-psychiatrist"),
—73% said that their pet communicated back to them,
—59% said that their pet understood them and was sensitive to their moods,
—50% said the pet stayed close when family members were anxious or upset,
—23% said the pet mimicked their emotions,
—11% said the pet expressed feelings that they could not or did not express, and
—4% said their pet developed an illness when family tension was high.

When asked to rate the importance of their pet at various times in their lives:

—75% said that their pet was of *great importance* to the family at all times,
—73% said at times of a temporary absence of a spouse,
—71% said during their free time and times of relaxation,
—70% said during the childhood period,
—68% said pets were of *great importance* when they were sad, lonely, or depressed,
—59% said at times when their marriage was without children,
—53% said at times when there was a temporary absence of children in the home,
—52% said during illness or death of family members,
—50% said during crises, separation, or divorce,

—48% said at times of moves and relocations (moving is a part of military life and the pet can serve as a support system and provide stability during the move),

—45% said pets were of *great importance* during the teenage period, and

—36% said during periods of unemployment.

When asked if they celebrated their pet's birthday, 34% said that they usually celebrated it, 32% said they sometimes celebrated it, and 34% said they never celebrated it.

Fifty-three percent of the 896 families reported that they had pictures of their pets displayed at home and 10% had then displayed at their job.

When asked who got the most strokes or recognition (physical touch, look, word, smile, gesture, or other act of acknowledgement) in the family, 37% said their spouse, 33% said the children, and 30% said the pet.

Dr. Murray Bowen considers the triangle to be the basic building block of any emotional system. A triangle is formed when the tension within a two person emotional system exceeds a certain level. Triangles are patterned ways of dealing with intense feeling states. These triangles can consist of three people or two people and an issue (or pet) within the family system. Increased closeness between any two family members results in increased distance from the third member of the triangle. Pets, like humans, can be triangled into a family system to relieve an uncomfortable situation. In terms of pets, triangles usually provide a display of affection, anger, or distancing. Triangling was described in the questionnaire as a process in which two persons transfer the tension or intense feeling between them onto a third person (or issue or pet). Respondents were asked to give an example of triangling that they thought involved the pets in their family.

When asked if the pet got brought in (triangled in) when there was tension between two family members, 44% said sometimes to always, with 8% saying always. Examples that were given included:

1. Situations in which the pet was described as acting as a peacemaker by trying to get the couple's attention away from their fighting.
2. Situations in which the dog was described as a diversion from a

crisis and thus served as a tension release. Pets provided comfort.

3. Situations in which a family member yelled or expressed anger or tension at the pet instead of another family member. Some described hitting the pet instead of the person they were really angry with.
4. Situations in which the pet would do something "cute" and people would forget they were angry.
5. Situations in which the pet was described as coming up during periods of tension and seeking petting and loving—this acted as a release from frustration and helped cool down the argument.
6. Situations in which the pet was described as sensing that things were not going well. They would do something silly and make family members laugh. This helped family members to develop a sense of balance again, and paying attention to the pet allowed them to get control of their feelings.

Several respondents reported examples of *not* triangling the pet in—they purposely put their pet in the backyard during their conflict because the pet always got upset and tried to interfere.

No respondent in this study described a situation in which they talked to their pet instead of other family members directly so that these other family members could hear. This had been reported as an example of triangling in the 1977 study (Cain, 1983).

When asked to describe the degree of loss felt by the family when they had a pet who died, was killed, or lost, 94% said that they experienced an important to extreme loss when they lost their pet. It has been recorded in the literature that family members describe the loss of a pet as a time of sadness, grieving, crying, mourning, and real depression (Nieburg and Fischer, 1982).

This study sample was a cross-section of people (896 family members) who shared their thoughts and ideas about *their* pets in *their* families. The majority (68%) indicated that pets were considered full family members, 30% said they were close friends, and 96% described their role in the family as very important. It is clear that pets contribute to the quality of family life in very positive ways. They seem to satisfy basic human needs for love and companionship.

The reasons for the strong emotional attachment between people and pets have been stated distinctly. According to various researchers, pets provide seven critical functions for family members: something to care for; something to keep us busy; something to touch; something to watch; something that makes us feel safe; something that provides a stimulus to exercise; and something that guarantees us companionship (Katcher and Beck, 1983).

This study was conducted to further knowledge about families and how they function. It will help family therapists to realize how important pets are to the family structure. Family therapists need to learn as much as possible about the family and how family members interact with each other. Pets can provide very important information about how the family system is organized or disorganized. Pets are an important part of the family system. Therefore, family therapists need to carefully consider pets in family treatment, and they need to be aware that the pet *is* a significant family member.

REFERENCES

Beck, A., and Katcher, A. *Between pets and people.* New York: G. T. Putnam's Sons, 1983.

Bowen, M. *Family therapy in clinical practice.* New York: Jason Aronson, Inc., 1978.

Cain, A. A study of pets in the family system. In A. Katcher and A. Beck, *New perspectives on our lives with companion animals.* Philadelphia: University of Pennsylvania Press, 1983.

Fogle, B. (Ed.). *Interrelations between people and pets.* Springfield, Illinois: Charles C. Thomas, Publisher, 1981.

Lynch, J. *The broken heart: The medical consequences of loneliness.* New York: Basic Books, Inc., 1977.

Nieburg, H., and Fischer, A. *Pet loss.* New York: Harper and Row, Publishers, 1982.

White, B. *Betty White's pet-love: How pets take care of us.* New York: William Morrow and Company, 1983.

The Social Meanings of Pets: Alternative Roles for Companion Animals

Jean E. Veevers

ABSTRACT. When companion animal interact closely with people, the roles they play may be categorized in terms of three major functions. The *projective function* involves the extent to which pets may serve as a symbolic extension of the self. The *sociability function* involves the role of pets in facilitating human-to-human interaction. The *surrogate function* involves the extent to which interaction with pets may supplement human-to-human interaction, or serve as a substitute for it.

A person publicly identified with a companion animal makes a symbolic statement of their personality and self-image. Whether or not this process is intentional, the presence of a pet and the way it is treated become factors which are taken into account in the assessment of the social self.

Pets facilitate interaction by being social lubricants. They provide a neutral subject of conversation, and perform a variety of functions as social catalysts.

Since interaction with companion animals can approximate human companionship, the presence of pets may serve to supplement the benefits usually derived from the roles of friend, parent, spouse, or child. Alternatively, pets may serve as surrogate antagonists. In the extreme, interaction with companion animals may not only supplement human companionship, but may actually replace it.

These three major functions are discussed with examples. Implications are noted for future research on companion animals.

INTRODUCTION

Since the early 1970's, there has been a growing appreciation of the social roles played by pets, and of the social and emotional benefits which may be derived from keeping companion animals. Awareness of these phenomena was initially sparked by Levinson's

Jean E. Veevers, is Professor, Department of Sociology, University of Victoria, Victoria, British Columbia, Canada.

seminal work on *Pet Oriented Child Psychotherapy* (1969), but quickly grew to include the possibility of beneficial effects for persons with special problems, such as those mentally or physically handicapped, emotionally disturbed, or severely neurotic or schizophrenic.

From there, it was a small step to conclude that if pets are beneficial for "special" populations, they may be beneficial for normal ones as well. Pets were perceived to contribute to human development in a number of ways, with special benefits accruing to children (Levinson, 1972). Attention was then directed to the potential role of pets as therapeutic agents for the elderly (Gee and Veevers, 1984b). If dependent populations benefit from animal companions, might not healthy adults do so as well? In recent years, attention has finally been given to the roles which companion animals may play for ordinary persons in ordinary families. The present paper is devoted to the social roles which companion animals may play in contemporary society.

Recent usage has tended to substitute the phrase "companion animal" for the term pet. However animals in the pet role are designated, they are characterized by several inter-related traits. They are kept for their intrinsic appeal, rather than their usefulness; they live in intimate association with their owners; and they are regarded as subordinates and treated as possessions (Veevers, 1984a). Although no one knows exactly the prevalence of pets in North America, a conservative estimate would be that about two-thirds of all households include a dog, and about one-third include a cat. Pet owners therefore represent a clear majority of persons, and their prevalence appears to be increasing (Gee and Veevers, 1984a). Given the many obvious and serious deleterious effects known to be associated with the presence of pets in urban areas, the advantages believed to be derived from them must be considerable. Social scientists are only beginning to consider the significance of pets to modern man, and their consequences in contemporary households.

When companion animals live in close association with their owners, interaction with them can have at least three separate functions for their owners. The *projective function* concerns the extent to which the selection of a pet is interpreted as making a statement about the owner. The *sociability function* concerns the extent to which having a pet acts as a social lubricant, and effects the quantity and quality of interaction with other humans. Finally, the *surrogate function* concerns the extent to which pet-human interaction may serve as a supplement to human-human interaction or even, in some extreme cases, as an alternative to it. These three functions will be described and discussed with examples from the burgeoning literature on the human-animal bond.

PETS AS STATEMENTS: THE PROJECTIVE FUNCTION

A person publicly identified with a companion animal makes a symbolic statement of their personality and self-image. Whether or not this process is intentional, the presence of a pet and the way it is treated become factors which are taken into account in the assessment of the social self.

The kind of pet a person selects, like the kind of car one drives, or the style of clothes one wears, is a way of expressing one's personality. The person who says: "Love me, love my dog." is making a statement of his right to individual preference. Casual observers of the social scene have often noted the projection of self onto pets as an expression of one's character and habits. Selecting a macho dog may be an attempt to project a macho image, whereas selecting a Persian kitten may be an attempt to project cute and defenseless feminine dependency. One study of dog owners, based on a small and unrepresentative sample, found that a Great Dane served as a symbol of "masculinity, power, strength, dominance, and virility," whereas a Chihuahua served as a symbol of femininity (Hartley and Shames, 1959, cited by Levinson, 1968:506). Many examples can be found of pets which seem to reflect the personality of their owners. The hypochondriac may extend his concern with health to his pet's health. Hostile dogs may be selected as a means of acting out one's own aggression and hostility (Rosenbaum, 1972:33).

Pets and Personality: Are Pet Owners Different?

The folk-wisdom suggestion that persons with pets are different from persons without them has received some tentative support from available research, but no conclusive evidence is yet available.

In any early study, Cameron et al. (1966) suggested that pet owners liked people less than non-owners. In later work (Cameron and Mattson, 1972), he suggested that pet-owners tended to claim less felt regard from others, tended to like pets more than people, and were generally less psychologically healthy than non-owners.

There are demonstrated relationships between personality characteristics and preferences in pet ownership. Kidd and Kidd (1980) found personality differences in dominance, nurturance and autonomy between cat lovers and dog lovers. In a later study, Kidd, Kelley and Kidd (1983) found personality differences among horse, turtle, snake and bird owners. The common-sense expectation that snake owners would be unconventional and novelty-seeking was in fact supported. Research by Allen (1982) also suggests the possibility of systematic differences in attitude patterns between dog owners and non-owners. These data provide tentative support for the speculations by Ball (1971) on cats, dogs, and people. Recent work begins to suggest a systematic relationship between personality and pet ownership, both in actuality and in hypothetical preference, but results are still inconclusive (Edelson and Lester, 1983).

Are Pet Owners Nicer?

The folk-wisdom further suggests that pet owners are not only different from non-owners, but are somehow nicer than them. Success in human-animal relationships is often viewed as predictive of success in human relationships as well. An early test of this hypothesis found that low expressed affection for dogs accompanies low affection for people and, in the case of men, low *desire* for such affection (Brown, Shaw and Kirkland, 1972). Guttman (1981:97) found non-owners to have a stronger tendency to be independent, to avoid permanent ties, and to be less disturbed by loneliness and by being alone. Another study found that college-age pet-owners tended to have higher empathy and interpersonal trust scores than non-owners (Hyde, Kurdek and Larson, 1983). Although there is some suggestion that pet owners are more socially oriented than non-owners, recent work (Ray, 1982) has failed to show a relationship between love of people and love of animals, suggesting that data on this topic also are still inconclusive.

Pets as Status Symbols

Whether or not pet possession says something about personality, it can say something about status. Pets are expensive. The demography of pet ownership shows that pets, especially large pets, are associated with large incomes and large homes (Gee and Veevers, 1984a). Kings and emperors collected elephants and lions as tribute: celebrities today keep ocelots of cheetahs. In 1974, 10,000 Americans owned big cats (Time, 1974:43). Some "preposterous" pets make a very definite status point, being something that only someone very powerful and independent could own (Muller, 1980). *Newsweek*, commenting on pet-set chic, observes that: "As status-conscious auto buffs snatch up Lamborghinis, the parvenus of pet-dom are drawn to the bizarre and the exotic for prestige. It's not who you are, it seems, but what you walk (*Newsweek*, 1974:74).

When a pet is viewed as a symbolic extension of the owner, then the pet not only lives with the owner, but at the same standard of living. Indulging one's pet becomes a way of indulging and of "being good" to oneself, and Americans spend billions every year doing just that. Pets can be humanized to the point where virtually all of the services which are available to people are available to animals— for a price. For examples, poodles routinely get their hair done at beauty parlors: shampoo, cut, blow-dry, manicure, the works. When they go, they can go by special limousine, wearing custom-made sweaters (*Time*, 1974:44). Other dogs not only go to school, but also to day care, to summer camp, or even to special restaurants (*Newsweek, 1974*). A plethora of examples of such excesses are documented by Szasz (1969), who argues that *Petishism* can be a form of fetishism in our society.

In an informal study, Harris (1983) found that, of 224 pet owners, only 0.4% said they choose a pet for its status function. Although pet owners may not be conscious of a status function, or may be un-willing to admit such motives, it is clear that having a pet, particu-larly an expensive, exotic, or difficult pet, proclaims the owner as a person of privlege. A companion animal, other than a guard dog, a seeing eye dog, or a hearing-ear dog, is an indulgence. Time spent with companion animals is one option for the use of leisure time; re-sources spent on them are one alternative for disposable income. An expensive and attractive animal is a personal accessory as surely as an expensive car or a cashmere sweater. Observing that it is as easy to love a Heinz 57 variety mutt as it is a championship Shih Tzu is like observing that one can tell time with either a *Timex* or a *Gruen*.

PETS AS SOCIAL LUBRICANTS: THE SOCIABILITY FUNCTION

Interaction with pets can serve to change the nature of interaction with other people. One function of pets is as a social lubricant, in-creasing the quantity and quality of social interactions. Several pro-cesses may contribute to an increase in sociability.

Pets Attract Attention

Before any kind of social interaction can take place, one person has to gain the attention of another. Being with a pet increases one's social visibility. Obviously, some animals perform this function better than others. Any large animal attracts attention, but even a small one may be a focus of interest if it is unusual, like a monkey, or threatening, like a snake. One function of animals is to increase the social visibility of their owners.

Pets and Interpersonal Appeal

Whatever the reality, a person with a pet is believed to be somehow "nicer" than someone who rejects animals. In our culture, love of children and love of animals are generally thought to be associated with a wide range of positive attributes. In a projective test, Lockwood (cited by Messant, 1982:106) found that subjects describing a scene which included animals found it less threatening than one without animals, and had a more positive perception of the character of people associated with animals than those without them. When W. C. Fields quipped: "Anyone who hates children and dogs cannot be all bad," he evoked a nervous laugh for his inversion of the popular wisdom. The politician who includes a cocker spaniel in the family portrait is still making a politically astute gesture.

Pets and Conversation

Sociability involves a considerable amount of small talk, which is an end in itself rather than a means of conveying information. "Shared sentiment makes pets a safe subject about which to talk in almost any social situation, however tense or awkward" (Feldmann, 1978:308). An animal, like an unusual *object d'art*, may be a focus of interest and a subject of casual conversation. Indeed, next to the weather, a pet may be almost the most neutral subject of conversation.

Pets as Ice-Breakers

The presence of a pet attracts attention to a person, predisposes the observer to respond positively to him or her, and then provides an occasion for a safe and neutral comment. The presence of a pet therefore serves as an ideal catalyst for initial contacts. This is especially true when some action by the pet provides an apparently unwilled provocation, for which the owner may or may not decide to take responsibility. In this regard, Goffman observes:

> A woman who carries on or with her a camera, a dog, a book, or almost any object, is providing reasons strangers can use as a basis of initiating a comment to her, and is thus in effect exposing herself. (Goffman, 1977:331)

Men as well as women are perceived as more approachable when they are accompanied by a pet. Messent (1982:106) reports that people walking with dogs are much more likely to be attended to than those without dogs. Owners are looked at more frequently, are greeted more frequently, and are engaged in more and longer conversations with strangers. In a Swedish study, reported motives for owning dogs included the opportunity to meet people (Messent, 1982:106). In this context, a dog on a leash may serve much the same sociability function as a pretty baby in a carriage, inviting attention, comment, and admiration.

Pets as Entertainers

Pets not only provide people with something to talk about, but also something to look and play with. One role of the pet is to entertain. Some pets may entertain just by looking cute. Others spontaneously cavort around, act silly, or are taught to do tricks and show off skills. Active pets perform an at-home circus, like a live television show, which is a source of interest and distraction. One theory suggests that part of the therapeutic value of pets is their ability to distract attention away from threatening stimuli, thereby allowing persons to deal with their anxieties more effectively (Brickel, 1982).

Pet Aficionados

Persons with special interests in specific kinds of animals are recognized social types who are "buffs" of one kind or another. "Dogdom" refers to those persons, collectively, who are interested in dogs (Stein and Urdang, 1971:422), and that interest provides many social contacts. The showing of dogs and cats accounts for a considerable amount of the social interaction of enthusiasts. In this capacity, dogs serve much like stamps for philatelists or art for connoisseurs. For some persons, such as breeders or trainers, business contacts become merged with friendship networks, and interaction with other animal lovers becomes their main source of social contacts.

Pets and Self-Disclosure

When psychologists want to know how a person feels, they often decrease the sense of threat by asking them to describe other people, thereby inadvertently revealing their own beliefs and attitudes by projecting them onto others. Describing companion animals is even less threatening, and may be equally revealing. When it is impolite or inappropriate to ask direct personal questions, inquiry may still be made regarding pets. This ploy, familiar to all skilled conversationalists and interviewers, may also have therapeutic implications. Thus, Schowalter (1983:72) conclude that: "The inquiry of patients about their experiences with animals is often a very fruitful approach for understanding their wishes, fears, and displaced feelings." Jurgreis (1965:246) recommends that:

> Therapists should not hesitate to discuss the family's relationships to their pets. Anecdotes of deep significance are often revealed. Families are also less guarded and defensive when talking about their animals, probably because humans are more tolerant of instinctual drives in animals than in humans. Drawing attention to the behavior of family pets is highly productive of useful therapeutic material. (Jurgreis, 1965:246)

Pets as Barriers

If pets usually serve to facilitate social interaction, in some circumstances they can also be used to inhibit it. Some pets are deliberately chosen for their effectiveness in keeping others away. Rosenbaum (1972:40) describes a man who owned snakes commenting with satisfaction that relatives no longer came around. Pets can be used as excuse to avoid dealing with other problems. For example, an elderly person may surround herself with dozens of cats or dogs, thereby becoming "too busy" to attend to other matters. An excessive number of animals, which usually means an unhygienic and unappealing household, may also serve to disassociate the owner from unwanted and intrusive friends or family members.

PETS AS PEOPLE: THE SURROGATE FUNCTION

When interaction with animals too closely approximates interaction with humans, we say the animals have been *anthropomorphized*, that is, have been granted human attributes. If that interaction takes the place of human interaction, we consider the animals to have become substitutes for humans, and designate them as *surrogates*.

What Makes a Surrogate?

To some extent, almost all interaction with companion animals involves some anthropomorphism, and can in some way be construed as a surrogate for human relationships. The differences among relationships are in the degree to which animals are treated as humans, and are used to replace them. A wide range of possibilities are observed in everyday life, but as yet there is no convenient scale for assessing the degree of anthropomorphism in a particular circumstance.

As early as 1956, Foote suggested, not entirely facetiously, that the dog was a "neglected member of the family." In assessing the degree to which pets are anthropomorphized, several factors might be taken into account.

Cannibalism

With the exception of a vocal minority who are vegetarians, most people in North America have no qualms with the concept of animals for food. However, the raising of animals for market, and their subsequent slaughter, is acceptable only if the animals are not viewed, in some important ways, as being like humans. To eat fish, poultry, swine, sheep, or cattle is acceptable. However, eating an animal in the social role of pet is defined as repulsive. Horsemeat, which is acceptable in Europe, does not find a market here. We view with extreme aversion the prospect of eating dogs, although dogmeat is a delicacy in Hong Kong and other parts of the far east (*Time*, 1974).

Dogs and cats are anthropomorphized to the extent that eating them is almost like anthropophagy. "Pet cannibalism is one of the few moral horrors which is not a crime" (Beck and Knatcher, 1983:55).

Bereavement

Another indicator of the extent to which pets may be viewed as human is manifest in the elaborate ceremonies which may mark their death. Persons grieve for their pets in much the same way as they do for the deaths of other friends (Shirley and Mercier, 1983). While this grief is usually less than for the passing of a human intimate companion, in some instances it can be excessive or even pathological (Keddie, 1977; Kay and Cohen, 1983). One study from Glasgow University reports than 18% of adults were seriously affected in coping with everyday life after their pet's death (Stewart, cited by Messent, 1982:105).

As human-like creatures, dead pets must be treated with respect. They cannot be re-cycled into pet food (Beck and Katcher, 1983:54). Cities have special pet cemeteries. One study reports that three-quarters of bereaved owners had some kind of funeral for their dead pet (Shirley and Mercier, 1983).

Human Names

Some cliché names for dogs, such as Rover, clearly show the animal is only an animal. One indicator of a tendency towards anthropomorphization might be giving the animal a human name. This is by no means a conclusive indicator, however. Harris (1983:1199) found that about a third of dogs and cats had human names, but failed to find any systematic relationship between this and nature of the human/animal relationship.

Talking with Animals

Talking to animals in "doggeral," a kind of baby-talk intended to supplement non-verbal communication, is a form of communicating with oneself: of making observations and comments outloud without expecting a verbal response (Hirsh-Pasek and Treiman, 1982). Talking to animals with the expectation that they do understand abstract thought, and can in effect talk back, is something else. Beck and Katcher (1983:44) report that 30% of their subject group of pet owners confide in their pets. Slovenko (1982) is not entirely face-tious when he suggests that a pet may be a confident, and that a case could be made for the propriety of treating interaction with a pet as "privileged" information, like privileged communication with a lawyer or physician. He cites a number of cases in which pets have played a role in legal decisions. When a pet is the recipient of seri-ous conversation and/or confidences, one must conclude he is being given a human-like role.

Social Ceremonies

When pets are considered to be human-like, there may be cele-brations of milestones in their lives. In a recent study by *Psychology Today* of over 13,000 pet owners, half reported they kept pictures of pets in their wallet or on display in the home; one quarter had had a drawing or portrait done of their pet, and one quarter celebrated the pet's birthday (Horn and Meer, 1984:56). Beck and Katcher (1983:49) report that 30% of their subjects celebrate their animal's birthday in some way.

Surrogate Friends

Whether or not a dog is man's *best* friend, he is certainly one of them. Attitudes towards animals can range from aesthetic to utili-tarian, but one important dimension is the humanistic one, in which pets are regarded with strong affection (Kellert, 1980). The owner may do with the pet many of the activities also done with human friends: talking, eating, grooming, walking, relaxing and sleeping. The role of friend is especially important for persons who for one reason or another do not have many human friends. There are no data to indicate whether or not specific kinds of people have prefer-ences for specific roles for animal companions. However, it seems likely that animals as friends would be most likely sought out by per-sons who do not have dense social networks.

Surrogate Mates

Sometimes the role of pets goes beyond the simple role of friend and beings to approximate more intimate and significant relation-ships. Pets can become as important as a husband or wife, and in some instances act as surrogate mates (Beck and Katcher, 1983:

59–77). When pets are a source of conflict with a mate, the preference for the animal companion over the marital one may become clear. A number of examples can be found in which someone, given a choice between dog or wife, chose the dog. A pet acquired after the death of a spouse may be vested with much of the affect that was formerly invested in the late husband or wife. Pets as surrogate mates may be of special value to the elderly, where the mate has died and no alternative mate is likely to be forthcoming (Gee and Veevers, 1984b).

Animal sexuality may be a vicarious form of human sexuality. Antelyes (1974) observes that pet dogs can function as human sex symbols. The sex life of a pet may serve as a projected sex life for the owner, serving to project his or her unresolved desires (Rosenbaum, 1972:35).

The literature on pets tends to avoid mentioning the possibility of pet animals as a focus of erotic attraction. One exception, Schowalter (1983) notes that although it undoubtedly takes place, scientific documentation is scanty. The prospect of human-animal contacts is real enough for it to be incorporated into religious and legal codes, usually with severe penalties. When bestiality does occur, it apparently involves atypical instances in the lives of a very few people. Kinsey et al. (1953:509) estimate that, in the United States, some kind of erotic animal contact has been experienced at some time by 8% of adult males and 3% of adult women.

If the occurrence of human-animal erotic contacts is rare, fantasy concerning this possibility apparently is not. It is a common theme in mythology, and is frequently staged in "hard-core" pornography. The persistence of such themes suggests that they must have some appeal to other than an idiosyncratic minority.

Surrogate Children

One of the most prominent stereotypes about childless couples is that they use pets as surrogates for the children they cannot have or do not want. There are certainly cases of childless couples who invest in a pet all the emotional value and maternal behavior which might otherwise do to a child (Rosenbaum, 1972:42). However, the limited data on childlessness and pets offer only limited support for this part of the conventional wisdom.

Childless couples are not more likely than other couples to keep pets. The reality is that most couples have both children and pets.

The probability of having a pet is greater, not less, if one has a child as well (Veevers and Gee, 1984a).

One exploratory study found that about two-thirds of childless couples had pets. Of these, about half had casual attitudes towards their companion animals. The remaining half did tend, in varying degrees, to place their pets in a child-like role (Veevers, 1980:34). Some actually refer to a dog or cat as their "baby," and are quite open about their substitution.

If pets are sometimes substitutes for children who are wanted, they can also be part of the process of deciding to remain childless. In some instances, experience with trying to raise a dog or other pet has increased awareness of the tribulations of parenthood, and reinforced a disinclination towards it (Veevers, 1980:36).

If pets act as children for the childless, they may also act as another child for parents. Koller notes in passing that one function of pets may be to prolong the parenthood role for middle-aged and elderly parents.

> The family pet *always* needs attention, and the pleasure it brings its keepers derives partly from the sustained dominance and importance of those who take care of it. The need to be needed is powerful, and parents whose children have grown up are gratified by this sustained dependence of their family pet over the years. (Koller, 1974:288)

The interchangeability of pets and children may also operate in reverse, in that sometimes children are treated as pets. Rollins et al. (1973:520–523) note that in some families, one child may be selected to fill the social role of pet. This child, the antithesis of a scapegoat, may be given special privileges, and seen as doing no wrong. He or she is fussed over, is used as a focus of attention, and is expected to perform an entertainment function, being ingratiating and eager to please.

Surrogate Parents

While laypersons viewing childless couples often consider them to be substituting a Siamese cat for a baby, they are less likely to recognize that the child may view a pet as a surrogate parent. Nana, the dog baby-sitter in *Peter Pan*, performed this role. The large and cuddly dog, with infinite tolerance for the tugging demands of a toddler, may extend to the child more patience and more contact comfort than the mother. Indeed, the parent who seeks out a pet for the child may recognize that while she is taking on the trouble of another "child," the child is also getting the benefit of another "parent."

Conventional wisdom asserts that having a pet is generally good for a child. Whether or not a pet is essential for personality development, it is assumed to be beneficial to it. A pet may act as a proxy with whom a child can practice a variety of interactions which are later incorporated into other social relationship. Caring for a pet may encourage a sense of responsibility, and provide naturalistic examples of problems concerning toilet-training and sexuality (Bossard, 1953).

Large pets may give children a feeling of strength and confidence through identification. They can also be a source of continuity. Not only does the pet always have time to spend with the child, when the parent may not, but the pet is believed to be permanent. It does not go out for the evening, but more importantly, it does not file for divorce. A pet may provide a sense of continuity during the adjustment of separation and divorce: it is one "parent" the child can count on (Schowalter, 1983).

Surrogate Enemies

When pets are considered as surrogates, they are usually pictured as being the recipients of human love, or least of affection. In reality, however, responses to pets can and does run the entire gamut of emotions. Pets can pitch-hit for people in hostile situations as well as in benevolent ones. In this context, it is relevant to note that, in a survey of dog-owners conducted by the American Humane Association, one owner in five reported he did not like his dog (Wilbur, cited by Kidd and Kidd, 1980:941).

The concept of displaced aggression is conventionally illustrated with reference to the frustrated person who rages inwardly and goes home to kick his cat. The Society for the Prevention of Cruelty to Animals has made us aware of the extent to which pent-up anger and frustration can be expressed against pets rather than people. One role of pets is to fill-in as surrogate enemies. Although abuse of pets meets with disapproval, it does not carry the same social stigma and possibility of reprisals as does aggression against people. In addition, pets have the added vulnerability of being readily available when the real source of rage, as for example the IRS, cannot be reached. As Schowalter (1983:70) notes:

> A pet may represent for the child a figure which is lower on the family totem pole, and no matter how put-upon or demeaned one feels, it is still often possible to kick the dog. (Schowalter, 1983:70)

Abuse of a "Scapegoat" Pet

In some families with disturbed children, one child is singled out as the family scapegoat, who is then held responsible for a variety of family ills. The scapegoat child is relatively powerless compared with his parents, his services are not essential, and he can be molded to accept his role (Vogel and Bell, 1968:416). The literature on child-abuse makes frequent reference to the role of the "scapegoat" child, who is punished for the disruption attributed to him. Abuse of the scapegoat child is often associated with unrealistic expectations, and with ineffective teaching and discipline techniques. A comparable pattern may emerge with a "scapegoat" pet. A recent study examined the role of pets in 53 child-abusing families. The pattern of pet ownership was similar to other families. "Of pet-owning child-abusers, 88% of the families in which physical abuse took place also had animals that were abused" (DeViney, Dickert and Lockwood, 1983:327). The parallels between the treatment of pets and the treatment of children in child-abusing families suggest that animal abuse may be a early warning signal of domestic violence. The veterinarian, alerted by persistent "accidental" injuries to pets, may be the first professional to suspect more serious trouble to come.

Hate Me, Hate My Dog

If a person becomes strongly identified with a companion animal, then they have given "hostages to fortune" comparable to a spouse or a child, in that threat or injury to the animal becomes comparable to threat or injury to oneself. A dramatic fictional example of this is given in Mario Puzo's *The Godfather* in which an offer that cannot be refused is accompanied by the severed head of a prize horse. Pets may become direct targets of abuse intended to cause the owner vicarious pain. In more conventional circumstances, the threat to take away a pet may become an important force for social control, or of attempted social control. One study reports that a high proportion of adolescent delinquents were closely attached to pets which were killed by a parent or guardian (Robin, cited by DeViney, Dickert and Lockwood, 1983:328).

Precursors of Violence

The acting out of aggressive impulses towards animals may sometimes provide an effective alternative to comparable violence against humans. There is some evidence, however, that such behavior may also be a precursor of subsequent violence towards other people. To take one graphic example, members of the Charles Manson family reported tortured and killed dogs, and drank the animals' blood (Sanders, 1971). MacDonald (1963) appears to have been the first person to systematically examine the hypothesis that animal cruelty was part of the "threat to kill," a possibility also noted by Mead (1964). Tapia (1971) found that children who were cruel to animals were also aggressive in other ways. Wax and Haddox (1974a, 1974b) found evidence that cruelty to animals, together with enuresis and fire-setting, formed a triad of danger signals predicting later violence in adolescent males. Sendi and Blombren (1975), however, did not find a systematic relationship in their study of homicidal adolescents. Felthous (1980) relates childhood cruelty to animals to other patterns of aggression in male psychiatric patients, and suggests paternal deprivation as a major underlying cause. Aggression towards companion animals may be a substitute for aggression against people, but it may also be a kind of "practice" which later escalates to more serious violence.

CONCLUSIONS AND IMPLICATIONS: THE SOCIAL IMPORT OF PETS

In North America, most households now own a pet, usually a dog and/or a cat, but occasionally a less conventional companion. The trend towards keeping companion animals is increasing, as is the quality of care which is given to them (Gee and Veevers, 1984a). Considering these phenomena, *Time Magazine* (1970) posed as a serious question: "Do cities really need dogs?" Their analysis of "man's worst friend" presents a convincing case of the irrationality of pet ownership. Cats and dogs are expensive to keep, time-consuming to care for, and difficult to manage. Pestilent pets spread disease and infection, pollute the environment, and deflect scarce resources away from human priorities (Veevers, 1984b). They are also here to stay. Given their persistence in the face of serious disincentives, we can only conclude that companion animals must do something which their owners believe to be beneficial. Moreover, those benefits must be believed to be substantial.

What do companion animals do to earn their keep? Basically, they are participant in three kinds of major roles. They provide a medium of expression for the personality and preferences of the owner; they facilitate sociability; and under some circumstances they provide a supplement to human companionship, or an alternative to it.

The traditional observation that more research is needed is especially cogent for the subject of the social meaning of pets. Attention needs to be focused on two interdependent dimensions basic to our understanding of this area: the interaction of humans with pets, and the way such interaction may affect or structure the interaction of humans with other humans. What, if anything, do attitudes about companion animals tell us about other attitudes? Do patterns of preference for pets, and ways of interacting with them, reflect basic personality, as the folk wisdom would suggest? If pets do play a role in the formation and/or stabilization of adult personality, how can pets be prescribed to intervene effectively in this process? If companion animals do prove to be therapeutic, what are the criteria most useful in matching pets with owners with specific problems? Finally, if companion animals are sought as surrogate humans, under what circumstances can pets satisfactorily fulfill these atypical and uncanny roles? How can surrogate animals be selected and managed to maximize the advantage which accure to their owners while minimizing the practical, psychological and social costs?

REFERENCES

Allen, R. D. The relationship between attitudinal patterns and pet-owner type. *Dissertation Abstracts International*, 1983, 44(5–A), 1379.

Antelyes, J. The pet dog: A human sex symbol? *Veterinary Medicine/Small Animal Clinician*, 1974, 69, 201–204.

Ball, D. Cats and dogs and people. *Transaction*, 1971, 8, 44–47.

Beck, A. and Katcher, A. *Between Pets and People: The Importance of Animal Companionship*, 1983, New York: G.P. Putnam's Sons.

Bossard, J. H. Domestic animals: Their role in family life and child development. Pp. 236–252 in J. Bossard (ed.), *Parent and Child: Studies in Family Behavior*. 1953. Philadelphia: University of Pennsylvania Press.

Brickel, C. M. Pet-facilitated psychotherapy: A theoretical explanation via attention shifts. *Psychological Reports*, 1982, 50:71–74.

Brown, L. T., Shaw, T. G., and Kirland, K. D. Affection for people as a function of affection for dogs. *Psychological Reports*, 1972, 31, 957–958.

Cameron, P., Conrad, C., Kirkpatrick, D. D., and Bateen, R. J. Pet ownership and sex as determinants of stated affect toward others and estimates of others' regard of self. *Psychological Reports*, 1966, 19, 884–886.

Cameron, P. M. and Mattson, M. Psychological correlates of pet ownership. *Psychological Reports*, 1972, 30, 286.

DeViney, E., Dickert, J., and Lockwood, R. The care of pets within child abusing families. *International Journal for the Study of Animal Problems*, 1983, 4, 321–329.

Edelson, J. and Lester, D. Personality and pet ownership: A preliminary study. *Psychological Reports*, 1983, 53, 990–991.

Feldman, B. M. Pets and mental health. *Cereal Foods World*, 1978, 23, 306–309.

Felthous, A. R. Aggression against cats, dogs and people. *Child Psychiatry and Human Development*, 1980, 10, 169–177.

Foote, N. N. A neglected member of the family. *Marriage and Family Living*, 1956, 18, 213–218.

Gee, E. M. and Veevers, J. E. Everyman and his dog: The demography of pet ownership. 1984a. Department of Sociology, University of Victoria, mimeographed.

Gee, E. M. and Veevers, J. E. The pet prescription: Assessing the therapeutic value of pets for the elderly. 1984b. Department of Sociology, University of Victoria, mimeographed.

Goffman, I. *Stigma: Notes on the Management of Spoiled Identity*, 1963, Englewood Cliffs, New Jersey: Prentice-Hall.

Guttman, G. The psychological determinants of keeping pets. Pp. 89–98 in B. Fogle (ed.), *Interrelations Between People and Pets*, 1981, Springfield, Illinois: Charles C. Thomas.

Harris, M. B. Some factors influencing selection and naming of pets. *Psychological Reports*, 1983, 53, 1163–1170.

Hirsh-Pasek, K. and Treiman, R. Doggerel: Motherese in a new context. *Journal of Child Language*, 1982, 9, 229–237.

Horn, J. C. and Meer, J. The pleasure of their company: A report on *Psychology Today's* survey on pets and people. *Psychology Today*, 1984, 18, 52–57.

Hyde, K. R., Kurdek, L., and Larson, P. Relationships between pet ownership and self-esteem, social sensitivity, and interpersonal trust. *Psychological Reports*, 1983, 52, 110.

Jurgreis, J. E. The active role of the family therapist. Pp. 187–205 in A. S. Friedman et al. (eds.), *Psychotherapy for the Whole Family*, 1965, New York: Springer Publishing.

Kay, W. T. and Cohen, S. P. Public health significance of grief in the loss of a pet. *Journal of the American Veterinary Medicine Association*, 1983, 183, 351.

Kellert, S. R. American attitudes toward and knowledge of animals: An update. *International Journal for the Study of Animal Problems*, 1980, 1, 87–119.

Keddie, K. M. Pathological mourning after the death of a domestic pet. *British Journal of Psychiatry*, 1977, 131, 21–25.

Kidd, A. H. and Kidd, R. M. Personality characteristics and preferences in pet ownership. *Psychological Reports*, 1980, 46, 939–949.

Kidd, A. H., Kelley, H.T., and Kidd, R. M. Personality characteristics of horse, turtle, snake and bird owners. *Psychological Reports*, 1983, 52, 719–729.

Kinsey, C.A., Pomeroy, W. B., and Martin C. E. *Sexual Behavior in the Human Female*, 1953, New York: Cardinal Pocket Books.

Koller, Marvin R. *Families: A Multigenerational Approach*, 1974, New York: McGraw-Hill.

Levinson, B. M. Interpersonal relationships between pets and human beings. Pp. 504–522 in M. W. Fox (ed.), *Abnormal Behavior in Animals*, 1968, Philadelphia: Saunders.

Levinson, B. M. *Pet-Oriented Child Psychotherapy*, 1969, Springfield, Ill.: Charles C. Thomas.

Levinson, B. M. *Pets and Human Development*, 1972, Springfield, Ill.: Charles C. Thomas.

Mead, M. Cultural factors in the cause of pathological homicide. *Bulletin of the Menninger Clinic*, 1964, 28, 11–22.

MacDonald, J. M. The threat to kill. *American Journal of Psychiatry*, 1963, 120, 125–130.

Messent, P. R. Review of international conference on human/animal companion bond held in Philadelphia, PA on October 5th–7th, 1981. *Royal Society Health Journal*, 1982, 102: 105–107.

Muller, P. Preposterous pets have always been our status symbols. *Smithsonian*, 1980, 83–90.

Newsweek. The pet set: Chic unleashed. *Newsweek*, 1974, September 9:74–78.

Puzo, Mario. *The Godfather.*

Ray, J. H. Love of animals and love of people. *Journal of Social Psychology*, 1982, 116, 299–300.

Rollins, N., Lord, J. P., Walsh, E., and Weil, G. R. Some roles children play in their families: Scapegoat, baby, pet, and peacemaker. *Journal of the American Academy of Child Psychiatry*, 1973, 12, 511–530.

Rosenbaum, J. I've got the meanst dog on the block. Pp. 27–49 in *Is Your Volkswagen a Sex Symbol?*, 1972, New York: Bantam.

Sanders, E. *The Family*. 1971. New York: Avon Books.

Schowalter, J. E. Clinical experience: The use and abuse of pets. *Journal of the American Academy of Child Psychiatry*, 1983, 22, 68–72.

Selby, L. A., Rhoades, J. D., Irvin, J. A., Carey, G. E., and Wade, R. G. Values and limitations of pet ownership. *Journal of the American Veterinary Medical Association*, 1980, 11, 1274–1276.

Sendi, I. B. and Blombren, P. G. A comparative study of predictive criteria in the predisposition of homicidal adolescents. *American Journal of Psychiatry*, 1975, 132, 423–427.

Serpell, J. A. Childhood pets and their influence on adults' attitudes. *Psychological Reports*, 1981, 49, 651–654.

Shirley, V. and Mercier, J. Bereavement of older persons: Death of a pet. *The Gerontologist*, 1983, 23, 276.

Slovenko, R. Commentaries on psychiatry and law—Shielding communications with a pet. *Journal of Psychiatry and Law*, 1982, 10, 405–413.

Speck, R. V. The transfer of illness phenomenon in schizophrenic families. Pp. 293–304 in A. S. Friedman et al. (eds.), *Psychotherapy for the Whole Family*. New York: Springer.

Speck, R. V. Mental health problems involving the family, the pet and the veterinarian. *Journal of the American Veterinary Medicine Association*, 1964, 145, 150–154.

Stein, J. and Urdang, L. *The Random House Dictionary of the English Language*, 1971. New York: Random House.

Szasz, K. *Petishism: Pets and Their People in the Western World*. New York: Holt, Rinehart and Winston, 1969.

Time. Do cities really need dogs? *Time Magazine*, 1970, 96 (July 20), 35.

Time. The great American animal farm. *Time Magazine*, 1974, 104 (December 23), 42–46.

Vogel, E. F. and Bell, N. W. The emotionally disturbed child as the family scapegoat. Pp. 412–427 in N. W. Bell and E. F. Vogel (eds.), *A Modern Introduction to the Family*. 1968, New York: The Free Press.

Wax, D. E. and Haddox, V. G. Enuresis, fire-setting and animal cruelty: A useful danger signal in predicting vulnerability of adolescent males to assaultive behavior. *Child Psychiatry and Human Development*, 1974a, 14, 151–156.

Max, D. E. and Haddox, V. G. Enuresis, firesetting and animal cruelty in male adolescent delinquents: A triad predictive of violent behavior. *Journal of Psychiatry and the Law*, 1974b, 2, 45–71.

Veblin, T. *The Theory of the Leisure Class*, 1899, reprinted with introduction by J. K. Galbraith, 1973, Boston: Houghton Mifflin.

Veevers, J. E. *Childless by Choice*, 1980. Toronto: Butterworths.

Veevers, J. E. What is a pet? Defining the concept of companion animal. 1984a. Department of Sociology, University of Victoria, mimeographed.

Veevers, J. E. Pestilent pets: Medical, social, environmental and political costs and problems of companion animals. 1984b. Forthcoming. Vogel, E. F. and Bell, N. W. The emotionally disturbed child as the family scapegoat. Pp. 412–427 in N. Bell and E. Vogel (eds.), *A Modern Introduction to the Family*. 1968. New York: Free Press.

Initiation and Maintenance of the Human-Animal Bond: Familial Roles from a Learning Perspective

Clark M. Brickel

ABSTRACT. This article examines how individuals acquire and maintain an emotional bond for animals throughout the life span. In contrast to accepted psychoanalytical explanations, a learning perspective is taken where persons are taught to love animals; emphasis for such teaching is placed within the family. Children are taught to relate emotionally to animals under a framework of social learning theory using classical, operant, and observational learning. After this emotional base has been established, and as individuals form independent cognitions about the world, animals represent *tabula rasa* stimuli upon which persons inscribe ideosyncratic content. Following childhood, maintenance issues are focused upon using a social role-activity theory rationale. At this stage pet-oriented role activities perform utilitarian functions, defining relationships between the individual, family, and society.

One hot summer day I was meandering aimlessly beside a little local creek when I came upon a stagnant pool. In the bottom . . . three catfish lay gasping out their lives. They interested me . . .

I had begun to like them, in an abstract sort of way, and wished to know them better. But the problem of where to keep them while our acquaintanceship ripened was a major one. . . . I was driven to the admittedly desperate expedient of finding temporary lodgings for them in the bowl of Granny's old-fashioned toilet.

Clark M. Brickel is with the Department of Psychology, University of Southern California, Los Angeles, California. The author is indebted to Brandt Smith for a critical review of the manuscript.

I was too young at the time to appreciate the special problems which old age brings in its train. It was one of these problems which was directly responsible for the dramatic and unexpected encounter which took place between my grandmother and the catfish during the small hours of the ensuing night. It was a traumatic experience for Granny, and for me, and probably the catfish too. Throughout the rest of her life Granny refused to eat fish of any kind and always carried a high-powered flashlight with her during her nocturnal peregrinations. As for myself, the effect was to engender in me a lasting affinity for the lesser beasts of the animal kingdom. (Mowat, 1963, pp. 6–7)

This gentle narrative reveals the glimmer of a lasting childhood experience, an experience leading to an enduring, affectionate association with animals. I would like to take the reader briefly across the chronological spectrum so that we may begin a joint speculation about the etiology of human-animal bonding.

Mr. J. was an average patient on the long-term, total care unit where I worked. This 75-year-old male, a victim of Organic Brain Syndrome, stared vacantly into space, hour after hour, wherever he was placed by nursing staff. He presented no behavioral problems, but the rudimentary self-care behaviors we acquire early in life had been lost by Mr. J., a consequence of gradual brain tissue deterioration. Dressing, eating, bathing, all were duties which could be carried out only with the aid of dedicated nursing staff.

Communication with this man seemed out of the question. In the footsteps of other staff I had carried out lengthy monologues with Mr. J., hoping to establish some degree of verbal contact, to no avail. I was consistently greeted with silence and two soft almond eyes which seemed to look through me.

Yet there were specific behaviors which I could not reconcile with Mr. J.'s overall behavior pattern. What prompted this otherwise low-functioning patient to save scraps from his meals for two cats kept on the ward? And when I later stood by this man with a small pet dog, what neurological activity sparked him to tug at the leash for the animal and activate his neglected vocal cords in a strained request for "Dog?" Why would this patient respond to animals when most other stimuli were ignored?

From a clinical standpoint such isolated behaviors appear remarkable and encouraging. If some behaviors consistent with the "real world'' can be engendered with the presence of animals, other behaviors can be generated. But the underlying questions are why a person will respond to animals when other entreaties at communication fail; when most synaptic passageways appear to have been erased, why will persons who suffer the ravages of debilitating functional or organic disorders still respond—and respond appropriately—to animals?

The most widely accepted explanation of the human-animal bond is best expressed in the work of Levinson (1972) (for an extensive listing of Levinson's works the reader is referred to Brickel, 1980–81). Levinson's thesis uses a ''natural psychoanalytic'' approach where animals are viewed as symbolically important to people, given that they are expressions of the unconscious self. Due to this symbolic importance people are attracted to animals and the more natural (primitive/unconscious/less urbanized) world they represent.

Interdisciplinary texts focusing on the human-animal bond (Anderson, Hart, & Hart, 1984; Fogle, 1981; Katcher & Beck, 1983) embrace this viewpoint. Relating to animals, and pet-keeping in particular, are both considered efforts to combine the conscious and unconscious in a controllable manner (Savishinsky, 1983), resolve our inner conflicts (Heiman, 1965; Rynearson, 1978), gain defense mechanisms (Ryder, 1973), or symbolically resolve conflicts through dreams and fantasy (Bettleheim, 1977; Van de Castle, 1983).

Theories arguing for an innate attraction to animals and their symbolic vitality are conceptually attractive. But learning theory offers an alternate perspective which is less complex, more precise, and contains a high degree of practical application in explaining human behavior. Because learning theory has been ignored in accounting for the human-animal bond, this paper will suggest a groundwork where human-animal relationships are seen as stemming from learning experiences encountered within the family. This position reflects two central concepts: (1) We perceive animals as our emotional wards. Animals represent a class of stimuli saturated with emotional properties. Generally speaking the emotional association between people and animals is a positive one, easily converted in specific associations with pets; (2) We *learn* to perceive animals in this manner, mainly within the family. We do not innately recognize any particular animal species as emotionally ally or enemy, but are taught, systematically and extensively, recognition of some learned emotional taxonomy. In our Western culture we learn that certain classes of animals (e.g., dogs and cats) exist primarily to be loved.

Other animals (e.g., snakes) are to be feared or avoided. Given the emotional plasticity of the human condition and the lack of innate love for any one type of animal, we cannot state that people love animals instinctively.

OVERVIEW

The first section of this paper will examine some ways that families teach their children to emotionally relate to animals. This initiation and maintenance of the human-animal bond takes place under a framework of social learning theory using classical, operant, and observational learning. The second section, in reference to the maturing individual, extends social learning theory into a more cognitively oriented social role-activity theory. While initiation of the bond is possible here, maintenance aspects are focused upon. It is proposed that in later stages of people's lives animals are integrated into role-activity and consequently perform utilitarian functions for the individual, partially defining relationships between the individual, family, and the larger society.

BOND INITIATION AND MAINTENANCE

I. Infancy Through Childhood

Because our society values animals, the family is a primary source in instilling in its younger members respect for animals. Families start teaching their children to like animals almost immediately. By the time most children have reached the age of two the idea that pets and other domesticated animals represent a rewarding, uniformly positive experience is firmly engrained. In the family parents are more successful than psychologists in shaping attitudes and behaviors. However psychologists have the ability to analyze and differentiate modes of learning application. Although unaware of the processes involved, parents effectively teach children to love animals using highly skilled and multiple doses of classical, operant, and observational conditioning.

Classical Conditioning

Classical conditioning deals with stimulus substitution where the presentation of some potent unconditioned stimulus (UCS) heralds the presentation of a neutral stimulus. Due to this paired presentation an association is established where the neutral stimulus acquires properties that elicit responses formerly generated only by the UCS. The neutral stimulus is now considered a conditioned stimulus (CS), which in turn may be paired with additional neutral stimuli for a chaining of learning effects. Responses remain stable; only the stimuli change. When a number of stimuli have acquired the ability to evoke the original response through such stimulus chaining, higher order conditioning is said to have taken place. The learning of such conditioned responses may be either behavioral or attitudinal. If we assume that parents or other family members have rewarding properties about them such as love or affection, and consequently influence the child to respond in a certain manner, we recognize that a foundation has been laid for classical conditioning.

The newborn infant is instantly exposed to a world of light filled with a chaotic array of sounds, odors, sights and movement. Harnessed by physical development of the nervous system the infant fights to make sense of this world. The chaos perceived by the infant gradually yields to orderly perceptual forms which are ultimately transformed into stimuli having symbolic meaning and emotional content. By the time this occurs the child has learned to associate its parents (originally neutral stimuli) with rewarding properties, e.g., they dispense food, security, and affection. These rewarding properties generate positive affective states and approach responses in the infant. In short, the infant tends to be happier in the presence of the family, as most babysitters know. The infant has learned to identify and love the parents.

With this in mind, consideration of higher order learning may take place. The parents are conditioned stimuli; their presence evokes conditioned responses in the infant. By presenting neutral stimuli to the infant parents link responses elicited by them to stimuli which they subsequently present. And parents consistently introduce animals to the developing child on two levels. The first level is subtle but effective. It concerns the common use of animal figures within the family's residence, with special attention paid to the child's milieu. Even the simplest of nurseries is stocked with a larder of animal representatives. The most obvious are stuffed toy animals manufactured from an unlimited selection of species. Lions, tigers, giraffes, every animal from ape to zebra finds its reincarnated image beside or in a child's crib. This symbolic appearance is not limited to dolls or other toys used to stimulate and amuse the child. Animal figures also appear on the child's wardrobe, furniture, eating utensils, sheets, pillowcases, and wallpaper (actually this process was probably started in the hospital where animal figures adorn children's wards). Hence to begin with, the child's home—its place of protection, nurturance and security—is definably stamped with the imprimatur of the animal kingdom. The developing child, having encountered a menagerie of animal figures in the home, learns to associate them with parents and home and feels comfortable around them.

In a more active manner family members engage the child in play or fantasy, using the animal as a catalyst, for example, where tickling is "done" by a toy bear, or the infant is lovingly stroked with the fur of some other toy animal. When this happens we witness the beginning of anthropomorphism, where human attributes are given to animals, and also see how the family prepares the child for future enjoyable interactions with real animals.

Functional concerns are also achieved with depicted animals. The child may be coaxed to eat with the use of a spoon, fork, plate, or glass portraying a particular animal. Again this animal figure may become endowed with the ability to think and give affection: "Johnny, see Mickey on the spoon? He loves you and wants you to eat all your food so you get strong." While such experiences are small in and of themselves, constant exposure to animals in the home environment combine with countless repetitions of small interactions between child and toy or utensil. This combination of events adds up to lasting learning experiences.

The second level of the child's introduction to animals within the family is significantly more active and concerns monitoring the child with live animals, usually pets. Parents intuitively know that if the child is to learn to love animals initial experiences must be positively rewarding, and great care is taken insuring that primary association with animals is emotionally gratifying for the child, and pleasant as possible for the animal.

The negative consequences of early classical conditioning with animals are well illustrated in the case of "Little Albert." Watson and Rayner (1920) paired the presentation of a white rat (neutral stimulus) with a loud, starting noise (UCS) to Albert, an unsuspecting 11-month-old infant. Not only did Albert subsequently display fear and avoidance behaviors in the presence of the rat, such conditioned responses generalized to other white furry objects including a rabbit, a cat, cotton, and human hair.

Parents will take an opposite mode with their conditioning because they seek to nurture approach behavior. Ideally the setting is calm and within the home. One of the parents gently holds and controls the animal, and some of the positive associations that the child holds for the parent are transferred to the pet. Parents control such interactions completely, readily interrupting if either child or pet appear uncomfortable or headed for some unpleasantness, and promptly rewarding both child and pet for successful behaviors.

Since the pet is in many senses a genuine family member (Cain, 1978), introductions and successive interactions must be pleasurable to insure future interactions. For example, with a pet next to her and a child on her lap, the mother may take the child's hand into her own, lift it up to her face, and gently stroke her face with the child's hand while saying something to the effect of "nice." The mother may then take the child's hand and stroke it over the animal, repeating her verbalizations. Consider that in this simple transaction the parent has paired herself with the pet, and that to some degree, responses associated with the mother will be transferred to the pet. The tactile qualities inherent in the mother will also be associated with the pet, and we know that stimulation of the skin is meaningful, builds cognitive associations, and can be remembered and sought for (Meichenbaum, 1977; Montagu, 1971). Finally we encounter the concept of "nice" shared between two very different organisms, gaining a sense of the etiology of semantic conceptualizations which, as Osgood, Suci, and Tannenbaum (1957) point out, occupy different dimensions of semantic space.

Observational Learning (Modeling)

Society passes on expectations and values to its members for internal consistency. If, due to conditioning processes society values animals for both biological and psychological reasons, efforts to have society's members share the value system can be expected. This seems to be the case. The mass media carry numerous human-interest stories emphasizing the affectional relationship people have with animals. The family unit is besieged with focal points in the news about the consequences of rewarding relationships with animals, e.g., stories about seeing-eye dogs, or instances where persons are saved from threatening circumstances by pets. Books and movies are presented to the public giving animals human attributes, rendering depicted animal characterizations as "superstimuli" that refresh and strengthen learned secondary associations with animals. These messages reinforce our values concerning pets and are quite direct regarding anticipated behaviors of care, affection, and admiration for them. The explicit communication is made that animals are to be loved and cared for, and that such actions will reward us with the affection of the animal and admiration from others. When persons who are exposed to such information integrate it into their behavioral and attitudinal repertoire without benefit of tangible external reinforcements, observational learning has taken place.

Observational learning is most sought by pet food manufacturers in commercials aimed at the public, where cats, with voiced over-dubbing, comment on their food preferences, or dogs go to unusual lengths to get at their kibble cuisine. Actors and actresses in such commercials display great emotional satisfaction with animals, plainly valuing them. These models, whom others admire or identify with, extol the virtues of animals, further reinforcing our shared value systems for them. The figurative message is "If you love your pet, maintain this object of affection with our product," or more literally, "Maintain your reinforcement source with this product."

Children receive messages involving the reinforcing aspects of animals on two primary levels, one being through the media which, when directed at children emphasizes animal characters, supplemented by schooling where animal graphics are heavily used in texts to facilitate learning, the other through modeling of significant others in the family. Learning acquisition does not require personal involvement, but can take place vicariously through observation of another's behaviors and the ensuing consequences. Not only can new response patterns be acquired via modeling, but emotional responses can be conditioned by witnessing others having pleasurable (rewarding) or painful (punishing) experiences. For example, Bandura, Grusec and Menlove (1967) and Bandura and Menlove (1968) demonstrated that behavioral avoidance of dogs in young children could be extinguished, and approach behavior elicited, when children observed others happily interacting with dogs. Such behavior was seen to generalize to different dogs and resulted in positive affect and joyful interactions. In another study (Bandura, Blanchard & Ritter, 1969), subjects who formerly avoided snakes overcame their fears and learned to enjoy handling them. Within a social learning theory approach this modeling process depicts a basic manner in which the foundation for animals as reward sources is built.

Within the family this modeling process is used extensively by parents who must teach their children about the environment. Parents commonly model pleasurable interactions with pets for the benefit of their children. They perform this in a systematic manner, insuring an event with pleasurable affective consequences. I have been enrolled in such activities by strangers who, toddler in hand, approached me inquiring about the temperament of my dog. When I responded that the dog was gentle, the parent, apparently satisfied that the dog was a good teaching instrument, would ask if the child could pet or hold the animal. Given my consent the parent invariably put the child down, crouched next to the dog, and proceeded to handle the dog *prior to* the child's actual participation. This would be accompanied by frequent verbalizations ("Nice doggy; how sweet!") and positive affect (smiling). Then the child would be invited to do the same.

If the child hesitated the parent again modeled the appropriate behavior. Once engaged with the dog the child displayed this accomplishment with the parent ("See?"), and both would continue to pet the dog, sharing the moment. If the dog responded by licking the child or exposing her belly to be rubbed (a likely occurrence) this was considered an "extra" by the parent and was dutifully remarked upon, "Oh, how cute. Isn't this doggy nice? She loves us." The child's continued interaction and positive affect would be verbally reinforced by the parent, "See? There is nothing to be afraid of; animals love you." Although this whole procedure could be enacted in a few minutes, the event undoubtedly left the child with a strong impression on the rewarding consequences of pet interactions. Here vicarious conditioning through modeling was a prelude to participant modeling, a more powerful experience than vicarious conditioning alone (Bandura, 1977).

The three outcomes of modeling processes (Bandura, 1969) lend themselves well to bond initiation and maintenance issues within the family. New learning is the first outcome and concerns initiation, as in the above example, where a child observes some agreeable animal interaction. Modeling also has inhibitory/disinhibitory effects, and this concerns reinitiation where the parent counteracts the negative experiences of a fearful child. A third outcome is response facilitation. This outcome deals with bond maintenance, and is relevant when a family purposely increases the number of household pets, thereby inviting the child's exposure to animals. Such diverse outcomes render modeling an effective parental tool for establishing children's emotional ties. There is little doubt that modeling strategies—live, participant, and symbolic—play a major role in conditioning children to love animals. Because of such conditioning people gain an awareness of animals as secondary reinforcers, an awareness that exerts considerable discriminative control over future behaviors.

Operant (Instrumental) Learning

Operant conditioning naturally follows classical and observational learning in sequence, since these earlier learning modes are particularly adapted to a child's limited capacities. A parent needs to closely monitor activities for positive outcomes. Accordingly, operant conditioning is facilitated by these earlier experiences, especially when the child has learned to identify animals as discriminative stimuli associated with secondary reinforcements. Under such conditions the child's responses to animals are shaped easily by the family, who reward the child for rudimentary approaches and successive approximations to pets. These child-pet interactions are monitored closely by the family, and animals are carefully screened out for undesirable learning experiences.

With operant or instrumental conditioning the emphasis is on respondent behaviors. The situation is where the individual child in this instance freely moves about busily responding to incoming stimuli. When an autonomous response is followed by favorable outcomes (reinforced), the operant behavior increases in frequency. For example, a young man who approaches a cat with intentions of petting it will continue approaching cats in the future if the outcome proves rewarding. The cat displays a sufficient amount of affection when petted, or its amiable female owner shows up. A scratch or bite on the cat's part, or a belligerent female owner, however, will diminish the future likelihood of such behavior.

An emphasis on respondent behavior means that two sources of secondary reinforcement must be considered equally. Reinforcements coming from people in the form of attention, praise or affection from family members have been stressed. However, since the child will eventually act independently of the family, animals must display those qualities that the child has been taught to consider reinforcing (e.g., warm, soft, playful, fun, or otherwise affectionate, and at the very least, interesting). Children find passive, inactive, and unresponsive animals only slightly more interesting than rocks, and will do everything they can to activate such beasts for their amusement. Hence the family shapes initial bonding activities, but it is up to the animals themselves to encourage bond maintenance.

Until the child is older then, most opportunities for operant conditioning are limited. Operant conditioning to animals is correlated with the child's degree of ambulation, social maturity, and familial freedom. Usually by the age of three operant conditioning is a prime component of the bonding process. Conditioning is still regulated in that the family monitors, or sets up and shapes child-animal interaction. Classes of animal stimuli (certain pets; animal toys) that have been judged as "safe" for the child can be played with freely. This family system operates in such a way so that all child-animal interactions are geared toward such positive concepts as gentleness, love, affection or fun.

Within the family these mainstream child-animal interactions are heavily reinforced. When little Johnny cries because one of his Teddy bear's limbs has fallen off, the parents quickly move to comfort both Johnny and the bear. If little Kathy plays satisfactorily with the family dog her parents may join in the fun, or at least stop what they are doing to observe and comment. When little Jay ceases eating the dog's food and instead takes efforts to feed the dog, parental approval is swiftly forthcoming and will be shared by other family members since responsibility is a sought for trait in the child's development. In each case the child is rewarded with powerful secondary reinforcers for animal interaction—hugs, kisses, and verbal praise. The effectiveness of such reinforcements in shaping behavior has been amply demonstrated (see for example, O'Leary & Wilson, 1975; Ullman & Krasner, 1965).

The development of operant responses is obviously not limited to situations in the family setting, or to any one chronological stage of development. They will be operational for the rest of the person's life. Exposure to this learning expands as opportunities for operant conditioning, under family scrutiny and independent of such monitoring, increase with age. Responsiveness to animals is encouraged by the environment when we consider children in rural areas. But urban children also are offered abundant opportunities for interaction. Many urban families keep pets. Even when the family does not keep pets, pet exposure will take place in the homes of friends and relatives. Zoos usually have "petting areas" or animal nurseries set aside where children are encouraged to touch, feed, and admire more exotic animals. So many experiences of these types take place that by the age of five, the child's emotions, attitudes, and behaviors towards a diverse animal menagerie have been shaped by the family. The child has learned to love animals, and is consequently drawn to their presence.

Quite often this approach behavior is strong enough to generate consternation in the parent whose child finds *all* animals attractive. Such children generalize their response patterns from the class of "safe" animals presented under controlled circumstances within the family, to the larger class of "strange" animals encountered outside of the family setting. The less sophisticated child has coded all animals as discriminative stimuli having favorable consequences when contacted. Recognizing the learning discrepancy, the parents must then set about refining the child's discriminating processes. Animal stimuli are subsequently broken down into those that may be approached with impunity, familiar pets; those that call for discretion, strange or sick pets; and those that must not be approached at all, guard dogs and wild animals.

Of the three learning procedures discussed, instrumental learning probably receives the most familial attention and direction. After the child's behavior is shaped to parental satisfaction the child is more or less free to interact with animals independently. Given this initial direction the child will do so. The future strength of emotional linkage to animals will depend upon whether subsequent animal contacts have positive or negative outcomes.

II. Adolescence Through Old Age

The previously discussed learning paradigms—classical, observational and instrumental—continue molding people's relations to pets, allowing both for long term bond maintenance and bond initiation in the later stages of life when bonding did not successfully occur in childhood. As found by Larsen et al. (1974) in regard to physical suffering, empathy for pets may be greater than for other people. This type of information substantiates the emotional depth of early learning experiences and their maintenance.

Because initiation of the bond takes place more commonly in childhood, the latter part of life concerns itself mostly with maintenance issues. Cognitions become increasingly important in our lives as we mature, and so maintenance of the bond from adolescence through old age becomes increasingly cognitively oriented. As individuals continue their maturation and formulate independent cognitions about the world, animals come to represent *tabula rasa* stimuli upon which persons inscribe their own symbolism and roles. This role-play with animals performs a more utilitarian function than earlier role-play by defining the individual's self-identity and relationships with family and society.

It is vital to note that an increased reliance on role activity for human-animal bond maintenance is not independent of conditioning processes, but is firmly based upon their continued engagement throughout the life-span and earlier emotional attachments generated by them. For example, Byrne and Clore (1970) describe an excellent paradigm of how our evaluations are based upon implicit affective responses learned in a context of classical conditioning:

> It is proposed that the evaluative meaning of any given stimulus is a positive linear function of the proportion of positive reinforcements associated with it. According to the model positive and negative reinforcements act as unconditioned stimuli which evoke implicit affective responses. Any discriminable stimulus associated with such unconditioned stimuli becomes a conditioned stimulus which elicits the implicit affective response. It is proposed that these implicit responses mediate verbal assessments . . . and other evaluative responses. (p. 103)

Following this model we understand that having been associated with innumerable reinforcements, pets become unconditioned stimuli that automatically evoke positive affective responses. Furthermore, neutral stimuli, people or objects, contiguous to animals, will, through association, in turn evoke positive affective responses and evaluations. These occurrences encourage maintenance of the human-animal bond through role-taking.

Social Role-Activity Theory

During the process of socialization all persons living within a culture learn and explore a variety of family related roles for purposes of social definition. Roles are defined by societies as proscribed behaviors that incur status; both duties and privileges follow these behaviors. But in role assumption people take on more than a set of behaviors. They take on attitudes regarding self, based on status, and expectations of how others value them. Roles can be either ascribed, bestowed or achieved through competition with others (Horton & Hunt, 1968).

Social role, as the major link of an individual's attachment to the larger social system, provides an image and self-definition, both of which ultimately impact feelings of self-value. If a person's role is ill-defined, ambiguous, or in conflict, a person undergoes a loss of status, and feels uncertain regarding her or his personal identity (Itzin, 1970). Positive self-feelings are retrievable through activity. Lemon, Bengtson, and Peterson (1972) indicate that activity provides role supports required to reaffirm self-concepts and enhance psychological self-maintenance. The more frequent and intimate the activity, the more potent its validating ability. Since social roles permit us to act upon the environment and strengthen self-ideas, the probability that alienation and negative self-imagery will develop decrease as activity increases (Maddox & Eisdorfer, 1962). Meaningful activity contributes to status, achievement, recognition, and ultimately, morale.

Social role-activity theory is commonly referred to in predicting successful aging (Kalson, 1976; Knapp, 1977), and can be generalized to all age groups. This theory holds that through meaningful activity a person's role and subsequent self-concepts of esteem, identity, and value are strengthened (Palmore & Luikart, 1972). Deny meaningful activity and losses of role and self-concept follow. It is assumed that people have a degree of role flexibility and will be maximally engaged in some roles while minimally involved with others. But roles differ in terms of importance. In examining role clusters, Havighurst (1957) extracted two general factors: (1) A family-centered configuration (parent/spouse/home maker/worker) consisting of thoroughly internalized first-order roles; (2) An extra-family centered configuration (user of leisure time/friend/citizen/association member) of a second order, being less deeply internalized, but still rewarding. These learned roles were so deeply internalized that they represented self-expectations. High levels of role performance were correlated with high adjustment.

With the onset of maturity interacting with animals comes to represent a functionally meaningful activity, allowing for the assumption of first or second order roles. Maintenance of the human-animal bond is therefore assured. Animals become the *tabula rasa* upon which the person inscribes, through activity, roles necessary for self-enhancement. Persons who are dissatisfied with their roles or undergo role conflicts experience manifestations of anxiety, e.g., withdrawal, depression. Therefore animals additionally take on a therapeutic stance in presenting opportunities for "trying on" new roles and working out role conflicts.

Our emotional development, from childhood through old age, is often buffeted by disagreeable events. The child experiences failure and success, rejection and acceptance, self-doubt and confidence. Negative experiences develop inner resources, but also produce tensions regarding self-concepts. In order to relieve such tensions role play with real or imaginary companions is important for the child. This play satisfies needs for companionship, self-aggrandizement, collaboration, and a release of forbidden impulses (Jersild, 1968). Pets satisfy such needs. A child who feels powerless before adults has a feeling of mastery over pets who may be assigned roles of peer or submissive sibling. The need to feel significant is met by directing a pet to sit or fetch or perform some trick. As children grow they take on a number of roles in play, feeling what it might be like to have a certain status. Pets invite such activities of fantasy. The child assumes roles of parent, teacher, or anything else with an animal and has no fear of rejection (Levinson, 1969). Success in this role play is virtually assured.

When the child begins passage into adolescence role-play and animal activities take on a more utilitarian nature. The teenager works at establishing new ties to the family under the dual siege of dramatic physiological changes and peer pressures. At the heart of this psychic storm lies a consuming struggle for self-identity. Animals are enlisted as sources of emotional support, since animal oriented activities help carve out definitions of self. Parents, family, and friends all change in the ways they relate to developing adolescents but animals do not. They provide emotional anchors during the tempest, giving comfort and solace through their stability. During calmer periods the adolescent can choose to enhance status among family and friends via the caretaking and training of animals. These activities allow for the growth of responsibility and establish role boundaries within the family.

Our psychologically ambiguous perception of animals makes them attractive for role-activity integration, insuring maintenance of the human-animal bond for older age groups. In essence, animals represent whatever we want them to, given our current needs and biases. Young and middle age adults satisfy many emotional needs through their interests in animals. Childless couples may enjoy "parenting" pets until they have children. Even persons who have never owned animals would like to have pets for their children (Wilbur, 1976), and so the possibility of familial expansion entails pet ownership and bond maintenance. Adult status needs are met by keeping exotic or expensive pets. Psychological transactions from family to independent living, and geographical transitions from area to area are eased with the presence of companion animals with whom owners share both active and quiet times. Role activity with pets is fulfilling since the pet-owner role encompasses other roles which fluctuate in terms of importance to the owner. Examples of such roles are friend, protector, companion, provider or parent, all significant roles modeled formerly within the family of origin, and duplicated with the pet's aid.

In reference to the elderly as a group undergoing systematic role loss, Rosow (1973) states that such losses result in diminished self-esteem, eroded images of self-identity, exclude the aged from meaningful social participation, and give rise to unstructured life styles which arouse anxiety. Engaging in pet related activities brings about a reacquisition of usefulness and purpose for the elderly. Depression levels can also be lowered (Brickel, in press; 1984). Pets that are interesting draw others to the pet owner, enhancing feelings of importance and social participation. In a similar manner, pets in the household serve as added incentive for children and grandchildren to visit. The responsibility of animal keeping helps individuals to feel needed and lends daily structure to the lives of persons who otherwise have minimal responsibility. Pets serve as "therapeutic distractions" (Brickel, 1982) for house-bound fragile elderly. As surrogate family members pets provide solace and continuity for persons who suffer the loss of a spouse or child. A number of pets will constitute a new psychological family or individuals who are separated from, or have lost, many family members. In general, activity with pet animals abridges negative consequences of old age, enhancing the probability of successful aging.

This spectrum of role activity with pets is family-originated. It does not diminish the human-animal bond but enhances and maintains it, accentuating the suppleness of animals to meet human psychological needs. Pets will be there in happy and sad times, and both laughter and tears will be shared with them. They will be loved intrinsically, or valued as objects for their monetary worth. Arguments for pure actualizing animal relationships, to the exclusion of "lower" utilitarian or object-oriented levels (Fox, 1981) are well intentioned, but do not fully consider the psychological status of people and their affiliation needs with animals.

We are taught to love animals in our youth and within our family. Frequently we need to love and be close to animals as we age, build new families, or reconstruct old ones. Our earlier emotional training becomes pragmatic when we use it to cognitively balance a more sophisticated psychological equilibrium. This earlier emotional training comes full circle when we pass it on within the family to our own children.

REFERENCES

Anderson, R. K., Hart, B., & Hart, L. (1984). (Eds.), *The pet connection.* University of Minnesota: CENSHARE.

Bandura, A. (1969). *Principles of behavior modification.* New York: Holt, Rinehart, & Winston.

Bandura, A. (1977). Self-efficacy: Toward a unifying theory of behavioral change. *Psychological Review, 84,* 191-215.

Bandura, A., Blanchard, E., & Ritter, B. (1969). The relative efficacy of desensitization and modeling approaches for inducing behavioral, affective, and attitudinal changes. *Stanford University, 13,* 173-199.

Bandura, A., Grusec, J., & Menlove, F. (1967). Vicarious extinction of avoidance behavior. *Journal of Personality & Social Psychology, 5,* 16-23.

Bandura, A., & Menlove, F. (1968) Factors determining vicarious extinction of avoidance behavior through symbolic modeling. *Journal of Personality & Social Psychology, 8,* 99-108.

Bettelheim, B. (1977). *The uses of enchantment.* New York: Vintage Books.

Brickel, C. M. (1980-81). A review of the roles of pet animals in psychotherapy and with the elderly. *International Journal of Aging and Human Development, 12,* 119-128.

Brickel, C. M. (1982). Pet-facilitated psychotherapy: A theoretical explanation via attention shifts. *Psychological Reports, 50,* 71-74.

Brickel, C. M. (1984). Depression in the nursing home: A pilot study using pet-facilitated psychotherapy. In R. K. Anderson, B. Hart, and L. Hart (Eds.), *The pet connection* (pp. 407-415). University of Minnesota: CENSHARE.

Brickel, C. M. (in press). Pet-facilitated psychotherapy. *Clinical Gerontologist.*

Byrne, D., & Clore, G. L. (1970). A reinforcement model of evaluative responses. *Personality, 1,* 103-128.

Cain, A. O. (1978). *A study of pets in the family system.* Paper presented at the meeting of the Georgetown Family Symposium, Washington, D.C., October.

Fogle, B. (1981). (Ed.), *Interrelations between people and pets.* Illinois: Charles C Thomas.

Fox, M. (1981). Relationships between the human and non-human animals. In B. Fogle (Ed.), *Interrelationships between people and pets* (pp. 23-40). Illinois: Charles C Thomas.

Havighurst, R. J. (1957) The social competence of middle-aged people. *Genetic Psychology Monographs, 56,* 297-375.

Heiman, M. (1965). Psychoanalytic observations on the relationship of pet and man. *Veterinary Medicine/Small Animal Clinician, 60,* 713-718.

Horton, P. B., & Hunt, C. L. (1968). *Sociology.* New York: McGraw-Hill.

Itzin, F. (1970). Social relations. In A. Hoffman (Ed.), *The daily needs and interests of older people.* Illinois: Charles C Thomas.

Jersild, A. T. (1968). *Child psychology.* New Jersey: Prentice-Hall.

Kalson, L. (1976). MASH: A program of social interaction between institutionalized aged and adult mentally retarded persons. *Gerontologist, 16,* 340-348.

Katcher, A. H., & Beck, A. M. (1983). (Eds.), *New perspectives on our lives with companion animals.* Pennsylvania: University of Pennsylvania Press.

Knapp, M. (1977). The activity theory of aging: An examination in the english context. *Gerontologist, 17,* 553-559.

Larsen, K. S., Ashlock, J., Carroll, C., Foote, S., Feeler, J., Keller, E., Seese, G., & Watkins, D. (1974). Laboratory aggression where the victim is a small dog. *Social Behavior and Personality, 2,* 174–176.

Lemon, B., Bengtson, V., & Peterson, J. (1972). An exploration of the activity theory of aging. *Journal of Gerontology, 27,* 511–523.

Levinson, B. M. (1969). *Pet-oriented child psychotherapy.* Illinois: Charles C Thomas.

Levinson, B. M. (1972). *Pets and human development.* Illinois: Charles C Thomas.

Maddox, G., & Eisdorfer, C. (1962). Some correlates of activity and morale among the elderly. *Social Forces, 41,* 254–260.

Meichenbaum, D. (1977). *Cognitive behavior modification.* New York: Plenum Press.

Montagu, A. (1971). *Touching.* New York: Harper & Row.

Mowat, F. (1963). *Never cry wolf.* New York: Dell Publishing.

O'Leary, K. D., & Wilson, G. T. (1975). *Behavior therapy: Application and outcome.* New Jersey: Prentice Hall.

Osgood, C. E., Suci, G. J., & Tannenbaum, P. H. (1957). *The measurement of meaning.* Illinois: University of Illinois Press.

Palmore, E., & Luikhart, C. (1972). Health and social factors related to life satisfaction. *Journal of Health and Social Behavior, 13,* 68–80.

Rosow, I. (1973). The social context of the aging self. *Gerontologist, 13,* 82–87.

Ryder, R. D. (1973). Pets in man's search for sanity. *Journal of Small Animal Practice, 14,* 657–668.

Rynearson, E. K. (1978). Humans and pets and attachment. *British Journal of Psychiatry, 133,* 550–555.

Savishinsky, J. S. (1983). Pet ideas: The domestication of animals, human behavior, and human emotions. In A. H. Katcher and A. M. Beck (Eds.), *New perspectives on our lives with companion animals* (pp. 112–131). Pennsylvania: University of Pennsylvania Press.

Ullman, L., & Krasner, L. (1965). (Eds.), *Case studies in behavior modification.* New York: Holt, Rinehart, & Winston.

Van de Castle, R. L. (1983). Animal figures in fantasy and dreams. In A. H. Katcher and A. M. Beck (Eds.), *New perspectives on our lives with companion animals* (pp. 148–173). Pennsylvania: University of Pennsylvania Press.

Watson, J. B., & Rayner, R. (1920). Conditioned emotional reactions. *Journal of Experimental Psychology, 3,* 1–14.

Wilbur, R. H. (1976). *Pets, pet ownership and animal control: Social and psychological attitudes, 1975.* Paper presented at the National Conference on Dog and Cat Control, Denver, Colorado, February.

The Companion Animal
in the Context
of the Family System

Cecelia J. Soares

ABSTRACT. The nature and possible value of the bond between humans and their companion animals has begun to receive attention from professionals involved in the behavioral sciences and in health care. A few investigators have specifically addressed the question of the role of the companion animal in the family system. This review summarizes a number of studies dealing with the relationship of companion animals with humans at different stages of life, as well as research concerning the possible role of the companion animal in both the functional and dysfunctional family system. The review concludes with an evaluation and discussion of research to date and suggestions for future investigations.

The bond between humans and the animals they have domesticated through the millenia has been recognized since ancient times. Earliest known fossil remains give evidence for domestication of dogs over 12,000 years ago; the cat has lived in association with man for at least 6,000 years (Messent & Serpell, 1981). In spite of the enormous numbers of people who currently own domestic animals of all kinds throughout the world, the nature of the bond between humans and their companion animals has only recently come to be of interest to professionals involved in the behavioral sciences and health care.

In particular, the work of Dr. Samuel Corson (1980) and Dr. Boris Levinson (1961, 1964, 1965, 1968, 1969, 1972, 1978) indicating that animals could have therapeutic value for disturbed children and adults catalyzed current interest in the human/animal relationship. In surveying the literature, however, one becomes aware

Cecelia J. Soares is Adjunct Professor and Department Chairman, Department of Pathology and Microbiology, Life Chiropractic College West; Visiting Lecturer, Department of Physiology-Anatomy, University of California, Berkeley, CA.

that there is relatively little information about events between normal pet owners and their pets. There are, in fact, only a few studies of normal human/companion animal interaction, and even fewer that examine this relationship in the context of the family.

This review will summarize literature pertaining to the relationship between companion animals and humans, particularly as that relationship exists within the family system. Since families which live with companion animals are by definition comprised of individuals, this article will also review studies which attempt to deal with the relationships between individual human beings and their animals first and then those which attempt to approach the more complex area of family/animal interactions.

RELATIONSHIPS BETWEEN COMPANION ANIMALS AND HUMANS

Physiological Effects of Companion Animals on Humans

One of the best-known studies of the physiologic effects of the presence of companion animals on humans is the study by Friedmann, Katcher, Lynch, and Thomas (1980). They showed that for white subjects the presence of a pet in the home was the strongest predictor of one-year survival following discharge from a coronary care unit. These researchers determined that the effect of pets was not due to the better health of the pet owners at the start of the study, nor due to pet owner's higher socioeconomic status, nor associated with only dogs as pets. Most importantly, "the effect of pets was not present only in those people who were socially isolated; it was independent of marital status and access to social support from human beings" (p. 211).

The last-mentioned finding suggested to Friedmann et al. that pets might have important effects on the lives of adults that are independent of and supplementary to human contact. Subsequently, other research revealed that the blood pressure of subjects fell below its resting level when they talked to or petted a dog (Lynch, Thomas, Long, Malinow, Chickadone, & Katcher, 1980), and that the mere presence of a friendly dog in the room resulted in lower blood pressures and heart rates in children while they were resting or while they were reading aloud (Friedmann, Katcher, Thomas, Lynch, & Messent, 1983). In the latter experiment, the investigators speculated that the presence of the animal caused the children to modify their perceptions of both the experimental situation and the experimenter by making them seem less threatening, in other words, that the presence of the animal reduced anxiety (p. 464).

The Relationship Between Companion Animals and Children

Dr. Boris Levinson has written extensively on the relationship of pets to child development and their use in the psychotherapy of disturbed children. He has theorized that pets are objects of fantasy and as imaginary companions for children; as agents through which children learn responsibility, develop a sense of identity, and develop independence; as sources of unconditional love and loyalty; and as stimuli for certain kinds of cognitive learning (Levinson, 1961, 1964, 1965, 1968, 1969, 1972, 1978). He relates these various childhood experiences with animals to a child's mastery of developmental tasks at various stages (Levinson, 1972, chapter 2).

Bossard and Boll (1966) have expressed similar concepts about the functions of pets for children. In addition, others have theorized about the benefits normal children can derive from association with animals. It has been suggested that a pet may act as a transitional object, defined by Winnicott (1953) as an object through which children can create ego boundaries, overcome insecurity, and widen their experience in the outside world.

More recently, Kellert and Westervelt (1983), in one of the only instances of quantitative research into the relationship between children and animals, studied the attitudes of 250 children, at several grade levels, towards animals. They found major differences among age, sex, ethnic, and urban/rural groups. In particular, they established three major age-related developmental stages in the way children relate to animals: (1) 6-9 years: major increase in affective relationship to animals; (2) 10-13 years: major expansion in cognitive understanding and knowledge of animals; (3) 13-16 years; dramatic increase in ethical concern and ecological appreciation of animals.

Relationships Between Companion Animals and Adults

A number of investigators have addressed the questions of the psychological relationship between pets and non-elderly adults. Various studies have shown the following to be the benefits of pets most frequently reported by their owners: provide companionship, provide an aid to health and relaxation of the owner, provide protection, provide a source of non-judgmental acceptance, love and loyalty, provide something for the owner to love and nurture, provide an outlet for playfulness (Bossard, 1944; Levinson, 1972, chapter 3; Petcare, 1977; Savishinsky, 1983). Voith (1983) has pointed out that the attachment between an adult and a companion animal may be so powerful that the adult will decide to keep the pet even though it has proven itself to be destructive or dangerous.

One study has indicated that dog ownership may contribute to ego strength, as measured by the Ego Strength scale of the Minnesota Multiphasic Personality Inventory (Harris, 1981). Another has demonstrated that pet owners who described pets as family members scored significantly higher in the Purpose in Life Test and the Health Opinion Survey (Wille, note 3). These results led the investigators to speculate that pet ownership, where there was a certain intensity of attachment to the pet, made a concrete contribution to the health and well-being of the pet owner.

The literature in the area of psychosocial benefits of pet ownership for normal individuals has been contradictory. Cameron, Conrad, Kirkpatrick, and Bateen (1966), and Cameron and Mattson (1972) concluded from their work that pet owners tended to feel less well-regarded by others, to value people less than animals, and to like animals better than people. However, most of the current research demonstrates opposite findings. Corson and Corson (1980) and Brown, Shaw, and Kirkland (1972) found that people who had high affection for dogs were high in affection for other people, while people low in affection for dogs were low in affection for others, and Mugford (1980) records results of Lee who found that interactive pet-owners were higher in their need for affiliation than non-interactive pet-owners. Lockwood (1983) reported that people associated with animals in scenes from the Thematic Apperception Test (TAT) were often judged by subjects to be friendlier, happier, more confident, and more relaxed than people not associated with animals in TAT scenes.

The studies of Salmon and Salmon (1983), working in Australia, have shown that a dog seems to have different characteristics to an owner, depending on the owner's life-stage. For example, ''single people tended to describe their dogs as less reliable; to young childless couples their dog was more active and rough; people with older children saw their's as more confident; widowed, separated, and divorced people saw theirs as more aggressive; whereas old childless couples described their dog as more reliable'' (p. 254). Their data analysis also yielded certain points of comparison between human-dog and human-human relationships, for example, "a pet is seen as a living creature with whom a person can share a relationship involving trust and the warm feelings of love and emotional support. This relationship also includes a recognition of intelligence on the part of the pet'' (p. 254).

To some extent, the benefits of pet ownership in adults seem to be correlated with socioeconomic status and residential environment. Ory and Goldberg (1983) found, for example, that in rural adult women with relatively high incomes, pet ownership was positively correlated with high morale, but in subjects with low incomes, pet owners had lower morale. Similar results were obtained in California with rural pet owners (Franti, Kraus, & Borhani, 1974).

Relationships Between Companion Animals and the Elderly

Many of the studies of elderly individuals and companion animals have been conducted in institutional settings. However, in order to maintain emphasis on the family context, this writer has decided to restrict discussion of the literature to that concerning the elderly person and the pet in the home.

Mugford and M'Comisky (1974) placed budgerigars with elderly people in home environments. They reported that those who received the birds showed consistent improvement in attitudes towards other people and towards their own mental health compared to elderly persons who received only plants. Ory and Goldberg (1983) found that although there was no relationship between the presence of household pets and reported happiness in elderly people, there was a definite positive correlation between happiness and the degree of attachment to the companion animal. The higher the socioeconomic status, the greater was the correlation. Although these studies, as well as those based on institutionalized geriatric populations, have indicated that there are psychological advantages associated with pet ownership for the elderly, the authors of such studies readily admit that present data do not permit determination of whether pet ownership per se produces benefits or whether it is simply a matter of healthier personalities choosing to own pets. In any case, it is interesting to note that the rate of pet ownership is actually highest, not among the elderly, but among those in the population who have the most human companionship, married couples with children

(Schneider & Vaida, 1975). Financial and housing considerations may well underlie these statistics.

Investigators studying attitudes towards pets and happiness among the rural elderly (Connell & Lago, 1983; Lago, Knight, & Connell, 1983) found that a favorable attitude toward a pet contributed more to the predictive power of a model used to explain differences in happiness scores of subjects than did social satisfaction of activities of daily living. The direction and magnitude of the effect depended on marital status in this study, a favorable attitude toward pets contributing to increased happiness in the unmarried subgroup, but not in the married subgroup.

THE COMPANION ANIMAL IN THE FAMILY SYSTEM

Over fifty percent of households in the English-speaking world keep pets (Fogle, 1983); in the United States, as of 1978, 41,000,000 of the 80,000,000 American families had at least one dog and 23,000,000 families owned cats (Perin, 1981). Given the relationships between humans and companion animals discussed above, it would seem inevitable that combining individuals of all ages into families along with their pets would greatly increase the complexity of these relationships as the people interact with each other and the pets within the context of a system.

Levinson (1964, 1968) has suggested that the role of the pet in the family depends upon the family structure, the emotional strengths and weaknesses of each family member, the emotional undercurrents within the family, and the social climate of the family. Bridger (1976) believed that there are two complementary dimensions of pet ownership which exist for the family itself: (1) that an animal can be the means by which a family can widen its social network, and (2) that an animal can make even a secure family setting a safer place to test out love and hate, preferences and rivalries, independence and cooperation, and destructive and creative feelings. Based upon the above, one would expect the role of the companion animal to vary according to the function or dysfunction of the family unit.

Functional Families

Voith (note 2) has reported, in her study of 500 pet owners, that 99 percent considered the dog to be a family member. This was borne out by family behavior in that 56 percent of owners allowed the dog to sleep on the bed with a human family member, 64 percent gave the dog tidbits from the table, 86 percent shared their snacks with the dog, and 54 percent celebrated the dog's birthday. Her population was a select one, however, all being clients at a major veterinary referral center, and there is no way to know if her respondents belonged to functional or dysfunctional families.

Macdonald (1981) studied child-parent pairs in Britain and discovered that when normal children interact closely with the family dog there is attachment such that the pet may function as a "significant other" for the child. Salmon and Salmon (1983) concluded from their work in Australia that the basis of the human/pet bond seems to correspond with human/human bonds. Other findings in their study indicated that companionship was the most important benefit from pet ownership both for single people and for those in families. In the lives of those without a complete family network, for example, widowed, separated, and divorced persons, a pet was more important, more of a friend, child, protector, and comforter; to those with children, the pet seemed to be another family member, primarily a playmate or friend for their children. In fact, "the functions of friendship for different family members were independent of one another. In other words, if the dog played a friendship role for the child(ren), it appears that it did not play this role for adults within the same family, and vice versa" (p. 258). There were many variations between individual families in their results, depending greatly on the life stage of the family and whether or not there were children, families without children describing their dogs in a more positive light than those with children, who seemed more aware of the problems in dog ownership.

Smith (1983) conducted an ethological study of dogs in homes, observing interactions between dogs and family members. Some of her observations showed that interactions were essentially proportional to the degree of attachment between dogs and family members, that interactions between dogs and family members contrasted with interactions between two humans in ways reflecting the fact that a person had less flexibility and more complexity to deal with when interacting with another person, and that the presence of children reduced the interactions of adult family members with dogs.

Cain (1983) reported a number of characteristics of pet relationships in 60 families according to a theory of family systems propounded by Dr. Murray Bowen, whose concepts she utilizes. A large variety of species of pets and types of families was represented in her sample. Eighty-seven percent of respondents considered their pet a member of their family, and 36 percent thought of it as a person. Subjects gave various reasons for obtaining a pet (e.g., rescue of an abandoned animal, protection, and so on), and 66 percent of respondents listed significant happenings in the family just before or at the time they acquired their pets (e.g., geographical moves, separation or loss, and so on). Subjects reported various areas of disagreement with regard to the function of the pet in the family (e.g., argument about pet discipline, argument about responsibility for pet care, and argument over space used by pets). Eighty-one percent of respondents reported pets as being sensitive to positive and negative feelings within the family, even to the extent of displaying physical signs when the family was tense or in conflict (e.g., diarrhea, refusal to eat). Thirty-six percent said pets "acted out" feelings being displayed in the family. Cain also presents a number of specific instances reported to her by families illustrating the various ways the pet was utilized to stabilize the family system when conflict arose, for example, a few respondents reported that they would talk to a pet instead of other family members, but so those other family members could hear what they were saying. In addition, Cain elicited other information about attitudes of family members towards loss of their pets.

Dysfunctional Families

Reports in the literature on the role of the animal in the dysfunctional family fall into two basic categories. One group of reports discusses the relationships of children from disturbed families with companion animals present in the home; the other group of reports focuses on the way in which the family pet may itself be drawn into the dysfunctional family system.

Van Leeuwen (1981) states from his experience as a child psychiatrist that he has observed that family disturbances over children and companion animals fall under three headings. First, the normal formation of attachments can go awry and result in anxious attachments and compulsive care-giving, often involving pathological mourning on the death of the pet. Second, fear of a parent may be displaced onto animals resulting in phobias. Third, unresolved fear and rage may be displaced or projected onto animals and result in cruelty towards them.

On the other hand, a study involving 500 abused and nonabused

adolescent children showed that most abused children had very positive experiences with their pets (Robin, ten Bensel, Anderson, &
Quigley, 1983). These authors reported that abused children, with
their characteristically low self-regard, are more likely than non-
abused children to experience pets as their sole love-objects and to
turn to them for love and support. Also, however, pets of abused
children are more likely than those of nonabused children to experience violence or death at the hands of someone other than the abused
child, and the abused child is less likely to have someone to talk to
regarding the loss of his or her pet. The authors concluded from
their work that, ''Pets clearly play a prominent part in the lives of
abused children. That relationship is characterized by deep feelings
of love, care, and empathy. What seems to divide those youths who
are sadistic to animals from those who are not is the extreme degree
of parental abuse'' (p. 116).

Several investigators who have attempted family therapy with disturbed families in the home setting have reported ways in which
companion animals become involved in the dysfunctional family
system. Speck (1965a), for example, states that,

> Behavior of these pets has often been revealing as an extension
> or indicator of human psychopathology . . . [for example] in
> families that have pets, the pet may become ill—either in con-
> junction with another family member or members, or as a sub-
> stitute for illness in one of the human members. At such times
> of distress the pet may die. (p. 204)

Friedman (1965a) has stated that, ''Pets display behavioral reactions that are extensions of the behavioral reactions of the family
members. Pets are very sensitive to emotionally charged affective
states within the family unit'' (pp. 251–252). Other therapists working with schizophrenic families reported their observation that ''a
pet's behavior on any particular evening [of therapy] was a direct
reflection of the feeling-tone of the family group'' (Jungreis &
Speck, 1965, p. 62). These authors also described specific animal/
human interactions within a disturbed family they were treating.
Friedman (1965b) also describes a family he treated in which social
phobia was a symptom which pervaded the family to such an extent
that the companion animals became involved and were reluctant to
go outside, and Speck (1965) reports repeatedly observing that pet
animals of the schizophrenic family

show fluctuations in both behavior and health coincidental with
the fluctuations in the behavior and health of the human family
members . . . observable animal behavior seems to have a direct relationship to the behavioral trends within the family . . .
if the family is angry with the therapist, the pet is apt to be angry also. (pp. 298–299).

In addition, some therapists observed that the family or a member
of the family used the pet to express resistance to therapy, for example by using the pet to occupy time or as an excuse to leave the room
(Sonne, 1965), or by using the animal to create havoc when the individual or family was under pressure from the therapist (Friedman,
1965a). Mitchell (1965) felt that companion animals were so integral to the dysfunctional family system that he included the human/
animal relationship as one of the five subsystems of which the family therapist should be aware. Along somewhat different lines, Holland and Perlmutter (note 1) reported a case where abnormal behavior of a family dog was the presenting sign of a family dysfunction,
and Mackler (1982) has observed that families with many pets are
often isolated and have a certain degree of psychosocial dysfunction.

DISCUSSION

One finds in the literature on the Human/Companion Animal
Bond widely differing modes of argument and evidence, from accounts of single events where humans and animals were brought together and individual case reports to true experiments with defined
protocols. Though this situation is because the study of the Human/
Companion Animal Bond is a small, new, highly complex interdisciplinary field of inquiry in which the generation of hypotheses and
formulation of methods to test them has just begun; nevertheless,
this situation makes cross-comparison of studies and reports extremely difficult. The parameters vary so widely from one investigation to the other. For example, the well-designed studies of Salmon and Salmon (1983) and Cain (1983), while investigating the
same general phenomenon, the pet in the family, were done in different countries, with different sample sizes, without defined parameters for what constituted a "family," and with one study re-
searching only the dog in the family while the other considered a

large variety of animals, from spiders and snakes to livestock. This is but one example of the wide variation in the literature in this field.

The following are suggestions for research which would begin to clarify the role of the companion animal in the context of the family system. (1) Baseline studies providing additional information about the nature of the attachment between pets and individual humans of all ages, and about the effects of companion animals on human personality development. This information is vital to the understanding of the role of companion animals in the more complex system of the family. (2) Studies of companion animals in all kinds of families, e.g., single individuals, childless couples, couples with varying numbers of children, single-parent and blended families, families with resident elderly members, families with physically or mentally disabled members. (3) Studies of differences between families with specific sociological variations e.g., socioeconomic status, ethnic background, rural/suburban/urban. (4) Studies of differences in the roles of companion animals of various species and breeds, and differences between families with varying numbers of pets. (5) Longitudinal studies of the roles of companion animals as families change over time. (6) Studies of the roles of companion animals in family systems with various types of dysfunction, especially related to the possible therapeutic value of a pet in the home.

There are many other possibilities for investigation into this area. However, it is crucial that the studies be designed with adequate numbers of subjects, that the extremely high number of potential variables be carefully controlled, or at least be taken into consideration in discussion of results, and that the data be objectively evaluated.

At this stage, the literature yields tantalizing hints of relationships between families and their companion animals and hints of the importance of these relationships. However, conclusions are inconclusive, in large part because of the uniqueness of every individual human and individual animal and the complexity generated by that uniqueness as people and their pets form interactional family systems.

REFERENCE NOTES

1. Holland, J.M., & Perlmutter, M. *A case study of a dysfunctional family system with the family dog behavior abnormality as the presenting sign.* Paper presented at the Conferences on the Human-Animal Bond, Irvine, California and Minneapolis, Minnesota, June, 1983.

2. Voith, V.L. *Behaviors, attitudes and interactions of families with their dogs*. Paper presented at the Conferences on the Human-Animal Bond, Irvine, California and Minneapolis, Minnesota, June, 1983.

3. Wille, R.L. *A study of the relationship between pet companionship and health status*. Paper presented at the Conferences on the Human-Animal Bond, Irvine, California and Minneapolis, Minnesota, June, 1983.

REFERENCES

Bossard, J.H.S. The mental hygiene of owning a dog. *Mental Hygiene*, 1944, *28*: 408–413.

Bossard, J.H.S., & Boll, E.S. *The sociology of child development*. New York: Harper & Row, 1966.

Bridger, H. The changing role of pets in society. *Journal of Small Animal Practice*, 1976, *17*: 1–8.

Brown, C.T., Shaw, T.G., & Kirkland, K.D. Affection for people as a function of affection for dogs. *Psychological Reports*, 1972, *31*: 957–958.

Cain, A.O. A study of pets in the family system. In A.H. Katcher & A.M. Beck (Eds.), *New perspectives on our lives with companion animals*. Philadelphia: University of Pennsylvania Press, 1983.

Cameron, P., Conrad, C., Kirkpatrick, D.D., & Bateen, R.J. Pet ownership and sex as determinants of stated affect toward others and estimates of others and estimates of others' regard of self. *Psychological Reports*, 1966, *19*: 884–886.

Cameron, P., & Mattson, M. Psychological correlates of pet ownership. Psychological Reports, 1972, *30*: 286.

Corson, S.A., & Corson, E.O. Pet animals as nonverbal communication mediators in psychotherapy in institutional settings. In S.A. Corson & E.O. Corson (Eds.), *Ethology and nonverbal communication in in mental health*. Oxford: Pergamon Press, 1980.

Fogle, B. *Pets and their people*. London: Collins Harvill, 1983.

Franti, C.E., Kraus, J.F., & Borhani, N.O. Pet ownership in suburban-rural area of California. *Public Health Report*, 1974, *89*: 473–484.

Friedman, A.S. Implications of the home setting for family treatment. In A.S. Friedman (Ed.), *Psychotherapy for the whole family in home and clinic*. New York: Springer Publishing Co., Inc., 1965.(a)

Friedman, A.S. The "well" sibling in the "sick" family: A contradiction. In A.S. Friedman (Ed.), *Psychotherapy for the whole family in home and clinic*. New York: Springer Publishing Co., 1965.(b)

Friedmann, E., Katcher, A.H., Lynch, J.J., & Thomas, S.A. Animal companions and one-year survival of patients after discharge from a coronary care unit. *Public Health Report*, 1980, *95*: 307–312.

Friedmann, E., Katcher, A.H., Thomas, S.A., Lynch, J.J., & Messent, P.R. Social interaction and blood pressure: influence of animal companions. *Journal of Nervous and Mental Disease*, 1983, *171*: 461–465.

Harris, J. Dogs contribute to ego strength. *The Latham Letter*, 1981, *3*: 13–15.

Jungreis, J.E., & Speck, R.V. The Island Family. In A.S. Friedman (Ed.), *Psychotherapy for the whole family in home and clinic*. New York: Springer Publishing Co., Inc., 1965.

Kellert, S.R., & Westervelt, M.O. Attitudes toward animals: Age related development among children. In R.S. Anderson, B. Hart, & L. Hart (Eds.), *The pet connection*. Minneapolis: Center to Study Human-Animal Relationships and Environments, 1983.

Lago, D.L., Knight, D., & Connell, C. Relationships with companion animals among the rural elderly. In A.H. Katcher & A.M. Beck (Eds.), *New perspectives on our lives with companion animals*. Philadelphia: University of Pennsylvania Press, 1983.

Levinson, B.M. The dog as co-therapist. *Mental Hygiene*, 1961, *46*: 59–65.

Levinson, B.M. Pets: a special technique in child therapy. *Mental Hygiene*, 1964, *48*: 243–248.

Levinson, B.M. Pet psychotherapy: use of household pets in the treatment of behavior disorder in childhood. *Psychological Reports*, 1965, *27*: 695–698.

Levinson, B.M. Interpersonal relationships between pet and human being. In M.W. Fox (Ed.), *Abnormal behavior in animals.* Philadelphia: W.B. Saunders, 1968.

Levinson, B.M. *Pet-oriented child psychotherapy.* Springfield, Ill.: Charles C. Thomas, 1969.

Levinson, B.M. *Pets and human development.* Springfield, Ill.: Charles C. Thomas, 1972.

Levinson, B.M. Pets and personality development. *Psychological Reports*, 1978, *42*: 1031–1038.

Lockwood, R. The influence of animals on social perception. In A.H. Katcher & A.M. Beck (Eds.), *New perspectives on our lives with companion animals.* Philadelphia: University of Pennsylvania Press, 1983.

Lynch, J.J., Thomas, S.A., Long, J., Malinow, K., Chickadone, G., & Katcher, A.H. Human speech and blood pressure. *Journal of Nervous and Mental Disease,* 1980, *168*: 526–534.

Macdonald, A. The pet dog in the home: a study of interactions. In B. Fogle (Eds.), *Interrelations between people and pets.* Springfield, Ill.: Charles C. Thomas, 1981.

Mackler, J.L. Teaching an old dog new tricks in family therapy. *Family Therapy*, 1982, *9*: 305–310.

Messent, P.R., & Serpell, J.A. An historical and biological view of the pet-owner bond. In B. Fogle (Ed.), *Interrelations between people and pets.* Springfield, Ill.: Charles C. Thomas, 1981.

Mitchell, H.E. The continuing search for a conceptual model of family psychotherapy. In A.S. Friedman (Ed.), *Psychotherapy for the whole family in home and clinic.* New York: Springer Publishing Co., 1965.

Mugford, R.A. The social significance of pet ownership. In S.A. Corson & E.O. Corson (Eds.), *Ethology and nonverbal communication in mental health.* Oxford: Pergamon Press, 1980.

Mugford, R.A., & M'Comisky, J.G. Some recent work on the psychotherapeutic value of caged birds with old people. In R.S. Anderson (Ed.), *Pet animals and society.* London: Balliere-Tindall, 1975.

Ory, M.G., & Goldberg, E.L. Pet possession and life satisfaction in elderly women. In A.H. Katcher & A.M. Beck (Eds.), *New perspectives on our lives with companion animals.* Philadelphia: University of Pennsylvania Press, 1983.

Perin, C. Dogs as symbols in human development. In B. Fogle (Ed.), *Interrelations between people and pets.* Springfield, Ill.: Charles C. Thomas, 1981.

Petcare: Pets as a social phenomenon—a study of man-pet interactions in urban communities. Petcare Information and Advisory Service, Melbourne, 1977.

Robin, M., ten Bensel, R.W., Anderson, R.K., & Quigley, J. Abused children and their pets. In R.S. Anderson, B. Hart, & L. Hart (Eds.), *The pet connection.* Minneapolis: Center to Study Human-Animal Relationships and Environments, 1983.

Salmon, P.W., & Salmon, I.M. Who owns who? Psychological research into the human-pet bond in Australia. In A.H. Katcher & A.M. Beck (Eds.), *New perspectives on our lives with companion animals.* Philadelphia: University of Pennsylvania Press, 1983.

Savishinsky, J.S. Pet ideas: The domestications of animals, human behavior, and human emotions. In A.H. Katcher & A.M. Beck (Eds.), *New perspectives on our lives with companion animals.* Philadelphia: University of Pennsylvania Press, 1983.

Schneider, R., & Vaida, M.L. Survey of canine and feline populations: Alameda and Contra Costa Counties, California. *Journal of the American Veterinary Medical Association*, 1975, *166*: 481–486.

Smith, S.L. Interactions between pet dog and family members: an ethological study. In A.H. Katcher & A.M. Beck (Eds.) *New perspectives on our lives with companion animals.* Philadelphia: University of Pennsylvania Press, 1983.

Sonne, J.C. Resistances in family therapy of schizophrenia in the home. In A.S. Friedman (Ed.), *Psychotherapy for the whole family in home and clinic.* New York: Springer Publishing Co., Inc., 1965.

Speck, R.V. The transfer of illness phenomenon in schizophrenic families. In A.S. Friedman (Ed.), *Psychotherapy for the whole family in home and clinic.* New York: Springer Publishing Co., Inc., 1965.

Van Leeuwen, J. A child psychiatrist's perspective on children and their companion animals. In B. Fogle (Ed.), *Interrelations between people and pets.* Springfield, Ill.: Charles C. Thomas, 1981.

Voith, V.L. Animal behavior problems: an overview. In A.H. Katcher & A.M. Beck (Eds.), *New perspectives on our lives with companion animals.* Philadelphia: University of Pennsylvania Press, 1983.

Winnicott, D.W. Transitional objects and transitional phenomena. *International Journal of Psychoanalysis*, 1953, *24*: 88–97.

Pets and the Socialization of Children

Michael Robin
Robert ten Bensel

ABSTRACT. Despite the widespread ownership of pet animals in American families, there is very little analysis of the role of pets in child development. This paper will examine the influence of pet animals on child development; the impact of pet loss and bereavement on children; the problem of child cruelty to animals and its relationship to child abuse; and the role of pets in both normal and disturbed families. The authors will also review their own research study of adult prisoners and juveniles in institutions in regard to their experiences with pet animals.

INTRODUCTION

Given the large numbers of children who have had pets, it is striking how little attention has been paid to the role pets play in the emotional and developmental lives of children. In addition to the mythological, symbolic and utilitarian aspects of the animal/human relationship, recent research has focused on the developmental aspects of this relationship. While there is a literature on the role of animals in myths, fairytales, dreams and nightmares, very little has been written on companion animals and children. This paper will focus on what is known about the normal developmental interactions between animals and children and the implications of this knowledge to the everyday lives of children. In addition to a review of the literature on companion animals and children, we will also report on our surveys of juveniles and adults in correctional institutions and their experiences with pet animals (Robin, ten Bensel, Quigley and Anderson, 1983, 1984; ten Bensel, Ward, Kruttschnitt, Quigley and Anderson, 1984).

Michael Robin and Robert ten Bensel are at the University of Minnesota, School of Public Health, Program in Maternal and Child Health, Box 197, Mayo Memorial Building, 420 Delaware Street Southeast, Minneapolis, Minnesota 55455.

COMPANION ANIMALS AND CHILDREN

Companion animals are a vital part of the healthy emotional development of children. As children develop, animals play different roles for the child at each stage of development. The period of childhood encompasses a number of developmental tasks—the acquisition of basic trust and self-esteem, a sense of responsibility and competence, feelings of empathy toward others and the achievement of autonomy—that can be facilitated for the child by a companion animal. The constancy of animal companionship can help children move along the developmental continuum and may even have an inhibiting effect toward mental disturbances (Levinson, 1970).

In what ways can a pet meet the mental health needs of a child? In the first instance, a pet is an active and energetic playmate, which facilitates the release of a child's pent-up energy and tension (Feldman, 1977). In general, a child who is physically active is less likely to be tense than one who is not. The security of the companion animal may encourage exploratory behavior, particularly for fearful children in unfamiliar situations. It may also serve as a bridge or facilitator towards relationships with other children. And for those living in situations without other children, a pet may be a substitute for human companionship. As one child said, "Pets are important especially for kids without brothers and sisters. They can get close to this animal and they both can grow up to love one another" (Robin, ten Bensel, Quigley and Anderson, 1983).

Caring responsibly for a pet will help a child experience the pleasures of responsible pet ownership. Levinson (1972) suggests that responsibility for pet care should be introduced gradually and that parents should recognize there will be periods when even for a conscientious child the care of a pet will be too much. Adolescents living in normal family environments more often shared the responsibility of pet care with other family members which became a source of mutual enjoyment (Robin, ten Bensel, Quigley and Anderson, 1983). The successful care of a valued pet will promote a sense of importance and being needed. By observing the pet's biological functions, children will learn about sexuality and elimination (Levinson, 1972; Schowalter, 1983).

In laboratory experiments, it was found that people of all ages, including children, use animals to feel safe and create a sense of intimacy. As Beck and Katcher (1983) have noted, pairing an animal with a strange human being apparently acts to make that person, or the situation surrounding that person, less threatening. For example, in an experiment where children were brought into a room with an interviewer alone or with with an interviewer with a dog, the children were found to be more relaxed as measured by blood pressure rates when entering a room with the interviewer and an animal (Beck and Katcher, 1983). In another study in England, Messant (1983) found people in public parks were considered more approachable for conversation when accompanied by a pet. In general, the presence of companion animals seems to have a relaxing and calming effect on people. When people talk to other people there is a tendency for blood pressure to rise; however, when people talk to or observe animals there is a tendency for blood pressure to lower.

Pets as Transitional Objects

It is widely accepted that the key factor in the relationship between children and companion animals is the unconditional love and acceptance of the animal for the child, who accepts the child "as is" and does not offer feedback or criticism (Levinson, 1969, 1972; Beck and Katcher, 1983). As Siegel (1962) has written, "The animal does not judge but offers a feeling of intense loyalty. . . . It is not frightening or demanding, nor does it expose its master to the ugly strain of constant criticism. It provides its owner with the chance to feel important." The simple, uncomplicated affection of an animal for his master was also noted by Freud in a letter to Marie Boneparte, "It really explains why we can love an animal like Topsy (or Jo-Fi) with such an extraordinary intensity: affection without ambivalence . . . that feelings of an intimate affinity, of an undisputed solidary. Often when stroking Jo-Fi, I have caught myself humming a melody which, unmusical as I am, I can't help recognizing as the aria from Don Giovanni: A bond of friendship units us both" (Freud, 1976).

Pets as Parents

Beck and Katcher (1983) have suggested that as children get older, the pet acquires many of the characteristics of the ideal mother. The pet is unconditional, devoted, attentive, loyal and non-verbal—all elements of the primary symbiotic relationship with the mother. From a developmental point of view, a major task of childhood is the movement away from the primary symbiotic relationship with the mother and the establishment of a separate and distinct identity (Erickson, 1980). This process of separation and individuation creates feelings of "separation anxiety" that occur throughout the life process, particularly at stressful times of loss or during new experiences (Perin, 1983). "One could regard the entire life cycle as constituting a more or less successful process of distancing from and introjection of the lost symbiotic mother, an eternal longing for the actual or fantasied ideal state of self" (Mahler, 1972).

Pets function, particularly for adolescents, as transitional objects, much like the blanket or teddy bear does for infants. As transitional objects, pets help children feel safe without the presence of parents. Pets are more socially acceptable as transitional objects for older children than are inanimate objects. Adolescence brings with it a changing relationship to pets, in large part due to this emergence of pets as transitional objects. At this period pets can be a confidant, an object of love, a protector, a social facilitator or a status symbol (Fogle, 1983). Moreover, the bond between children and pets is enhanced by its animate quality. The crucial attachment behaviors of proximity and caring between children and pets forms an alive reciprocating alliance (Bowlby, 1969). The relationship is simpler and less conflicted than are human relationships.

Like other transitional objects, most of the shared behaviors between animals and children are tactile and/or kinetic rather than verbal. Levinson (1969) has stated that pets may satisfy the child's need for physical contact and touch without the fear of entanglements that accompany contact with human beings. Children have a great need for empathetic listening and association with others. It is the non-interventiveness and empathy that makes animals such good companions. Pets are often perceived by children as attentive and empathetic listeners. As one child wrote, "My dog is very special to me. We have had it for seven years now. When I was little I used to go to her and pet her when I was depressed and crying. She seemed to understand. You could tell by the look in her eyes" (Robin, ten Bensel, Quigley and Anderson, 1983).

Pets as Children

Along with the parental role, pets simultaneously or alternately function as children for the pet owner (Beck and Katcher, 1983). This idea was expressed by the prophet Nathan during antiquity (2

Sam. 12:3): "The poor man had nothing save one little ewe lamb, which he bought and nourished up; and it grew up together with him, and with his children; it did eat of his own morsel, and drank of his own cup, and lay in his bosom, and was to him as a daughter." Midgley (1984) notes in her discussion of this passage that the lamb was not a substitute for the poor man's children as he had children. His love for the lamb was nonetheless the kind of love suited to a child. The lamb was a live creature needing love, and was able to respond to parental cherishing. The helplessness of the animal drew out from the man nurturing and humane caring.

Fogle (1983) notes that studies in New York State show that pets can elicit maternal behaviors in children as young as three years old. In fact, according to Beck and Katcher (1983), much of the usual activity of children and pet animals resembles a parent/child relationship with the animal representing the child as an infant. Children unconsciously view their pets as an extension of themselves and treat their pets as they want to be treated themselves. This process is what Desmond Morris has called "infantile parentalism," suggesting this is one way children cope with the loss of their childhood (Morris, 1967). Schowalter (1983), for example, discussed the case of a five-year-old insecure boy referred for psychiatric care due to his habit of petting his goldfish. For this boy, petting the fish helped him feel both caring and cared for. Gradually he was able to transfer his affection toward a dog. With increased parental nurturance, he became more confident and outgoing.

Sherick (1981) also presented a case of a nine-year-old girl whose pets became symbolic substitutes for her ideal self. The sick pets that she cared for and nursed back to health represented the cared-for, protected and loved child that she longed to be. The girl's mother was a vain woman concerned with appearances who turned most of her maternal instincts toward the family pet rather than her daughter. The girl's behavior toward her pet was an unconscious effort to model "good enough" mothering to her mother. Searles (1960) points out that many children grow up with parents unable to nurture them, because of their own disturbance, but who can show affection to an animal. The child then grows up thinking if only he or she were an animal then they might receive parental love. Kupferman (1977) presented a case of a seven-year-old boy whose ego development was so faulty that he took on the identity of a cat and meowed to his psychiatrist.

Pets and Families

The role of a pet in a family will be dependent upon the family's structure, its emotional undercurrents, the emotional and physical strengths and weaknesses of each of its members, and the family's social climate (Levinson, 1969). When a pet is acquired by a family a variety of changes frequently occurs in family relationships and dynamics. Cain (1983) found in her study of pets in family systems that families reported both positive and negative changes after acquiring a pet. Some families reported increased closeness expressed around the care of a pet, more time spent together playing with a pet, more happiness of family members, and less arguing. However, other families reported more arguing and problems over the rules and care of the pet and less time spent with other family members; for example, children spent less time with their parents and husbands spent less time with their wives (Cain, 1983).

Pets become, according to the theory of Murray Bowen, part of the "undifferentiated ego mass" of the family and form part of the emotional structure of that family (Bowen, 1965). Many people indeed consider their pet as a member of the family. In Cain's survey of 60 families, 87 percent considered their pet as a member of the family (Cain, 1983). Ruby has also noted that most families include their pets in their family photographs (Ruby, 1983). Family members not only interact with their pets in their own characteristic manner, but they also interact with each other in relationship to the pet. In some families, pets become the major focus of attention and assume a position even more important than human family members (Levinson, 1969).

As Levinson has cautioned, pets may be involved in family pathology (Levinson, 1969). For example, one young woman committed suicide after being ordered by her parents to kill her pet dog for punishment for spending the night with a man. The woman used the same gun on herself that she used to kill her dog (Levinson, 1969). In another case, Rynearson (1978) discussed a severely disturbed adult woman who as a child had a profound fear of her parents and siblings. She turned to her cat as a confidant with whom she shared her troubles. One day her younger sister was scratched by the cat and the woman watched her enraged mother kill the cat with a shovel and then her mother turned to her and said, "Never forget that you are the one who really killed her, because you weren't watching her closely—it's all your fault."

Children can involve their animals psychodynamically in their use of such defense mechanisms as displacement, projection, splitting and identification (Schowalter, 1983). There are times when a child living in a disturbed family will become overly attached to a pet to the detriment of human relationships. Such children have a basic distrust of people which becomes overgeneralized. This basic distrust of human attachments contributes to the intense displacement of attachment to a pet who is consistently receptive as a source of love and caring. In anxiously attaching to the animal, a child can gratify part of the self without risking interpersonal involvement. Disturbed children with limited ego strength will turn to their pets for warmth and caring to meet their regressed, insatiable need for closeness and love (Rynearson, 1978; Levinson, 1972).

In a study of 269 disturbed children institutionalized for delinquency problems, 47 percent said pets were important for children growing up because they provided someone for them to love. For the control group of students in regular public schools, a pet was important to them because it taught responsibility. For many abused and disturbed children, a pet becomes their sole love object and a substitute for family love. As one boy said of his pet, "My kitty was the joy of my life. It never hurt me or made me upset like my parents. She always came to me when she wanted affection." Another boy wrote, "My favorite pet was my dog Bell. I loved her very much. I took care of her all the time and never mistreated her. Sometimes she was the only person I could talk to." Overall, abused and disturbed children in this study were more likely to talk to their pets about their problems. Pets became their sole source of solace at times of stress, loneliness or boredom (Robin, ten Bensel, Quigley and Anderson, 1983).

PET LOSS

For many children, the loss or death of a companion animal is the first experience with death and bereavement. In fact, it is often stated that one of the most important aspects of pet ownership for children is that it provides the child with experiences of dealing with the reality of illness and death which will prepare them for these experiences later in life (Fox, 1983). By fully experiencing the grief of losing a pet, the child learns that death is a natural part of the life process, is painful, but is tolerable and does not last forever. A child can learn that death is permanent and that dead animals will not come back to haunt them. The children can also be taught that guilt feelings following the death of a loved object are common and can be overcome (Levinson, 1972).

There is a tendency, however, to minimize a child's grief over a lost pet. In the vast literature on children and bereavement there are few references to bereavement from pet loss (Nieburg, 1982). The death of a pet has been considered an "emotional dress rehearsal" and preparation for greater losses yet to come (Levinson, 1967). However, there are strong indicators that the loss of a pet is more than a "rehearsal," and it is a profound experience in itself for many children.

In a study of 507 adolescents in Minnesota, over one-half had lost their "special pet" and only two youths reported feeling indifferent to the loss (Robin, ten Bensel, Quigley and Anderson, 1983). Most of the youths whose pets had died had deep feelings of regret and sadness such as those who wrote, "My sorrows are very deep for my special pet, but I know she is in some place where she is treated very well. And I know she is thinking of me because I always think of her." And, "I was sad that he had to be put to sleep but I was glad that he didn't die painfully."

Stewart (1983) also surveyed 135 schoolchildren in central Scotland on their experiences and feelings toward pet loss. She asked the children to write about their pets and how they felt if their pet had died. She found that 44 percent had pets that died and two-thirds of these children expressed profound grief at their loss, such as the child who said, "I didn't believe it, I didn't know where I was." In most cases, the children got over the loss, usually with parental support. But in all the bereavements that seemed unresolved the parents were unwilling to have another animal.

How a child reacts to the loss of a pet depends largely on his or her age and emotional development, the length of time the child had the pet, the quality of the relationship, the circumstances surrounding the loss of the pet, and the quality of support available to the child. Pre-school children are less likely to become deeply attached to their pets, and are less likely to view the pet loss as irrevocable. According to Nieburg and Fischer (1982), children under five years usually experience the pet loss as a temporary absence, and from five years to nine years or so, pet loss is not seen as inevitable and is believed possible to avoid. Stewart (1983) found that school-aged children often expressed profound grief for a short time, and then seemed to quickly adapt to normal, especially if a new animal was introduced. Most young children miss their deceased animals, but more as a playmate than as an object that satisfies basic emotional needs.

It is usually adolescents who have the most profound experiences with pet loss. From early adolescence on, children begin to develop an adult perception that death is final, permament and inevitable (Nieburg and Fischer, 1982). Adolescents tend to take longer to get over their grief, in part because their relationships with pets tends to be more intense at this age (Stewart, 1983; Nieburg and Fisher, 1982). How a young adolescent will react to pet loss will depend on the circumstances surrounding the death of a pet. A pet may be lost in a variety of ways such as old age or illness, being run over, theft, given away or traumatic death. Unfortunately, there are very few empirically based epidemiological studies on the nature of pet loss. In Minnesota it was found that abused and disturbed youths suffered more pet loss, had their pets for shorter times, and were most likely to have had their pet killed accidentally or purposely more than any other factor (Robin, ten Bensel, Quigley and Anderson, 1983, 1984). Most of those children whose pets were traumatically killed were saddened by the loss of their pet, and, in a few cases, were angry and revengeful toward the person who killed their pet. For example, one child wrote, "He was 11 years old and my mother had my little brother and Duke started being grouchy and nipping at people. So my brother-in-law shot him. It really hurt bad, like one of my brothers died. It was really hard to accept" (Robin, ten Bensel, Quigley and Anderson, 1983). Another child wrote, "My sister was taking it for a walk and this man drove over it, then backed over it and then drove over it again. I was hurt very bad. I hated that man. I cried for two days straight" (Robin, ten Bensel, Quigley and Anderson, 1983). Not only did abused and disturbed youths experience more traumatic pet loss than did the controls, they were also less likely to have someone to talk to about their grief. Only 56 percent of those youths whose pets died traumatic deaths had someone to talk to about their grief, as compared to 79 percent of the control group who had support after traumatic pet loss.

Most mental health practitioners indicate that the forms of bereavement from pet loss are similar to those of human loss (Levinson, 1967). Some children might be surprised and embarrassed by the intensity of their grief and feel the need to conceal their grief from the outside world. Parents should be sensitive to the child's

grief and not minimize or ridicule its impact. Some young children
tend to view the death of a pet as punishment from their misdeeds. If
so, children should be assured that they were not to blame for their
pet's death. Given that our society has no public rituals for the death
of pets, families may enact funerals to acknowledge the importance
of the pet to the family (Levinson, 1967; Nieburg and Fischer,
1982). Children should also be offered a replacement pet; however,
there is disagreement if the replacement should be deferred for a
time (Levinson, 1981; Nieburg and Fischer, 1982) or take place immediately (Stewart, 1983).

CHILDHOOD CRUELTY TO ANIMALS

Interest in childhood cruelty to animals grew out of the notion that
cruelty to animals has a disabling effect on human character and
leads to cruelty among people (ten Bensel, 1984). This idea was ar-
ticulated by Saint Thomas Aquinas (1225–1274) who said: "Holy
scriptures seem to forbid us to be cruel to brute animals . . . that is
either . . . through being cruel to animals one becomes cruel to human beings or because injury to an animal leads to the temporal hurt
of man" (Thomas, 1983). Likewise the philosopher Montaigne
(1533–1592) wrote that "men of bloodthirsty nature where animals
are concerned display a natural propensity toward cruelty" (Montaigne, 1953).

Until the seventeenth and eighteenth centuries, there was relatively little awareness that animals suffered and needed protection because of this suffering. This new sensibility was linked to the growth
of towns and industry which left animals increasingly marginal to
the production process. Gradually society allowed animals to enter
the house as pets, which created the foundation for the view that
some animals at least were worthy of moral consideration (Thomas,
1983). The English artist, William Hogarth (1697–1764) was the
first artist to both condemn animal cruelty and theorize on its human
consequences. His *Four Stages of Cruelty* (1751) was produced as a
means of focusing attention on the high incidence of crime and violence in his day. The four drawings trace the evolution of cruelty to
animals as a child, to the beating of a disabled horse as a young man,
to the killing of a woman, and finally to the death of the protagonist
himself. As Hogarth declared in 1738, "I am a professional enemy
to persecution of all kinds, whether against man or beast" (Lindsay,
1979).

The link between animal abuse and human violence has been made more recently by Margaret Mead (1964) when she suggested that childhood cruelty to animals may be a precursor to anti-social violence as an adult. Hellman and Blackman (1966) postulated that childhood cruelty to animals, when combined with enuresis and fire-setting, were indeed effective predictors of later violent and criminal behaviors in adulthood. They found that of 31 prisoners charged with aggressive crimes against people, three-fourths (N = 23) had a history of all or part of the triad. The authors argued that the aggressive behaviors of their subjects were a hostile reaction to parental abuse or neglect. Tapia (1971) found additional links between animal abuse, child abuse, and anti-social behavior. Of 18 young boys who were identified with histories of cruelty to animals, one-third had also set fires, and parental abuse was the most common etiological factor. Felthous (1980), in another study, found that Hellman and Blackman's behavioral triad did have predictive value for later criminal behavior. He found extreme physical brutality from parents common, but he felt that parental deprivation rather than parental aggressiveness may be more specifically related to animal cruelty.

Kellert and Felthous (1983) also found in their study of 152 criminals and non-criminals in Kansas and Connecticut an inordinately high frequency of childhood animal cruelties among the most violent criminals. They reported that 25 percent of the most aggressive criminals had five or more specific incidents of cruelty to animals, compared to less than six percent of moderate and non-aggressive criminals, and no occurrence among non-criminals. Moreover, the family backgrounds of the aggressive criminals were especially violent. Three-fourths of all aggressive criminals reported excessive and repeated abuse as children, compared to only 31 percent for non-aggressive criminals and 10 percent among non-criminals. Interestingly, 75 percent of non-criminals who experienced parental abuse also reported incidents of animal cruelty.

These studies identified extreme parental cruelty as the most common background element among those who abuse animals. As Erich Fromm has noted in his study, *The Anatomy of Human Destructiveness* (1973), persons who are sadistic tend themselves to be victims of terroristic punishment. By this is meant punishment that is not limited in intensity, is not related to any specific misbehavior, is arbitrary and is fed by the punisher's own sadism. Thus, the sadistic animal abuser was, himself, a victim of extreme physical abuse.

While most children are usually sensitive to the misuse of pets, for some abused or disturbed children, pets represent someone they can gain some power and control over. As Schowalter (1983) has said, "No matter how put upon or demeaned one feels, it is still often possible to kick the dog." Cruelty to animals thus represents a displacement of aggression from humans to animals. Rollo May (1972) suggests that when a child is not loved adequately by a mother or father, there develops a "penchant for revenge on the world, a need to destroy the world for others inasmuch as it was not good for him." Severely abused children, lacking in the ability to empathize with the sufferings of animals, take out their frustrations and hostility on animals with little sense of remorse. Their abuse of animals is an effort to compensate for feelings of powerlessness and inferiority.

A weakness of the previous studies of childhood cruelty to animals is that they did not consider the patterns of pet ownership among their subjects. These studies did not distinguish if the abused animal was the child's own animal or if the child had ever had a companion animal and what the nature of that relationship might have been. Other than a passing comment by Brittain (1970) in his study of the sadistic murderer, little mention has been made of the child and his relationship to animals prior to the incident of cruelty. Brittain wrote, "There is sometimes a history of extreme cruelty to animals. Paradoxically they can also be very fond of animals. Such cruelty is particularly significant when it relates to cats, dogs, birds and farm animals, though it can also be directed toward lower forms of animal life, and the only animal which seems to be safe is the one belonging to the sadist himself." It is with these ideas in mind that we studied adult prison populations along with abused adolescents institutionalized for delinquency and emotional disturbances to determine their patterns of pet ownership and their feelings toward their pets.

In our study of 81 violent offenders imprisoned in Minnesota, 86 percent had had a pet sometime in their life that they considered special to them. Overall, 95 percent of the respondents valued pets for companionship, love, affection, protection and pleasure. Violent offenders were more likely to have a dog in their home while growing up. The control group had more animals as pets other than dogs or cats, but the offender group had more "atypical" pets such as a baby tiger, cougar, and wolf pup. When we asked what has happened to the special pet, over 60 percent of both groups lost their pets through death or theft; however, there were more pets that died of gunshots in the inmate group. In addition, the offender group tended to be more angry at the death of the pet. Strikingly, among the violent offenders, 80 percent wanted a dog or cat *now* as compared to 39 percent of the control group. This suggests something about the deprivation of the prison environment as well as the possibility of therapeutic intervention with pets among prison populations. Like the Kellert and Felthous study (1983), this study also found that most violent offenders had histories of extreme abuse as children (ten Bensel, Ward, Kruttschnitt, Quigley and Anderson, 1984).

We also surveyed 206 teenagers between the ages of 13 and 18 living in two separate juvenile institutions and 32 youth living in an adolescent psychiatric ward in regard to their experiences with pets. We compared them to a control group of 269 youths from two urban public high schools. Of the 238 abused institutionalized youths we surveyed, 91 percent (N = 218) said that they had had a special pet and of these youths 99 percent said they either loved or liked their pet very much. Among our comparison group 90 percent (N = 242) had had a special pet and 97 percent said they either loved or liked their pet very much. This suggests that companion animals do indeed have a prominent place in the emotional lives of abused as well as non-abused children. It is also a corrective to those who suggest that pet ownership in itself will prevent emotional or behavioral disturbances in children. Merely having a special pet played no part in whether or not a child was eventually institutionalized (Robin, ten Bensel, Quigley and Anderson, 1983, 1984).

In considering the issue of abuse of animals, the authors found that the pets of the institutionalized group suffered more abuse; however, the abuser was usually someone other than the child. In a few instances, youths had to intervene against their parents to protect their pets. As one youth wrote, 'He jumped on the bed and my mom beat him and I started yelling at her because she was hurting my dog.'' Another child wrote, ''My dad and sister would hit and kick my cat sometimes because he would get mad when they teased him. I got mad and told them not to hurt him because he's helpless'' (Robin, ten Bensel, Quigley and Anderson, 1983, 1984).

Of those youths who indicated that they mistreated their pets, sadness and remorse were the most common responses. For example, one child said, ''I remember once I was punished for letting the dog out and so I hit him for that. I felt real bad after that and comforted it a lot." All of those who mistreated their pets, except for one youth, indicated that they loved or liked their pets very much and felt bad about hurting their pets. Only one youth said he did not care that he hurt his pet. There was no self-reported evidence of sadism toward pets.

There were several instances of pets being harmed or killed as punishment to a child. According to Summit (1983), threatening to harm a child's pet is a common technique of child abusers to keep the child quiet about the abuse. In a recent child sexual abuse case discovered in a Los Angeles day care center, the adults involved allegedly silenced the children by butchering small animals in front of the children and threatening to do the same to their parents if they revealed the abuse. Mental health practitioners should routinely ask young people if anyone has ever hurt or threatened to hurt their animal.

Lenore Walker (1983) has suggested in her study on domestic violence that the best predictor of future violence was a history of past violent behavior. In her definition she included witnessing violent acts toward pets in the childhood home. At this point, without further studies, it is unclear what role, if any, violence toward pets plays in the emotional and behavioral disturbances of adolescents. Nonetheless, the abused institutionalized population experienced more violent pet loss than did the comparison group. They showed no evidence of callousness toward the sufferings of their pets and seemed to be troubled by the mistreatment of their pets.

CONCLUSION

Pets clearly play an important role in the lives of children. The relationship is characterized by deep feelings of love and care. It is enhanced by children's empathy toward the feelings of animals and their intuitive sense of having a common status with animals. As Freud (1953) wrote, "Children show no trace of arrogance which urges adult civilized men to draw a hard-and-fast line between their own nature and that of all other animals. Children have no scruples over allowing animals to rank as their full equals. Uninhibited as they are in the avowal of their bodily needs, they no doubt feel themselves more akin to animals than to their elders, who may well be a puzzle to them."

REFERENCES

Anderson, R.K., Hart, B., and Hart, L. The pet connection: Its influence on our health and quality of life. Minneapolis: CENSHARE, 1984.

Beck, A., and Katcher, A.H. Between pets and people: The importance of animal companionship. New York: G.P. Putnam's Sons, 1983.

Bowen, M. Family psychotherapy with a schizophrenic in the hospital and in private practice. In I. Borzormenyi-Nagy and J.L. Framo (Eds.), *Intensive family therapy.* New York: Harper and Row, 1965.

Bowlby, J. Attachment and loss. In *Attachment*, Vol. I. London: Hogarth Press, 1969.

Brittain, R.P. The sadistic murderer. In *Medicine, Science and the Law*, 1970, 10:198–207.

Cain, A. A study of pets in the family system. In A. Katcher and A. Beck (Eds.), *New perspectives on our lives with companion animals.* Philadelphia: University of Pennsylvania Press, 1983.

Erickson, E. *Identity and the life cycle.* New York: W.W. Norton, 1980.

Feldmann, B.M. Why people own pets. In *Animal Regulation Studies*, 1977, 1:87–94.

Felthous, A. Aggression against cats, dogs and people. In *Child Psychiatry and Human Development*, 1980, 10:169–177.

Fogle, B. (Ed.) *Interrelations between people and pets.* Springfield, Illinois: Charles C. Thomas, 1981.

Fogle, B. *Pets and their people.* New York: The Viking Press, 1983.

Fox, M. Relationships between the human and non-human animals. In B. Fogle (Ed.), *Interrelationships between people and pets.* Springfield, Illinois: Charles C. Thomas, 1981.

Freud, S. Letter to M. Boneparte. In I. Simitis-Grubrich (Ed.), *Sigmund Freud.* New York: Harcourt Brace Jovanovich, 1976.

Freud, S. *Totem and taboo.* Standard edition. London: Hogarth Press and the Institute of Psychoanalysts, 1953, 1–161.

Fromm, E. *The anatomy of human destructiveness.* New York: Holt, Rinehart and Winston, 1973.

Hellman, D., and Blackman, N. Enuresis, firesetting and cruelty to animals: A triad predictive of adult crime. In *American Journal of Psychiatry*, 1966, 122:1431–1435.

Katcher, A.H. Interactions between people and their pets: Form and function. In B. Fogle (Ed.), *Interrelations between people and pets.* Springfield, Illinois: Charles C. Thomas, 1981.

Katcher, A.H., and Beck, A. (Eds.) *New perspectives on our lives with companion animals.* Philadelphia: University of Pennsylvania Press, 1983.

Kellert, S., and Felthous, A. Childhood cruelty toward animals among criminals and non-criminals. Manuscript submitted for publication, 1983.

Kupferman, K. A latency boy's identity as a cat. In *Psychoanalytic Study of the Child*, 1977, 32:193–215.

Levinson, B. *Pet-oriented child psychotherapy.* Springfield, Illinois: Charles C. Thomas, 1969.

Levinson, B. The pet and the child's bereavement. In *Mental Hygiene,* 1967, 51:197–200.

Levinson, B. Pets, child development, and mental illness. In *Journal of the American Veterinary Medical Association*, 1970, 157:1759–1766.

Levinson, B. *Pets and human development.* Springfield, Illinois: Charles C. Thomas, 1972.

Levinson, B. Pets and personality development. In *Psychological Reports*, 1978, 42:1031–1038.

Lindsay, J. *Hogarth: His art and his world.* New York: Taplinger Publishing Co., 1979.

Mahler, M.S. On the first three subphases of the separation-individuation process. In *International Journal of Psycho-Analysis*, 1972, 53:333–338.

May, R. *Power and innocence.* New York: W.W. Norton and Co., 1972.

Mead, M. Cultural factors in the cause of pathological homicide. In *Bulletin of Menninger Clinic,* 1964, 28:11–22.

Midgley, M. *Animals and why they matter.* Athens: University of Georgia Press, 1984.

Montaigne, M. de. *The essays of Montaigne.* New York: Oxford University Press, 1953.

Morris, D. *The naked ape.* New York: McGraw-Hill, 1967.

Nieburg, H.A., and Fischer, A. *Pet loss: A thoughtful guide for adults and children.* New York: Harper and Row, 1982.

Perin, C. Dogs as symbols in human development. In B. Fogle (Ed.), *Interrelations between people and pets.* Springfield, Illinois: Charles C. Thomas, 1981.

Robin, M., ten Bensel, R.W., Quigley, J., and Anderson, R.K. Childhood pets and the psychosocial development of adolescents. In A. Katcher and A. Beck (Eds.), *New perspectives on our lives with companion animals.* Philadelphia: University of Pennsylvania Press, 1983.

Robin, M., ten Bensel, R.W., Quigley, J., and Anderson, R.K. Abused children and their pet animals. In R.K. Anderson, B. Hart, and L. Hart (Eds.), *The pet connection: Its influence on our health and the quality of life.* Minneapolis: CENSHARE, 1984.

Ruby, J. Images of the family: The symbolic implications of animal photography. In A. Katcher and A. Beck (Eds.), *New perspectives on our lives with companion animals.* Philadelphia: University of Pennsylvania Press, 1983.

Rynearson, E.K. Humans and pets and attachment. In *British Journal of Psychiatry,* 1978, 133:550–555.

Schowalter, J.E. The use and abuse of pets. In *Journal of the American Academy Child Psychiatry,* 1983, 22:68–72.

Searles, H.F. *The nonhuman environment.* New York: International University Press, 1960.

Sherick, I. The significance of pets for children. In *Psychoanalytic Study of the Child,* 1981, 36:193–215.

Siegel, A. Reaching severely withdrawn through pet therapy. In *American Journal of Psychiatry,* 1962, 118:1045–1046.

Stewart, M. Loss of a pet—loss of a person: A comparative study of bereavement. In A. Katcher and A. Beck (Eds.), *New perspectives on our lives with companion animals.* Philadelphia: University of Pennsylvania Press, 1983.

Summit, R. The child sexual abuse accommodation syndrome. In *Child Abuse and Neglect,* 1983, 7:181.

Tapia, F. Children who are cruel to animals. In *Child Psychiatry and Human Development,* 1971, 2:70–77.

ten Bensel, R.W. Historical perspectives on human values for animals and vulnerable people. In R.K. Anderson, B. Hart, and L. Hart (Eds.), *The pet connection: Its influence on our health and quality of life.* Minneapolis: CENSHARE, 1984.

ten Bensel, R.W., Ward, D.A., Kruttschnitt, C., Quigley, J., and Anderson, R.K. Attitudes of Violent criminals towards animals. In R.K. Anderson, B. Hart, and L. Hart (Eds.), *The pet connection: Its influence on our health and quality of life.* Minneapolis: CENSHARE, 1984.

Thomas, K. *Man and the natural world.* New York: Pantheon Books, 1983.

Walker, L. The battered women syndrome story. In D. Finkelhor (Ed.), *The dark side of families.* Beverly Hills: Sage Productions, 1983.

The Preadolescent/Pet Bond
and Psychosocial Development

Janet Haggerty Davis
Anne McCreary Juhasz

ABSTRACT. Human/animal bond research has revealed that a pet's roles in a human being's life are influenced by individual perception of the pet's attributes. By extrapolating from this conclusion, the companion animal's role in the preadolescent's psychosocial development is delineated. A pet is classified as a developmental resource during preadolescence since it is perceived as a responsibility and a friend. Perception of a pet is influenced by the demands of development and thus should change over time. A static relationship indicates cause for concern.

In our society, the child and his or her pet form a natural partnership. Youngsters and animals are often associated in children's books, in popular literature, and in the media (Bossard & Boll, 1966). However, the psychosocial relationship between the young and pets is not a widely researched topic (MacDonald, 1979). Thus, there is a need to explore the role of companion animals for children of different ages.

The purposes of this paper are to identify the companion animal's ascribed roles as represented by research from the field of the human/animal bond; to delineate those roles within the context of the preadolescent's developmental status; and to propose a conceptual structure within which the preadolescent's relationship with a companion animal can be examined. It is suggested that a pet owner can use his or her pet to meet certain psychosocial needs which arise during the preadolescent developmental period. This phenomenon occurs when the young pet owner perceives the companion animal as a viable resource for meeting the demands of continuing growth.

Jane Haggerty Davis is Assistant Professor, Public Health Nursing, University of Illinois, Health Sciences Center, Chicago. Anne McCreary Juhasz is Professor, Department of Foundations in Education, Loyola University of Chicago.

The significance of exploring the preadolescent-pet relationship is highlighted by statistics on pet ownership. In the United States more than half of the childrearing households own a pet (Purvis & Otto, 1976). In England, 51% of the pet-owning families also have children (Pedigree Petfoods, 1980). These figures attest to the popularity of companion animals in Western cultures. However, research on the human/animal bond is a relatively recent development.

RESEARCH ON THE HUMAN/ANIMAL BOND

Research on the human/animal bond addresses two major components of the relationship between human beings and companion animals; the therapeutic role of pets, and the implications of pet ownership for impaired and well populations. A spectrum of investigative approaches is evident in the literature. These approaches include case studies, surveys, quasi-experimental and experimental designs. Most of the research focuses on attitudes and behavioral responses toward pet animals although a few studies have included physiological measures. Adults, adolescents, preadolescents, and children are represented in the samples studied.

Adults and Companion Animals

Adults have been studied in relation to pets most often in therapeutic settings. A number of studies have identified significant mental health improvements in institutionalized adults and the aged associated with animal-facilitated therapy (Brickel, 1979; Corson & Corson, 1980; Corson, Corson, Gwynne, & Arnold, 1977; Doyle, 1975; Fields, 1977; Francis, Turner, & Johnson, 1983; Lee, 1979; Robb, Boyd, & Pritash, 1980). The results of this research suggest that a pet can be a useful therapeutic agent for socially isolated, ill, and disabled adults. The conclusions drawn from the findings are that companion animals provide impaired individuals with a channel for communication with other human beings; they also elicit a sense of control from and improve the self-esteem of dependent persons.

The nonsignificant results of Robb's (1982) animal-facilitated therapy program demonstrate that some patients may not respond to this type of therapy. The sample in this study consisted of relatively stable (physically and psychosocially) male patients who were involved in a variety of other recreational and therapeutic activities.

The animal-facilitated therapy employed was evaluated as an inconsequential experience for the subjects. Based on these findings it might be concluded that animal-facilitated therapy is an effective therapeutic approach only for more severely impaired and isolated groups.

This conclusion is challenged by the findings of Thompson, Kennedy and Igou (1983) which revealed that only their moderately impaired subjects had significant changes on a posttest score of psychosocial functioning after participating in animal-facilitated therapy. The very impaired subjects in their study demonstrated no significant changes. These findings suggest that animal-facilitated therapy is more appropriate for relatively stable patients.

The conflicting implications gleaned from research on animal-facilitated therapy call attention to the fact that the therapeutic effects of pets apparently are related to individual patient characteristics such as clinical diagnosis. A more accurate picture of the value of animal-facilitated therapy may emerge with a deeper emphasis on personal characteristics which would include history of pet ownership. An additional consideration related to the effects of animal-facilitated therapy is that such programs are an addition to the patient's therapeutic regieme. Animal-patient intervention has been used in conjunction with other therapist-patient interventions, it has not replaced them. The animal is generally used as a stimulus for therapeutic change in patients by serving as an animate object of interest and by providing tactile comfort. Research in the field has not controlled for the interactive effects of several therapeutic procedures being simultaneously implemented but has acknowledged that animal-facilitated therapy is a supportive, not an autonomous program.

One study has identified the role of the family pet for non-institutionalized, impaired adults. Middle-aged patients with medical diagnoses of a chronic disease and a depressive reaction were surveyed by McCulloch (1981) in relation to the value of pet ownership for such persons. Of the 31 subjects, 20 reported that their pet helped their morale and 26 identified their pet as an important source of companionship during illness. Encouraging a sense of humor was the most valued attribute of the pet. Overall, the pet served as a social support.

Less well researched than the therapeutic role of pets is the significance of pet ownership for the well adult population. Studies in this area have produced mixed results with the pet itself having little significant impact on its owner's life (Lago, Knight, & Connell, 1983; Ory & Goldberg, 1983). The strength of human relationships apparently affects the owner-pet relationship. However, most pet owners do consider their pet to be an important member of the family (Cain, 1978; Willie, 1982).

In stark contrast to the pet having a small role in an owner's quality of life are the findings of Mugford and M'Comisky (1975). They conducted a field experiment in an urban community in England which tested the effects of pet birds on the social attitude of the elderly. Thirty subjects between the ages of 75 and 81 who lived alone and did not own pets prior to the study were interviewed for attitude toward others and self-concept. Subjects in the experimental groups received either a begonia or a small bird while the control group received only the interviewer's attention. The subjects were again interviewed 5 months later and only the bird owners demonstrated significant improvement in attitude toward others and self-concept. The begonia owners and the control group had no significant improvement in their measures. The owners became very attached to their pets and the bird was a popular topic of social conversation for the elderly subjects. The investigators suggest that pets can be positive influences on the aged because ownership activities facilitate socialization.

The cardiovascular effects of contact with pets have been documented in both physically sick and well populations. Friedmann, Katcher, Lynch and Thomas (1980) found that pet ownership was a significant factor in cardiac disease survival. Over a 2-year period 96 patients with a diagnosis of cardiac disease (angina pectoris or myocardia infarction) were interviewed as part of a social survey which included social contacts, living situation, psychological mood status, and pet ownership. One year later it was found that 28% of the sample without pets had died as compared to only 3% of the pet owners. Pet ownership accounted for a significant amount of the variation in survival rates and this relationship was not dependent on the type of pet owned, nor was it dependent on the severity of the subject's disease. No one interpretation accounts for these results although inherent differences in personality between owners and nonowners has been offered as an explanation.

A physiological component of the pet's influence is suggested by the results of another study. The effects of pets on well human beings as measured by blood pressure readings were identified in 35 dog owners. The blood pressures of the subjects were found to be significantly lower when they stroked their animals than when they read a story aloud to another person. The researchers propose that interaction with a pet might be less threatening than some types of interactions with other human beings (Friedmann, Katcher, Meislich, & Goodman, 1979).

Presently, research on the relationship between non-institutionalized adults and companion animals is suggestive rather than conclusive. The pet appears to be regarded as a family member but this role is of nebulous significance. Pet ownership has been found to affect an owner's self-concept and survival of cardiac disease. Tactile interaction with a companion animal is apparently related to a feeling of security. Exactly why pets have beneficial effects on human beings remains unclear which indicates a need for explanatory theory development in the field of human/animal bond research.

Children and Companion Animals

Children and companion animals have been studied in a variety of settings. Pets are frequently a component of educational and therapeutic programs in special care settings for young people because it is felt that animals are useful teaching and socialization tools (Ferguson, 1981; Levinson, 1968, 1972; Ross, 1981). The following group of studies illustrate how animal-facilitated therapy has assisted emotionally disturbed children.

Levinson (1969, 1970, 1972) is a leading researcher in the use of pets, particularly a dog, during psychotherapy for children. His research consists of 23 psychiatric case histories of youngsters aged 3 to 15 who demonstrated improved psychosocial functioning after animal-facilitated therapy was initiated. Levinson posits that a companion animal is successful in facilitating therapeutic goals because of the way in which the young perceive pets. Unlike the adult therapist, who is seen as an authoritative figure, a child sees a pet as accepting and dependent. This perception increases the child's sense of control and self-confidence. The young patient feels safe in communicating to a pet and trusts the animal to act as a mediator with the therapist. The child-pet relationship is used by the therapist as a bridge to other interventions. Animal-facilitated therapy is not limited to the use of domesticated animals.

At the World Dolphin Foundation in Miami neurologically impaired persons were observed to respond postively when watching the resident dolphins. Smith, Truby, and Phillips, motivated by this observation, selected 8 autistic youngsters (aged 10 to 17) and exposed them to 6 play sessions with the dolphins. The investigators videotaped the sessions and found that all of the subjects demonstrated prolonged attention spans when in the presence of the dolphins and several demonstrated increased verbalization and interactive play. Exactly why the dolphins affected the subjects' social skills is still being analyzed (Smith, 1983).

In addition to mental health effects, the physiological effects of pets on the young have been documented. The blood pressures of 26 male and female children (average age 12) were found to be significantly lower when a dog was present in an experimental setting than when it was absent. The subjects' blood pressures were measured when they were resting and when they read a story aloud. The children did not touch or interact with the dog during the experiment. The investigators suggest that the dog changed the subjects' perceptions of the setting, making it less anxiety provoking which resulted in lower blood pressures (Friedmann, Katcher, Thomas, Lynch, & Messent, 1983).

How adolescents and children actually perceive companion animals has been explored in several studies. Male and female adolescents (n=507) who were patients in a psychiatric hospital, students in a school for delinquents, or were attending regular high schools were surveyed for their relationships with a family pet. Of the total sample, 91% had a special pet at some time during their lives; 72% loved their pet and 25% liked it. The delinquents, more often than the other subjects tended to play alone with the animal. Another difference between the groups was that the delinquents and the hospitalized subjects emphasized more strongly the role of the pet as a love object and a confidant. Based on these findings the researchers suggest that the owner-pet relationship can be a substitute for other social relationships (Robin, ten Bensel, Quigley, & Anderson, 1983).

The status of the pet as a transitional object was identified by Wolfe (1977). Her sample was comprised of 22 young male and female adolescents. Those subjects who were characterized as being sensitive and nurturant did use their pet as a comforting object during episodes of stress. These individuals perceived the pet as a faithful and empathetic creature.

Juhasz (1983) conducted an exploratory study on factors in self-esteem of early adolescents (12 to 14-year-old males and females) which revealed the importance of a pet for this age group. In the course of the study, the subjects were asked to list things that made them feel satisfied and good about themselves. In this category pets were ranked below parents but above other adults in the subjects' lives such as teachers.

Bucke (1930) investigated the thoughts, reactions, and feelings of 1,200 male and female pet owners aged 7 to 16 toward their pets. After a qualitative and quantitative analysis, his results revealed that the sample perceived their pets as companions, confidants, and playmates. They also identified pets as responsive creatures who were dependent on human beings.

Kellert (1983) surveyed 267 students in the second, fifth, eighth, and eleventh grades regarding their attitudes toward domesticated and wild animals. The majority of the sample (87%) owned a pet. The most typical perception of animals was that they are anthropomorphic beings; the subjects also appreciated animals more for their recreational and emotional attributes than for practical reasons such as a source of food. The female subjects had more affection for pet animals than did the male subjects.

Bryant (1982) found that 83% of her 7 to 10-year-old subjects felt that their family pet was a special friend to them. Another finding of this study was that for the 10-year-old subjects the incidence of intimate talks with a pet reliably predicted a measure of empathy. Children from large families had lower competitive attitudes if they reported having intimate talks with a pet on a routine basis.

MacDonald (1981) surveyed 10-year-old males and females (n = 31) to identify their relationship with a family dog. The most frequent child-pet interactions were playing with the dog, exercising the dog, and talking to the dog. The majority of the sample felt that their dog understood the content of human communication.

Parents have noted that the family pet provides their children with an opportunity to witness certain significant life events such as birth, illness and death. They also feel that the requirements of pet care foster individual responsibility in a youngster (Salmon & Salmon, 1983). Parents generally evaluate the pet as an educational instrument (Cain, 1978). Moreover, companion animals have been used to formally instruct children about mutual respect and concern for others (Lapp & Scruby, 1982).

In summary, research has revealed that for the young a pet is both a playmate and a responsibility. Additionally, adults use pets to teach children responsibility. Children frequently classify their pet as a social companion and confidant. From these conclusions it can be seen that young subjects are able to specifically identify a pet's role in their lives. There are some differences related to age, sex, and personality traits in how young people perceive a companion animal.

A Companion Animal's Ascribed Roles

The human/animal bond is a multifaceted relationship which has psychosocial and physiological dimensions. Taken together, research literature in the field ascribes the following roles to pets: socialization facilitator, stress reducer, personal responsibility, and social companion. How these roles impact on a human being seems to be determined by individual perception of the pet's attributes. Certain pet roles may be central to one person's sense of well-being and extraneous to another's. Since individual perception is molded by a number of external and internal factors, it is evident that the human/animal bond is a complex phenomenon. By beginning with an analysis of the pet's roles for the well, young owner, clarification of the pet's significance for this group can be initiated.

THE ROLE OF THE PET DURING PREADOLESCENCE

Several authors have suggested that the pet has its strongest impact on an owner during the middle childhood years due to the developmental characteristics of this period (Gesell, Ilg, & Ames, 1956; Jenkins, Shacter, & Bauer, 1966; Levinson, 1978). Unlike the younger child, the preadolescent is able to think logically and no longer imbues animals with magical qualities (Piaget, 1962). Thus the preadolescent period provides a rich background upon which the significance of pets can be examined.

Characteristics of the Preadolescent

The preadolescent period is considered to span the middle years of childhood, from the ages of 9 to 12. During this time the individual is expanding his or her identity foundations. Peers, more so than parents, become an important frame of reference and friends are generally of the same sex. The preadolescent enjoys boisterous outdoor activities as well as quiet indoor hobbies such as starting collections. He or she has begun to assume more responsibilities for chores and may seek jobs in the neighborhood in order to earn spending money. The preadolescent is learning how to leave the comfort and security of the family and the primary grades in order to prepare for the demands of adolescence and high school (Thornburg, 1974).

The view that preadolescence is a distinct developmental period in an individual's life is based on the premises that the preadolescent has specific psychosocial needs and developmental tasks to accomplish and is in a specific stage of personality evolution. An assumption underlying these premises is that human development is a hierarchical process. Preadolescence is built on the experiences of earlier years and in turn, growth during preadolescence forms the foundation of adolescence. From adolescence, the individual's development culminates during the years of adulthood.

Erikson and Sullivan have formulated stage theories of psychosocial development which address the preadolescent period. These two theories will be used to identify the developmental concerns of the preadolescent. Based on these distinguishing characteristics, it is proposed that interaction with pets serves specific purposes in fostering healthy psychosocial development during the middle years of childhood.

Developmental Tasks

Erikson's developmental theory reflects a psychodynamic influence through its concern with ego maturation. It is a life-span approach which delineates qualitatively unique stages of ego development in chronological order. The child of between 6 and 12 years is in the developmental stage of "industry versus inferiority" according to Erikson. It is during this time that the individual learns feelings of achievement from completing tasks well. He or she is developing a new strength, a sense of competence from achievement outside the family system (Erikson, 1959).

During the middle years of childhood a person's "sense of individual identity," also referred to as ego identity or self-concept is strongly tied to school performance (Erikson, 1959). This academic performance is judged in several ways, each of which is potentially stressful. First, the student is compared with a peer group (Blaesing & Brockhaus, 1972), secondly, the teacher verbally evaluates the student (Williams & Workman, 1978), and lastly, the student is faced with external evidence of personal worth in the form of grades (Whaley & Wong, 1979). Concern about academic performance is a major worry during the preadolescent years (Gesell, Ilg, & Ames, 1956).

A crisis in ego identity can occur if the individual fails to develop a sense of pride in personal achievements. This failure can compromise the individual's progress into a healthy adulthood. By not achieving a sense of "industry," the preadolescent is ill-prepared to meet the demands of adolescence, the next developmental stage (Erikson, 1963).

Personality Development

Sullivan (1953b) has postulated an interpersonal theory of personality development which includes age-related stages. According to his theory, the way in which a person develops and maintains a sense of self is related to perceptual feedback from others (Riddle, 1972). That is to say, how others perceive an individual and how the individual interprets these communicated perceptions affect the self-image. Sullivan (1953a) calls this process "reflected appraisal."

The self-concept is based on an internal processing of the external environment. That environment contains different significant figures throughout the life cycle, persons who are important frames of reference at different ages. For the preadolescent the important figure is a special friend. A salient characteristic of this type of friend is emphathetic understanding. The friendship functions to validate the personal worth of each partner. Sullivan terms this reciprocity "collaboration" (Sullivan, 1953a).

The preadolescent naturally chooses friends who complement his or her personal needs (Ausubel, 1958). A best friend would be described as congenial, authentic, and able to establish a sense of intimacy in the friendship (Bigelow & LaGaipa, 1980). A specific friendship involves self-disclosure and the sharing of confidences. Disruption of an intimate friendship can be quite anxiety provoking for the preadolescent; not only is the nurturing aspect of the relationship lost, but the confidentiality of shared feelings is also at risk. If the preadolescent does not have a "collaboration" friendship personality development is considered stifled because the individual is lacking an age-appropriate significant figure. This deficit hampers present as well as future personality development (Sullivan, 1953a).

Companion Animals

The developmental concerns of the preadolescent as presented by Erikson and Sullivan are met through an internal processing of external social system resources. The owner-pet dyad is one type of social system within which development can be examined. Interaction with a pet on a daily basis has several features which might serve as resources for psychosocial growth.

One aspect of interaction with companion animals concerns human-pet play. People usually consider most of what they do with a pet to be playful activities. Play involves mental health considerations as it often provides a safe outlet for the expression of feelings (Monte, 1980). The expression, "I was only playing" succinctly summarizes the commonly accepted view that play is not considered to be an overtly serious endeavor but that true feelings do emerge in the process of play. Consequently, how a playmate reacts to the verbal and non-verbal expression of feelings affects the cathartic aspect of the play situation.

A companion animal has several characteristics which make it an ideal playmate. First of all, it is a consistently available companion which is never too busy to play. The pet is automatically a subordinate to its owner and the preadolescent finds it easier to express feelings to a nonauthoritative playmate such as a friend or younger sibling (Siegel, 1962; Stephenson, 1973). An animal can certainly be trusted not to "tell" confidences shared during play which is another useful characteristic. Besides play, pets can facilitate other developmental processes.

An individual's self-esteem or self-image may be positively affected by a relationship with a pet. In the animal's view the young owner is omnipotent. Unlike human beings, an animal is unable to perceive human inadequacies (Levinson, 1969). Also, a pet does not make interpersonal demands which the young owner cannot fulfill (Levinson, 1969). Human-pet relationships are not stressed by the anxiety of personal inadequacy or failure which accompanies other personal relationships (Bruner, 1983). Consequently, the preadolescent-pet relationship promotes self-assurance and confidence in the owner.

In essence, the pet functions as an ego-extension relative to self-esteem. As an ego-extension the animal is subjectively incorporated into the preadolescent's sense of self and is felt to represent positive dimensions of the self-image (Rosenberg, 1979). When the pet serves as a responsive source of approval, it is enhancing and maintaining the preadolescent's self-image.

A pet may make a preadolescent owner feel cared for, but the pet itself also requires care and attention (Schowalter, 1983). Interest in caring for pets has been noted to peak during the middle years of childhood (Gesell, Ilg, & Ames, 1956; Jenkins, Shacter, & Bauer,

1966). The young person who is able to demonstrate competence to his or her own caretakers and parents by taking on the responsibilities of pet care such as feeding and grooming can develop a sense of pride in his or her accomplishments (Bossard, 1944; Van Leeuwen, 1981). In contrast to human values, an animal does not impose standards of quality on the young owner's performance of tasks (Fox, 1981). Being able to meet the needs of a dependent creature is an important achievement.

In conclusion, it appears that the owner-pet relationship is tailored for the needs of the preadolescent. The pet is a trustworthy companion, it communicates regard for its owner, and it fosters responsibility. These features address the preadolescent's need to develop a positive self-concept through accomplishing tasks and to perceive that a close friend values and shares the individual's self-worth.

A CONCEPTUAL STRUCTURE

Can a pet actually affect the preadolescent's development? A synthesis of the human/animal bond literature suggests that in light of developmental needs, the companionship and responsibility aspects of pet ownership are important parts of the preadolescent-pet relationship. However, how the pet contributes to an individual's growth depends on one pivotal factor which is, the individual's perception of the pet.

Based on human/animal bond research, the following is proposed. When a person perceives a companion animal as a viable resource for meeting the demands of continuing growth, then the animal is contributing to a person's development. The pet is classified as a developmental resource due to its ascribed roles which reflect an element of accessible support. Human beings apparently value pets as supportive entities. The pet's value as a developmental asset will fluctuate, depending on the individual needs, age, and sex of the owner. Therefore, the owner-pet bond is optimally a flexible affiliation.

When the preadolescent's social system cannot or does not meet the developmental needs of middle childhood, the pet owner may then turn to a companion animal to provide intimate friendship and a feeling of achievement. At times it is appropriate for the preadolescent to use a companion animal in this manner since personal needs can exceed the resources of external social systems. Conversely, if the preadolescent is unable or unwilling to leave the security of the pet, this indicates a deficit in the individual's ability to meet the abiding challenges of growth. For healthy development, the pet serves in a supportive capacity to other social bonds. The owner-pet bond which supports sound development does not exclude human relationships. When the pet becomes the exclusive support for the preadolescent, two areas of concern emerge: is the external social system deficient in providing the owner with resources for addressing developmental concerns? and; is the owner deficient in internally processing social resources to meet developmental demands?

Implications

An analysis of the preadolescent/pet bond suggests several implications for adults who are involved with young people. It would be expected that the preadolescent pet owner will identify his or her pet as "something that makes me feel good about myself." The companion animal's character naturally contributes toward a sense of personal satisfaction during the middle years of childhood. Next, the intensity of the owner-pet attachment can be scrutinized. From a developmental perspective, the healthy owner-pet relationship is evidenced by variability in attitudes and behavioral responses toward the pet over time. A rigid relationship indicates limitations in growth potential relative to developmental progress.

It is important that adults recognize the valuable role a pet can play in the development of the preadolescent. The pet can make a substantial contribution to an individual's healthy progression into adulthood. Acknowledging that the developmental outcomes of the preadolescent period can be affected by the owner-pet bond accords that relationship the respect it deserves.

REFERENCES

Ausubel, D.P. (1958). *Theory and problems of child development.* New York: Grune & Stratton.

Bigelow, B.J., & LaGaipa, J.J. (1975). Children's written descriptions of friendship: A multidimensional analysis. *Developmental Psychology, 11*, 857–858.

Blaesing, S., & Brockhaus, J. (1972). The development of body image in the child. *Nursing Clinics of North America, 7*, 597–608.

Bossard, J.H.S. (1944). The mental hygiene of owning a dog. *Mental Hygiene, 28*, 408–413.

Bossard, J.H.S., & Boll, E.S. (1966). *The sociology of child development.* New York: Harper.

Brickel, C.M. (1979). The therapeutic roles of cat mascots with a hospital-based geriatric population: A staff survey. *The Gerontologist, 19*, 368–372.

Bruner, J. (1983). Play, thought, and language. *Peabody Journal of Education, 60*(3), 60–69.

Bryant, B.K. (1982). Sibling relationships in middle childhood. In M.E. Lamb & B. Sutton-Smith (Eds.), *Sibling relationships: Their nature and significance across the lifespan* (pp. 87–122). Hillsdale, NJ: Lawrence Erlbaum.

Bucke, W.F. (1930). Cyno-psychoses: Children's thoughts, reactions, and feelings toward pet dogs. *Pedagogical Seminary and Journal of Genetic Psychology, 10*, 459–513.

Cain, A.O. (1978, October). *A study of pets in the family system.* Paper presented at the Georgetown Family Symposium, Washington, DC.

Corson, S.A., & Corson, E. O'L. (1980). Pet animals as nonverbal communication mediators in psychotherapy in institutional settings. In S.A. Corson & E. O'L. Corson (Eds.), *Ethology and nonverbal communication in mental health* (pp. 83–110). Elmsford, NY: Pergamon Press.

Corson, S.A., Corson, E. O'L., Gwynne, P.H., & Arnold, L.E. (1977). Pet dogs as nonverbal communication links in hospital psychiatry. *Comprehensive Psychiatry, 18*, 61–72.

Doyle, M.C. (1975). Rabbit-therapeutic prescription. *Psychiatric Care, 13*, 79–82.

Erikson, E.H. (1963). *Childhood and society* (2nd ed.). New York: Norton.

Erikson, E.H. (1959). *Identity and the life cycle: Selected papers.* (Psychological Issues Monograph No. 1). New York: International Universities.

Ferguson, H. (1981). *The use of pets in Canadian residential care facilities for children.* Unpublished master's thesis, University of Manitoba.

Fields, S.T. (1977). Pet-person social interaction in institutional settings: An ethnomethodological analysis. *Dissertation Abstracts International, 78*, 6941A. (University Microfilms No. 7805838).

Fox, M. (1981). Relationships between the human and nonhuman animals. In B. Fogel (Ed.), *Interrelations between people and pets* (pp. 23–40). Springfield, IL: C.C. Thomas.

Francis, G., Turner, J.T., & Johnson, S.B. (1983). *Domestic animal visitation as therapy with adult home residents.* Manuscript submitted for publication.

Friedmann, E., Katcher, A.H., Lynch, J.J., & Thomas, S.A. (1980). Animal companions and one year survival of patients discharged from a coronary care unit. *Public Health Reports, 95*, 307–312.

Friedmann, E., Katcher, A.H., Meislich, D., & Goodman, M. (1979). Physiological response of people to petting their pets. *American Zoologist, 19*, 915.

Friedmann, E., Katcher, A.H., Thomas, S.A., Lynch, J.J., & Messent, P.R. (1983). Social interaction and blood pressure. *Journal of Nervous and Mental Disease, 171*, 461–465.

Gesell, A., Ilg, F.L., & Ames, L.B. (1953). *Youth. The years from ten to sixteen.* New York: Harper.

Jenkins, G.G., Shacter, H.S., & Bauer, W.W. (1966). *These are your children* (3rd ed.). Glenview, IL: Scott & Foresman.

Juhasz, A.M. (1983). *Problems in measuring self-esteem in early adolescents.* Unpublished manuscript, Loyola University of Chicago.

Kellert, S.R. (1983). *Attitudes toward animals: Age-related development among children.* Manuscript submitted for publication.

Lago, D.J., Knight, B., & Connell, C. (1983). Relationships with companion animals among the rural elderly. In A.H. Katcher & A.M. Beck (Eds.), *New perspectives on our lives with companion animals* (pp. 328–340). Philadelphia: University of Pennsylvania Press.

Lapp, C.A., & Scruby, L. (1982). Responsible pet relationships: A mental health perspective. *Health Values: Achieving High Level Wellness, 6*(4), 20–25.

Lee, D. (1979). Birds as therapy at Lima State Hospital for the criminally insane. *Bird World, 1*(6), 14–16.

Levinson, B.M. (1968). Household pets in residential schools. *Mental Hygiene, 2*, 411–414.

Levinson, B.M. (1969). *Pet-oriented child psychotherapy.* Springfield, IL: C.C. Thomas.

Levinson, B.M. (1970). Pets, child development, and mental illness. *Journal of the American Veterinary Medicine Association, 157*, 1759–1766.

Levinson, B.M. (1972) *Pets and human development.* Springfield, IL: C.C. Thomas.

Levinson, B.M. (1978). Pets and personality development. *Psychological Reports, 42*, 1031–1038.

MacDonald, A.J. (1981). The pet dog in the home: A study of interactions. In B. Fogel (Ed.), *Interrelations between people and pets* (pp. 195–206). Springfield, IL: C.C. Thomas.

MacDonald, A.J. (1979). Review: Children and companion animals. *Child Care, Health and Development, 5*, 359–366.

McCulloch, M.J. (1981). The pet as prothesis—defining criteria for the adjunctive use of companion animals in the treatment of medically ill depressed outpatients. In B. Fogel (Ed.), *Interrelations between people and pets* (pp. 101–123). Springfield, IL: C.C. Thomas.

Monte, C.F. (1980). *Beneath the mask* (2nd ed.). New York: Holt, Rinehart, & Winston.

Mugford, R.A., & M'Comisky, J.G. (1975). Some recent work on the psycho-therapeutic value of cage birds with old people. In R.S. Anderson (Ed.), *Pet animals and society* (pp. 54–65). London: Baillere Tindall.

Ory, M.G., & Goldberg, E.L. (1983). Pet possession and well-being in elderly women. *Research on Aging, 5*, 389–409.

Pedigree Petfoods (1980). *Pets and the British.* Leicestershire: Pedigree Petfood's Education Center.

Piaget, J. (1962). The stages of the intellectual development of the child. *Bulletin of the Menniger Clinic, 26*, 120–128.

Purvis, M.J., & Otto, D.M. (1976). *Household demand for pet food and the ownership of cats and dogs: An analysis of a neglected component of U.S. food use.* St. Paul: University of Minnesota, Department of Agriculture and Applied Economics.

Riddle, I. (1972) Nursing intervention to promote body image integrity in children. *Nursing Clinics of North America, 7*, 651–661.

Robb, S.S. (1982). *Pilot study of pet-dog therapy for elderly people in long-term care.* (Available from S.S. Robb, Pittsburg VA Medical Center, University Drive, Pittsburg, PA 15240).

Robb, S.S., Boyd, M., & Pritash, C.L. (1980). A wine bottle, plant, and puppy. *Journal of Gerontological Nursing, 6*, 721–728.

Robin, M., ten Bensel, R., Quigley, J.S., & Anderson, R.K. (1983). Childhood pets and the psychosocial development of adolescents. In A.H. Katcher & A.M. Beck (Eds.), *New perspectives on our lives with companion animals* (pp. 436–443). Philadelphia: University of Pennsylvania Press.

Rosenberg, M. (1979). *Conceiving the self.* New York: Basic Books.

Ross, S.B. (1981). Feelings and their medical significance. *Ross Timesaver, 23*, 13–16.

Salmon, P.W., & Salmon, I.M. (1983) Who owns who? Psychological research into the human-pet bond in Australia. In A.H. Katcher & A.M. Beck (Eds.), *New perspectives on our lives with companion animals* (pp. 244–265). Philadelphia: University of Pennsylvania Press.

Schowalter, J.E. (1983). The use and abuse of pets. *Journal of the American Academy of Child Psychiatry, 22*, 68–73.

Siegel, A. (1962). Reaching the severely withdrawn through pet therapy. *American Journal of Psychiatry, 118*, 1045–1046.

Smith, B.A. (1983). Project Inreach: A program to explore the ability of Atlantic Bottlenose dolphins to elicit communication responses from autistic children. In A.H. Katcher & A.M. Beck (Eds.), *New perspectives on our lives with companion animals* (pp. 460–466). Philadelphia: University of Pennsylvania Press.

Stephenson, P.S. (1973). Working with 9-to-12-year-old children. *Child Welfare, 52*, 375–382.

Sullivan, H.S. (1953a). *Conceptions of modern psychiatry.* New York: Norton.

Sullivan, H.S. (1953b). *The interpersonal theory of psychiatry*. New York: Norton.

Thompson, M., Kennedy, R.W., & Igou, S. (1983). Pets as socializing agents with chronic psychiatric patients: An initial study. In A.H. Katcher & A.M. Beck (Eds.), *New perspectives on our lives with companion animals* (pp. 427–430). Philadelphia: University of Pennsylvania Press.

Thornberg, H.D. (Ed.). (1974). *Preadolescent development*. Tucson: University of Arizona Press.

Van Leeuwen, J. (1981). A child psychiatrist's perspective on children and their companion animals. In B. Fogel (Ed.), *Interrelations between people and pets* (pp. 175–194). Springfield, IL: C.C. Thomas.

Whaley, L.F., & Wong, D.L. (1979). *Nursing care of infants and children*. St. Louis: C.V. Mosby.

Williams, R.L., & Workman, E.A. (1978). Development of a behavioral self-concept scale. *Behavior Therapy, 9*, 680–681.

Willie, R.L. (1982). A study of the relationship between pet ownership and health status. *Proceedings of the 5th Annual Research Conference, VA Medical District #17, 1*, 14.

Wolfe, J. (1977). The use of pets as transitional objects in adolescent interpersonal function. *Dissertation Abstracts International, 38*, 2391B. (University Microfilms No. 7724135).

Pets, Early Adolescents, and Families

Anita Miller Covert
Alice Phipps Whiren
Joanne Keith
Christine Nelson

ABSTRACT. This paper reviews the patterns and effects of early adolescents' involvement in the care of animals and the relationship between that experience and selected family and individual variables. It provides baseline data on early adolescents and animal involvement concerning: species of animals, family income, family relationships, parental views of animal raising, animal owner self-esteem and self-management, and the view of youth on the benefits of animal involvement.

Domestication of animals for food and labor as well as for companions has long been established. Humans have had a prolonged interaction with animals from antiquity (Reed, 1959). Animals first provided basic resource needs of humans for food, clothing and shelter (Levinson, 1969), and later evolved to meet the psychological needs of their owners (Mugford, 1977). Where once animals served primarily as food, co-hunters, herders and protectors, broad cultural changes in the way individuals live have contributed to the rise in importance in the role of the animal as a companion and social interaction facilitator.

Bryant (1972) summarized the pervasive influence of animals on language, arts, economic and interpersonal behavior as well as our laws and observed that the phenomena which he aptly calls the "zoological connection" deserves increased research attention as an area of social causation. Levinson (1982) identified four major areas of investigation of animal human interaction that he believed would be useful.

Anita M. Covert, Alice P. Whiren, Joanne Keith, and Christine Nelson are in the Department of Family and Child Ecology, College of Human Ecology, Michigan State University, East Lansing, MI 48824-1030.

(1) the role of animals in various human cultures and ethnic groups over centuries; (2) the effect of association with animals on human personality development; (3) human-animal communication; and (4) the therapeutic use of animals in formal psychotherapy, institutional settings and residential arrangements for handicapped and aged populations. (p. 283)

Using an ecosystems perspective of the family (Bubolz et al., 1979), it is important to study the effects of animals in the family system and upon the development of family members. The purpose of this study is to examine the pattern and effect of early adolescents' involvement in the care of animals and the relationship between that experience and selected family and individual variables.

CHILDREN CARING FOR ANIMALS

A substantial proportion of children studied have been involved in interaction with animals. Bowd (1982), in interviewing 37 kindergarten children from middle and lower-class families noted that 86 percent of them had pets in the family and that 46 percent had multiple pets. Salomon (1981) whose Canadian sample was predominately middle class, also found a high incidence of pet ownership with 53 percent of the children owning a pet at the kindergarten level and 90 percent at the sixth grade. The peak ownership level in her study was 94 percent for 10 year olds.

The reported choice of animal or animal preference favors the traditional companion animal in frequency as might be expected. In the Salomon study (1981), furry animals were very important with most children either expressing a desire to have one or already owning one. Proportionally more of the younger children had fish than mammals. Cats and dogs were popular at all ages and with both boys and girls. Burke (1903) had earlier observed that girls preferred cats, his observations being based upon a sample of nearly 3,000 children's essays on a preferred pet.

Mention of domesticated animals other than traditional companion animals and horses is rare. Bowd (1982) observed that only 38 percent of the young children he interviewed were aware of the role of human care in the distinction between domestic and wild animals. The preponderance of all the literature on companion animals and pets seems to focus upon the dog. Some studies either sample dog owners and generalize to pet owners, or fail to mention the species of animal (Bowd, 1982; Hyde, Kurdek, and Larson, 1983; Keddie, 1977). The degree of relevance of animal species or breed upon the human-animal bond is yet to be fully explained though Kidd and Kidd (1980) have noted differences in owner personality between dog and cat lovers, and Serpell (1981) observed a relationship between childhood experiences and adult attitudes, and pet preferences. It is unclear from these pieces of research how many children from all segments of our society have pets and what species of animals these youths have. Do children care for animals other than dogs and cats? Is there a sex difference among animal ownership for different species? Do girls prefer cats as Burke found, do more boys own dogs, what about large animal ownership? Is there an age difference?

Research Questions: To what extent do early adolescents care for an animal? What is the distribution of animal species for boys and girls?

THE FAMILY

Cultural folk wisdom in America has supported the decisions of families to include pets in the household. Pets are also considered to be social assets (Luborsky et al., 1973). In fact, pet owners frequently view their pets as family members (Smith, 1983; Cain, 1983; Ruby, 1983; Hichrod, 1982) showing great attachment to them and treating them as if the animals could communicate (Cain, 1983) and as if they were empathic (Fox, 1981).

On the other hand, not all families have or want pets, for as Guttman (1981) noted, non-pet owners perceive animals as a burden or responsibility, or cause of household untidiness. Guttman found that pet owners more than non-pet owners object to being alone and often have pets for sociability. Non-pet owners still have positive attitudes toward pets and think animals are fine for someone else. Nevertheless, not all pets are problem free. They may put a burden on family finances, compete for time with social and business commitments and cause problems for the owner, the owner's family and neighbors (Mugford, 1981).

Why do some families choose to have pets while others do not? Does a family system with pets have better family relations than non-pet families?

Research Questions: Are there differences between families whose early adolescents have cared for an animal and those families which have not? Do early adolescents who have an animal feel closer to their parents?

BENEFITS FOR CHILDREN AND FAMILIES

Feldman (1970) compiled a short list of owners' needs for a pet from the literature: "(1) friend and partner, (2) self-identity and self-esteem, (3) facilitation and catalysis, and (4) childhood development" (p. 306.) This list is not unlike the sample of 50 parents who voluntarily replied to Salomon's (1981) open-ended query as to why they had allowed or encouraged their children to have pets. The parents reported that they believed that the pet was an unconditional friend, playmate or listener, that the pet developed a sense of responsibility, that the child's experience was broadened by giving the child an opportunity to make empirical observations of life processes, and that the child developed a respect for animals. Feldman's listing focused on outcomes while Salomon reported processes clearly related to those outcomes.

Potential benefits for children who have pets have been proposed for all age groups (Levinson, 1972). The role of the pet as the "transitional object" (Winecott, 1953) of early life that bridges the gap between self and other, the companion that provides nonjudgmental interaction and affection (Subman, 1981; Levinson, 1967), the animal provides for the child's management of negative feelings (Rynerson, 1978; Schowalter, 1983), the friend that supports the child's ability to cross boundaries in peer interaction (Feldman, 1978), the joyful playmate (VanLeeuwen, 1981) have all been suggested.

What research has been done on these suggestions? Those benefits derived through pet facilitated therapy have been discussed elsewhere (Allen, 1983). Fewer studies of the benefits to normal, healthy children have been reported.

Salomon (1980) provided anecdotal support from her sample of elementary school children for the roles of companion, playmate, confidante, object for love and affection, and object for responsible care and addition from the child. Hyde, Kurdel and Larson (1983) found young adult pet owners showed greater empathy and interpersonal trust when compared to non-pet owners, but did not find a difference in self-esteem.

A group of 507 adolescents that included normal high school youths as well as emotionally impaired and delinquent youth voluntarily replied to an open ended questionnaire on the role of pets in their lives (Robin et al., 1983). The most common benefit identified was companionship and friendship. The response that the pet was a member of the family was more common in public school youth than the other two groups. Delinquent youth tended to play alone with their pets and use the pet as a confidante three times more frequently than public school youth; they also reported that their pet protected them from physical harm more frequently than public school youths. When asked why pets were good for children, this adolescent group reported in order to frequency: (1) companionship and fun to be with; (2) a source of learning about responsibility and animal life; and (3) as someone to love and be loved by. All the respondents perceived benefits deriving from having a pet with the pet playing a special role in the lives of delinquent and impaired youth.

Benefits for physical health have been reported for adults, though there seems to be a lack of comparable studies using children as subjects (Katcher, 1981; Friedmann et al., 1980).

There have been many suggestions as to the benefits of animal care for children, but very little research has been conducted which can be generalized to most children.

> Research Questions: Do parents see caring for an animal as important? Is there a difference in self-esteem and self-management between early adolescents who have cared for an animal and those who have not? What are the benefits of caring for an animal as perceived by early adolescents? Do early adolescents perceive the death of a pet as stressful? Do early adolescents use pets to reduce their stress?

SAMPLE

The research reported here is a secondary analysis using the Michigan Early Adolescent Survey which surveyed Michigan youth 10-to 14-years-of-age. A sample of 285 Michigan families was interviewed. Early adolescents chosen for this study were selected using a stratified multistage cluster approach. Twenty-five clusters were assigned 12 interviews each which totaled 304 families. Counties were assigned random numbers based upon population. Two densely populated counties, Wayne and Oakland, had more interviews than could possibly be conducted, consequently, substitutions were made based on similarity of demographics. In each of the 20 counties selected, school districts were assigned random numbers based upon their numbers of students. Two school districts from each county were randomly selected. Lists of youths in grades 5, 6, 7, and 8 were obtained, and equal numbers of males and females from each grade were randomly selected.

Each youth was interviewed in his/her home and a questionnaire was administered to each parent separately in two-parent homes and to the parent in one-parent homes. The interviews dealt with several topic areas in addition to that which is presented in this paper. Each interview took about an hour to complete.

Description of Families

Of the early adolescents who completed the survey 50.5 percent were females. Approximately three-fourths of the youth sampled were evenly split into ages eleven, twelve and thirteen. The remaining one-fourth was evenly divided between 10 and 14 year olds. These early adolescents were distributed evenly over the 5th, 6th, 7th, and 8th grades.

Eighty-two percent of the sample was white. Almost 19 percent was black. The remaining families were Mexican-American and other ethnic groups. Thirty percent of the families in this study reported a family income of $20,000–$30,000. Another 30 percent reported an income of $30,000–$55,000. Four percent were over $55,000. A little over 30 per cent reported income under $20,000.

Many more early adolescents (94.8%) lived with their natural mother than lived with their natural father (75.5%). Adoptive parents make up 2 percent of the mothers and 2.5 percent of the fathers. Step-parents make up 1.2 percent of the mothers and 4.7 percent of the fathers.

Over 50 percent of the fathers reported having a high school education or having attended college (but not graduating). Almost one-third were college graduates and/or had attended professional school. Two-thirds of the fathers were in the age group 36–50 years of age.

Seventy percent of the fathers were employed by others, most of them in skilled work, professional or management positions.

FINDINGS

For each of the findings discussed below, a correlation coefficient was computed. For Bernoulli variables, Phi Coefficients were computed. In other cases, Pearson Product Moment Correlation Coefficients were computed.

Early Adolescents Caring for Animals

When these early adolescents were asked if they had cared for an animal for a long period of time, i.e., a month or more, 89.4 percent said that they had. One out of ten early adolescents indicated that they had never cared for an animal. Table 1 shows the breakdown of species of animal by sex of the adolescents. It shows that a variety of species are cared for by adolescents. Dogs were the most frequently owned animal with about 40 percent of the youths listing dogs. When considering the sex of the animal owner, only cat owners and large animal owners show a significant difference with more cat owners being girls and more large animal owners being boys. There was no difference in animal ownership based on age. Youths of all grades 5 thru 8 equally owned animals.

Table 1: SEX OF ANIMAL OWNERS

	Boys n=141	Girls n=144	r
Dog	83.1%	77.3%	-.07
Cat	48.0	60.2	.12*
Rabbit or Hamster	34.0	34.0	-.00
Fish or Bird	29.8	31.9	.02
Large Animal (Calf, goat, sheep, pig)	16.3	9.7	-.10*
Horse	13.1	17.9	.07
Any animal	89.4	87.5	-.03

* p <.05

Families of Animal Owners

When examining the question of whether or not families of animal owners differed from non-animal owners, we examined the family income and family residence. As Table 2 shows as income increases animal ownership by early adolescents increases.

Specifically, as income increases, fish/bird and dog/cat ownership increases. No significant differences were found generally between animal owners in rural and urban areas. Although as we would expect, horse and large animal owners live in rural areas. (See Table 3.)

When the youth were asked to describe their relationships with their mothers and with their fathers, there was no significant differences between animal owners and non-animal owners. When each parent was asked to describe his/her relationship with his/her child, again no significant differences were found between animal owners and non-animal owners. (See Table 4.) Animal ownership does not seem to be related to the family's perception of closeness of family relationships.

Benefits for Early Adolescents and Families

Parents view caring for animals as beneficial. When parents were asked what skills were important for their child to learn, 94 percent of the mothers and fathers said that it was important.

Table 2: FAMILY INCOME

	Low (less than $20,000) n=86	Med. ($20-30,000) n=81	High (over $30,000) n=98	r
Any Pet	82.6%	91.4%	93.9%	.15**
Dog or Cat	72.1	82.7	85.7	.14**
Rabbit or Hamster	34.9	29.6	37.8	.03
Fish or Bird	23.3	30.9	39.8	.15**
Large Animal (Calf, Pig, Sheep, Goat)	10.5	13.6	13.3	.03
Horses	17.4	11.3	18.0	.01

** p <.01

TABLE 3:   RURAL/URBAN FAMILIES

	Rural (farm or small town) n=152	Urban (over 5,000) n=126	r
Any Pet	91.4%	86.5%	-.08
Dog or Cat	82.2	78.6	-.05
Rabbit or Hamster	36.8	31.7	-.05
Fish or Bird	28.3	34.9	.07
Large Animal (Calf, pig, sheep, goat)	22.4	1.6	-.31***
Horse	23.9	5.6	-.25***

*** p <.0001

Table 4: YOUTH'S RELATIONSHIP WITH MOTHER

Pet Ownership

Relationship	no n=29	yes n=247
poor	0.0	.8
fair	3.4	4.0
good	34.5	29.6
very close	62.1	65.6

no significant differences found

YOUTH'S RELATIONSHIP WITH FATHER

Pet Ownership

Relationship	no n=26	yes n=235
poor	0%	1.7%
fair	3.8	12.3
good	61.5	35.3
very close	34.6	50.6

no significant differences found

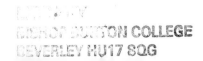

Self-Esteem

Using Coopersmith's Self-Esteem Scale (1967), a .13 Pearson Correlation Coefficient was found (significant at .05). Specifically for species, dog owners had a higher self-esteem with a correlation coefficient of .11 (significant at .05). It appears that early adolescent animal owners have higher self-esteem than non-animal owners.

Considering club membership as a measurement of sociability, more animal owners than non-animal owners are club members. Also examining sociability, youth were asked if they had participated in four leadership activities. No difference was found between animal owners and non-animal owners.

Self-Management

Using a six-item scale, each parent was asked about the level of his/her child's self-management skills. The scale had a reliability of .70. Generally, animals owners did not seem to have higher self-management skills. However, mothers reported that rabbit/hamster owners did have higher self-management skills ($r = .11$, significant at .05). There were no differences reported by fathers.

Adolescents Perceive Gain from Animals

What do adolescents perceive they gain from animals? Generally adolescents reported gaining responsibility, friendship/love/fun, and knowledge about animals. More rabbit/hamster owners reported gaining responsibility than other pet owners. More dog, horse, and fish/bird owners reported gaining friendship/love/fun than other pet owners. (See Table 5.)

Adolescents, Stress, and Pets

In answer to the question "Did you receive or lose a pet in the last year?", 55.5 percent of the early adolescents said "yes." Of these youths, 59.5 percent said that this affected them "a lot," 29.1 percent said this affected them "a little," and 11.5 percent said this affected them "not at all." Owners of large animals had a stronger correlation than the other species (significant at .01). Sex of owner did not seem to make a difference.

When these early adolescents were asked if they played with a pet

Table 5: WHAT ADOLESCENTS SAY THEY GAIN FROM ANIMALS

	Boys n=141	Girls n=144
Friendship	31.9%	27.1%
Knowledge	31.9	36.1
Responsibility	38.3	45.8
Getting Along w/others	5.0	4.9

ADOLESCENTS GAIN BY SPECIES OF ANIMAL

Species	Friendship %	Friendship r	Knowledge %	Knowledge r	Responsibility %	Responsibility r	Getting Along %	Getting Along r
Dog	87.8	.13*	85.3	.10	78.4	-.04	71.4	-.05
Cat	57.9	.06	57.9	.06	53.8	-.006	53.8	-.002
Rabbit/ Hamster	40.5	.09	35.1	.02	41.7	.14*	50.0	.08
Fish/Bird	38.1	.10*	37.1	.10*	35.8	.09	21.4	-.05
Lg. Animal	17.9	.09	15.5	.05	17.5	.11*	14.4	.01
Horse	23.8	.16**	17.4	.04	13.7	-.05	18.2	.02

* $p < .05$
** $p < .01$

when they were upset 48.5 percent said "yes" and 26.1 percent said "sometimes." There was no correlation between species of pet and use of pet for stress reduction. Neither was there any correlation between sex of early adolescent and use of pet for stress reduction.

SUMMARY

1. 89.4 percent of the early adolescents have cared for an animal for a long period of time.

2. Early adolescents owned a large variety of pets. Dogs were the most frequently owned pet with cats, rabbit/hamster, fish/bird, large animals, and horses following in that order.

3. Girls had more cats than boys. Boys did not seem to have more dogs than girls. Boys had more large animals than girls.

4. There did not seem to be a relationship between the youth's age and pet ownership.

5. As income increased, pet ownership increased. Specifically, as income increased, fish/bird ownership and dog ownership increased.

6. Youth with horses or large animals for pets were more likely to live in rural areas.

7. Pet ownership did not seem to suggest a better perceived relation with parents.

8. Parents viewed caring for animals as beneficial.

9. Early adolescent animal owners were more likely to have a higher self-esteem.

10. An animal owner was more likely to be a club member.

11. Early adolescent animal owners were not reported by their parents to show more self-management than non-animal owners.

12. When the youth were asked what they had gained from their pet, they reported gaining responsibility, friendship/love/fun, and knowledge. Dog, horse, and fish/bird owners were more likely to say friendship/love/fun. Rabbit/hamster owners were more likely to say something which indicated learning responsibility.

13. The death of a pet was very stressful.

14. Early adolescents used pets for stress reduction.

DISCUSSION AND IMPLICATIONS

The findings for early adolescents confirm Bowd's findings (1982) with kindergarten children and Salomon's findings (1981) with grade 6 early adolescents that 85–90 percent of children had pets. Just as Burke (1903) found, these findings suggest that girls had more cats than boys. This research further suggests that early adolescents had many species of animals in addition to dogs and cats which have been traditionally studied. While Levinson (1982) indicated that all studies separate companion animals from domestic animals, this study found the positive benefits occurred for both companion and domestic animal owners. The animal/human bond appears to have occurred with both companion and domestic animals.

Early adolescents whose families were better off economically were more likely to have an animal. There seems to be a direct relationship between parent's income and the opportunity to obtain the benefits of animal ownership.

While pet owners did not seem to have better relationships with their parents than other adolescents, they did seem to have higher levels of self-esteem. Animal ownership seems to affect the individual more than the family, but more consideration of this is needed with a closer examination of other family system variables. Youths said they gain responsibility, friendship/love/fun, and knowledge from their pets. Again, these seem to be individual benefits.

Early adolescent animal owners also indicated that their pet was both a source of stress and used for stress reduction. This area needs a more careful examination of the specific causes of stress and the process used when pets become stress reducers.

This study provides baseline data which because of random selection of subjects can be generalized to early adolescents. The next step would be a more indepth examination of the relationship between early adolescents and pets. For example, this study found that early adolescents care for a variety of species of animals, but it did not examine the degree of involvement. Are youths more involved with furry animals, with household pets, with small pets? Does the degree of involvement matter for a general population rather than a clinical population? Would we find that youths who are highly involved with their pets are more responsible or possibly less sociable?

REFERENCES

Allen, R. M. 1983. "Therapy, maintenance, and human/animal bond: a selected, annotated bibliography." *Veterinary Medicine/Small Animal Clinician*. (June) 893–899.

Bowd, A. D. 1982. "Young children's beliefs about animals." *Journal of Psychology*. 110: 263–266.

Bridger, H. 1976. "The changing role of pets in society." *Journal of Small Animal Practice*. 17:1–8.

Bubolz, M. M., Eicher, J. B., & Sontag, M.S. 1979. "The human ecosystem: a model." *Journal of Home Economics*. Spring.

Burke, W. F. 1903. "Cyno-psychoses. Children's thoughts, reactions, and feelings toward pet dogs." *Pedagogical Seminary*. 10:459–513.

Bryant, C. D. 1979. "The zoological connection: Animal-related human behavior." *Social Forces*. 58:2 (December) 399–421.

Cain, A. O. 1983. "A study of pets in the family system." In A.H. Kalihere and A. M. Beck (eds). *New Perspectives on Our Lives With Companion Animals*. University of Pennsylvania Press, Philadelphia.

Coopersmith, S. 1967. *The Antecedents of Self-Esteem*. San Francisco: W. H. Freeman.

Fox, M. 1981. "Relationships between the human and non-human animals." In Fogel (Ed.) *Interrelationship between people and pets*. Charles Thomas, Springfield, Illinois.

Friedman E., Kakher, A., Lynch, J., Thomas, S. "Animal companions and one-year survival of patients after discharge from a coronary care unit." *Public Health Reports*. 95:(4) 307–12.

Guttmann, G. 1981. "The psychological determinants of keeping pets." In Fogel (Ed.) *Interrelations between People and Pets*. Charles Thomas, Springfield, Illinois.

Hyde, Kurdek, Larson. 1983. "Relationships between pet owners and self-esteem, social sensitivity, and interpersonal trust." *Psychological Reports*. 52:110.

Kidd, A., & Kidd, R. 1980. "Pearsonality characteristic and preference in pet ownership." *Psychological Reports*. 46:939-949.

Keddie, K. 1977. "Pathological mourning after the death of a domestic pet." *British Journal of Psychiatry*. 131:21-5.

Levinson, B. 1972. *Pets and Human Development*. Charles Thomas, Springfield, Illinois.

Levinson, B. M. 1969. *Pet-Oriented Child Psychotherapy*. Charles C. Thomas, Springfield, Illinois.

Levinson, B. M. 1982. "The future of research into relationships between people and their animal companions." *International Journal of the Study of Animal Problems*. 3:4.

Levinson, B. 1968. "Interpersonal relationship between pet and human being." In W. M. Fox et al. (Eds.) *Abnormal Behavior in Animals*. Philadelphia: W. B. Saunders.

Levinson, B. 1967. "The pet and the child's bereavement." *Mental Hygiene*. 51:197-200.

Luborsky, L., Todd, T. C., & Kalcher, A. H. 1973. "A self-administered social assets scale for predicting physical and physiological illness and health." *Journal of Psychosomatic Research*. 17:109-20.

Mugford, R. 1977. "Problem dogs and problem owners: The behavior specialist as an adjunct to veterinary practice." In Fogel (Ed.) *Interrelations between People and Pets*. Charles Thomas, Springfield, Illinois.

Mugford, R. A. 1977. *The contribution of pets to human development*. Pedigree Pet Foods. Milton Mowloray, Leicestershine, England.

Reed, C. A. 1959. "Animal domestication in the prehistoric new East." *Science*. 130: 1629-1639.

Robin, M., Tenbensel R., Quigley J., & Anderson, R. 1983. "Childhood pets and the psychosocial development of adolescents." In A. H. Kalcher and A. Beck (Eds.). *New Perspectives on Our Lives with Companion Animals*. University of Pennsylvania Press Philadelphia.

Ruby, J. 1983. Images of the family: The symbolic implications of animal photography." In A. K. Katcher and A. M. Bech (Eds.). *New Perspectives on our lives with Companion Animals*. University of Pennsylvania Press, Philadelphia.

Rynearson, E. K. 1978. "Humans and pets and attachment." *British Journal of Psychiatry*. 133:500-5.

Salomon, A. 1981. "Animals and children: The role of the pet." *Canada's Mental Health*. 9-13.

Savishinsky, J. S. 1974. "The child is father to the dog: Canines and personality processes in an Artic community." *Human Development*. 17:460-466.

Schowalter, J. E. 1983. "Clinical appearance the use and abuse of pets. *Journal of the American Academy of Child Psychiatry*. 68-72.

Serpell, J. 1981. "Childhood pets and their influence on adult attitudes." *Psychological Reports*. 49:651-654.

Smith, S. 1983. "Interactions between pet dog and family members: An ethological Study." In A. K. Katcher and A. M. Beck (Eds.) *New Perspectives on Our Lives with Companion Animals*. University of Pennsylvania Press, Philadelphia.

Van Leeuwen, J. 1981. "A child psychiatrist's perspective on children and their companion animals." In Fogel (Ed.) *Interrelations between People and Pets*. Charles Thomas, Springfield, Illinois.

Winnuott, D. W. 1953. "Transitional objects and transitional phenomena." *International Journal of Psychoanalysis*. 24:88-97.

Pets and Family Relationships Among Nursing Home Residents

Joel Savishinsky

ABSTRACT. An anthropological study of pet visiting programs to three nursing homes reveals five aspects of how elderly residents deal with their past and present ties to their families. (1) Sessions trigger childhood memories and family reminiscences associated with animals. (2) Pet loss and human loss are spoken about as interrelated experiences. (3) Animal visits highlight and help counteract the decline of domesticity that people go through in institutions. (4) Residents explore their ties to pets they have had to give up and their relationships with family members currently caring for these animals. (5) The occasional visits of people's kin during pet sessions indicates the role of animals in domestic interaction and the reaction of family members to the situation of their institutionalized relatives. These findings are compared with other studies on the ties between pets and the elderly.

INTRODUCTION

In the life history of an individual, significant attachments can develop with people, places, objects, songs, colors, or any other element of experience with which memories are associated. The family relationships which shape a person's character are naturally a rich source for such associations. Domestic life, however, can include not only people, but also events, rituals, foods, furniture, photographs, and, for many individuals, pets. Domesticated animals are, by definition, creatures who have been attached to the *domus* or home, and pets are those animals who usually live within the walls of a house and share the intimate lives of its residents. Approximate-

Joel S. Savishinsky, is Professor and Chairperson of the Department of Anthropology at Ithaca College, Ithaca, NY 14850. The research reported here has been supported by grants from Ithaca College and the National Endowment for the Humanities. The help to Stephanie Schaaf and Dr. Janet Kranz of the Department of Preventive Medicine at the New York State College of Veterinary Medicine, Cornell University, and of the administrators, staff, residents, and volunteers of Ithacare, Lakeside Nursing Home, and the Reconstruction Home, is gratefully acknowledged.

ly 55% of American households have a dog, cat, or other companion animal, a figure which suggests the widespread presence of pets as "members of the family" (Pet Food Institute, 1983).

The significance of pet-keeping in modern society has received a considerable amount of attention in recent years. It has been highlighted in popular journalism and films, as well as in scholarly conferences and publications (e.g., Anderson, 1975; Fogle, 1980; Katcher and Beck, 1983; Anderson, Hart and Hart, 1984). Many claims have been put forth concerning the therapeutic and educational value of pet ownership. Companion animals have been introduced into clinical and institutional settings to enhance the treatment and well-being of handicapped, developmentally impaired, emotionally disturbed, elderly, hospitalized and imprisoned populations. It has been suggested that pets facilitate self-acceptance and self-confidence among such people, promote the development of their social skills and relationships, and serve as a medium for interpersonal contact and communication.

In the larger society, companion animals are presumed to benefit people in many stages and areas of life. They are seen as helping to educate children about sex, birth, death, biology, and responsibility. They are credited with providing the young and the mature alike with warmth and companionship; a hedge against loneliness and depression; a stimulus to activity and exercise; a sense of security and safety; a shared focus of family concern; a way to relax and reduce stress; a link to the natural world; an opportunity to nurture and be nurtured; a means to create contacts and common interests with other people; and a source of pride, status, and self-esteem (Levinson, 1972; Fox, 1981; McCulloch, 1982). While many advocates of pet ownership are also quick to warn that pets are not a panacea for human suffering and social ills, their caveats come in the midst of a growing chorus of praise for the purported benefits of human-animal ties.

The perception that animals promote the fulfillment of human needs has led to an increase in pet-facilitated therapy programs. Elderly people are among the prime recipients of these efforts, and programs have been geared both to aged individuals who live in their own homes (e.g., Mugford and M'Comiskey, 1975; San Francisco SPCA, 1982; Connell and Lago, 1983), and to those who reside in retirement communities, geriatric facilities, or nursing homes (Corson and Corson, 1980; Bustad, 1980; McCulloch, 1984). Contacts with pet animals are designed to address some of the significant losses that aged people commonly experience, including diminished companionship, a decrease in tactile experience, a decline in stimulating leisure activities, and reduced ties with family and friends. Since many elderly people have also had to give up their own pets upon moving into housing units or institutions designed for their age group, animal visitations are also meant to fill part of the gap created by this additional, involuntary loss. Pet programs thus center on the disruptions in family and personal life that accompany aging, and they constitute one social attempt to reconstruct a balance of domestic experiences caused by the diminution of earlier family relationships.

Despite the upsurge in pet programs for the elderly and other disadvantaged populations, there have been relatively few studies that document and evaluate the human impact of these efforts. Much of the pet therapy research that has been done is either clinical or experimental in nature or it has relied primarily on survey data. Various research reports have been criticized for being overly anecdotal, inconclusive, or lacking in effective sampling or control measures (Beck and Katcher, 1984). Furthermore, few studies have emphasized ongoing participation in, and observation of, companion animal programs in the institutional settings they are designed to humanize. This essay describes the results of one long-term, intensive research project being conducted on the Cornell Companion Animals Program (CCAP), a university-based, volunteer organization that provides weekly pet visitations to various nursing and educational institutions in Tompkins County, New York. The findings presented here center on three nursing homes and the reactions of their elderly residents to the visiting animals and the volunteers who bring them. Of particular importance are the ways in which residents' responses to people and pets reveal features of their past and present ties to their own families. Several of the domestic issues raised by the animals' presence are discussed here, and the results of the research are compared with the findings of other studies on pets and the elderly.

METHODS, OBJECTIVES AND BASIC FINDINGS

The CCAP was begun in the summer of 1982 with the basic goal of providing pet companionship to people whose living situation would normally preclude such contacts for them. At the time of its inception, the organization was conducting visits to three nursing homes, but it has since expanded its coverage to include six geriatric and custodial facilities, several Headstart and day-care centers, a school for children with physical and learning disabilities, a day treatment program for developmentally impaired adults, and a home for troubled adolescents. The program is sponsored by the Department of Preventive Medicine at the New York State College of Veterinary Medicine at Cornell University. While it has a paid, part-time director, the organization relies heavily on a cadre of some 85 volunteers drawn from Ithaca College, Cornell University, and the larger Ithaca community. These individuals are divided up into small groups of 5 to 15 people, each of which is assigned to visit a specific institution every week. The volunteers conduct their visitations using either their own pets or borrowed animals which have been offered to CCAP by people in the community.

Since December 1982, along with several of my students, I have been doing an anthropological study of CCAP's programs in the three nursing homes that the organization has been visiting since its start. Our research has several goals: (a) to describe and analyze the human impact of the pet sessions; (b) to identify the ways in which the program's operation differs among the three facilities; (c) to evaluate the organization's success in meeting its goals; and (d) to make recommendations that would help strengthen and improve the program's effectiveness.

Our methodology has emphasized the anthropological techniques of direct participant-observation, unstructured interviewing, and the collection of life history materials. We accompany volunteers to weekly pet sessions, working alongside them with our own animals. In our behavior, we duplicate the variously active and nondirective approaches that we have seen other volunteers employ in relating to people. The life history materials gathered from participating residents help us to understand more fully their previous ties to animals, their family and personal backgrounds, and their perceptions of institutional life. In addition, we attend the various training, educational, and social events that CCAP sponsors for its volunteer members so as to assess the structure and content of people's experiences within the organization. Finally, to gain a comparative perspective on the impact of the animal visits, we have done participant-observation on non-pet related recreational activities at the three homes under study, and have also been involved in CCAP sessions at other geriatric facilities. The latter two sets of data provide controls against which we can compare the pet visits with people's experiences in other programs and institutions.

Our research indicates that the pet sessions achieve their basic goal of fostering human-animal contact, but that they accomplish this in distinct ways at each of the homes. These differences have been detailed elsewhere (Savishinsky et al., 1983; Savishinsky, 1983–1984), but can be briefly summarized here. At two of the facilities, Ithacare and the Reconstruction Home, with maximum populations of 73 and 72 individuals, respectively, people are seen by small numbers of volunteers and animals in a group format; pet sessions are held in a large room to which interested residents are brought. Lakeside Nursing Home, the third and largest institution, has a capacity of 260 people: here a greater number of pets and volunteers move around the building separately and at their own pace, usually visiting individual residents in their own rooms or lounge areas. Approximately 10% of the people residing at Ithacare and the Reconstruction Home participate each week, while some 30% of Lakeside's population is contacted during an average visit. The differences in size of the volunteer groups and the resident populations at the three facilities, and the distinct formats followed in contacting the latter, yield different statistical profiles of "average" pet sessions (Table 1).

The distinctive experiences generated by these visits are qualitative, as well as quantitative in nature. At the Reconstruction Home and Ithacare, residents' contacts with pets and visitors are of longer duration and more public in nature, while those at Lakeside are briefer, but more intense and private. There is a core of steady volunteers, animals, and residents who regularly participate in sessions at each home, lending visits a degree of continuity and familiarity. Female volunteers outnumber their male counterparts at all the homes, ranging from a ratio of 2:1 at Lakeside to one of 5:1 at Ithacare. At the Reconstruction Home and Ithacare, residents are themselves "volunteers" in the sense that they have agreed to come to sessions; while at Lakeside, volunteers must approach people who may or may not want to be visited. At the latter facility, therefore, CCAP members have to deal with occasional rejection, an experience that program volunteers at other institutions do not have to confront.

Significant numbers of people at each of the homes are not reached by CCAP visitors because of disinterest, dislike of animals, ignorance of the sessions, administrative restrictions on the movement of pets within the facility, or time limitations which prevent volunteers from contacting them. At all three facilities, however, we found that

TABLE 1

STATISTICAL COMPARISON OF SESSIONS
AT THREE NURSING HOMES

	Reconstruction Home	Ithacare	Lakeside Nursing Home
Maximum Size of Facility's Population	72	73	260
Average Number of Residents Seen Per Session	7.6	6.4	78
Percentage of the Population Seen Per Session	11%	9%	30%
Average Number of Volunteers Per Session	3.4	4.5	8.8
Average Number of Animals Per Session	4.2	4.3	8.4
Ratio of Volunteers and Animals to Residents	1.0 volunteer and 1.2 animals to 2.2 residents	1.0 volunteer and 1.0 animal to 1.4 residents	1.0 volunteer 1.0 animal to 8.9 residents

participating residents enjoy and appreciate the visits and relate their significance to previous ties they have had with animals either in their childhood or adult phases of their lives. Floor staff also tend to respond favorably to the sessions, citing their positive impact on residents and acknowledging their own pleasure, as pet owners, in seeing animals used in an innovative way.

For many of the residents, the human contact with volunteers that the sessions offer becomes at least as important for them as the animal companionship being provided. This is manifested in several ways. First, some patients pay little attention to, ignore, or even reject the animals, but interact readily with the people who bring them. Second, volunteers and residents with a long history of involvement in the program often develop close, enduring ties with one another that then become a major feature of the weekly sessions for them. Third, certain residents who are initially noncommunicative or highly repetitive in what they share become more open and discursive in their talk as the weeks go by. Volunteers and residents who are experienced in the program rarely limit their conversations to the animals that are present, but speak about a broad range of personal and topical subjects. We have also found that some institutional staff turn to volunteers they have gotten to know for support in dealing with the problems, frustrations, and human losses inherent in their job.

These ongoing, progressive, and occasionally intense ties with residents and staff are among the richest emotional rewards emphasized by volunteers when evaluating their role. However, volunteers also sometimes experience such relationships as an unexpected commitment or burden whose intimacy, expectations, and demands they have not anticipated taking on as part of their work. Since many of the residents participating in the program are frail and elderly, and all of them are people dealing with the difficulties of being institutionalized, long-term volunteers also have to contend with their deterioration, their depressions, and, inevitably, some of their deaths. These difficult experiences are one factor contributing to a turnover rate of approximately 30% among the volunteers in the first year of CCAP's operation. Our recommendations have included the design of better training programs to prepare volunteers for their work, and the creation of more effective support systems that would allow them to cope with the practical and emotional demands of their experience.

PET VISITS AND FAMILY ISSUES

The weekly pet visits promote a great variety of social, physical, and verbal interactions at the facilities. Residents enjoy the tactile stimulation of contact with animals, an experience that restores an element of touch to the lives of people who are more often handled than led. Furthermore, pet sessions involve social encounters not only between volunteers and residents, but between the latter and staff, and between individuals and their fellow residents. By providing a shared source of approved interest, animals thus crystallize an increase in sociability among several categories of people.

The presence of pets also makes animals an obvious and easy topic of conversation. More noteworthy and more unexpected is the frequency with which certain other subjects are voluntarily raised by residents. Many of their conversations, initially centered on the animals, eventually shift to a concern with their former pets and, from this, their reflections on a range of personal and family issues. The latter include: (a) childhood memories and family reminiscences associated with animals; (b) pet loss and human loss as interrelated experiences; (c) the decline of domesticity that people go through as a result of being institutionalized; and (d) residents' ties to pets they had to give up when moving into the home, and their relationships with those family members who are currently caring for these animals. Of related significance are (e) the occasional, coincidental visits of people's kin to the facilities while sessions are in progress there. Our presence at the latter times allows us to monitor the reactions that these family members have to the pet activities being conducted for their institutionalized relatives. These five domestic issues and situations are either centered on or prompted by the animals, and the content of these experiences is elaborated on below.

Childhood Memories and Family Reminiscences Associated with Animals

Every participating resident has had one or more pets at some stage in life. Without any urging from volunteers, many people immediately respond to the presence of an animal by recounting stories of these earlier relationships. In particular, pets trigger childhood memories through which people detail the membership and lifestyles of the families they have grown up in.

While conversations have many idiosyncratic elements, certain patterns and sequences tend to recur. In one pattern, residents begin talking about a pet that is in the room and then proceed to relate something about an animal that they had as a child or adolescent. This generates discussion about what their family or household had been like at the time they owned that particular pet, and they then follow this up with anecdotes of family history from that stage of life. When reminiscing, many people tend to talk more about their childhood than their adulthood. Such individuals are more likely to discuss ties to their parents than their relations with their spouses or their own children. For these people, then, animals are most likely to conjure up youthful associations rather than memories from other periods of development. Several factors help to explain this. Some lifelong pet owners indicate that their most intense and personalized ties to animals occurred in childhood, while a small number of individuals indicate that they only had pets as children, not as adults.

The images that people have of their childhoods, families, and later life are expressed in certain themes that run through their conversations. Major emphases include the role that pets have played in household humor and people's occupations, personal accomplishments, shared marital experiences, moments of moral ambiguity, and painful memories. Many residents, for example, portray their pets as the source of domestic comedy. With considerable relish, one woman recalled:

> My father didn't want any kittens. So he was always giving the females away. But those "males" we kept just went right on having kittens. He never could tell the difference between males and females. He would get angry and we would laugh.

People from rural backgrounds often combine their memories of pets with stories of their working experiences with farm animals. Such associations range from the prosaic to the sensual. Some talk with pride, as well as nostalgia, about the physical demands of farming and husbandry. Personal accomplishments are sometimes directly linked to work with animals. One man frequently repeats the story of the large number of acres he plowed with his horse when a teenager, always adding, "I was the only one of my brothers who could control that animal." Another man, afflicted by a stroke-related speech impairment, occasionally expresses himself in poetry, often choosing animals for his subject:

> I can remember
> When I milked the cows
> It made me feel good
> Especially on a warm day.

Through the process of recall and retelling, then, many people achieve a renewed appreciation of their own occupations and work histories.

A small number of married couples jointly reside in two of the three homes. They often participate in animal visits together and speak at great length about the pets they have owned. Some of them have a stock set of stories about their animals which they tell to all new volunteers. In certain tales, one member of the couple has some favorite lines that he or she reserves for the telling, and so the spouses relate these anecdotes like a well-practiced ensemble. The pets that widows and widowers in the homes speak of are also connected by them to their deceased spouses. Single, married, and widowed individuals frequently have photographs of former pets on their walls or in albums, and these are shown to visitors with considerable enthusiasm. Since these pictures usually juxtapose kin or spouses with animals, the pet stories that accompany them broaden out into marital and family histories. Using the photographs as a point of departure, a person will describe the houses and vacation spots his family lived in with the pet, the children born during an animal's life, the favoritism that a spouse or child felt for a particular pet or, reversing the emphasis, the animal's partiality for a certain individual. Such reminiscences constitute more than travelogues or a series of tableaux: people weave into them an affirmation of marital and domestic life, drawing, in part, on the animals who shared the family's more positive and memorable moments.[1]

Narratives prompted by pets frequently exhibit a strong moral content. At a simple level, residents compare the behavior of animals and people in order to highlight the nature of human frailties and virtues. One person confessed: "I love animals so much (especially cats) because they don't talk back." At a deeper level, in discussing how members of their families have treated animals, residents often try to draw lessons about the personalities and values of these individuals. The theme of "kindness and cruelty" underlies many of their tales, highlighting, in some instances, an ambiguity that defies resolution. One woman, raised on a farm, compared her brother's gentleness with horses to the harsh way her father handled these animals. His severity, she said, has puzzled her throughout life. At the heart of the paradox for her was the warm and nurturant way her father dealt with his hunting dogs. "You'd think someone who loved one kind of animal would be gentle with all kinds. But I guess not." Another woman pictured animals as exemplars of a kind of domestic moral order that her own grandfather had lost sight of:

> My father was a farmer, and my grandfather before him. My grandfather, though, was not very good. He refused to believe that cows had any mind of their own. He killed a calf once, right in front of its mother. I tell you, that cow never forgave him. That particular cow was a great milker, probably a champ! Every time after my grandfather had killed her calf, whenever he'd milk her, she stuck her foot in the bucket of milk.

Residents, then, tell stories such as these as more than just pieces of family history: they are moral tales through which the characters of their kin can be described and judged.

Reminiscing can be a painful, as well as a meaningful process, and one conversational technique that residents employ to soften the sadness for themselves is to switch back and forth between personal issues and pet topics when they talk. For example, when one man was recounting to a volunteer the harsh discipline and academic failures he went through in elementary school, he periodically interrupted himself to pet the dog at his side and speak for a few moments about her coat, color, and demeanor. These digressions were not the product of a meandering or unfocused mind. Rather, the alternation of subjects made it easier for this resident to address and return to the difficult memories that were emerging. In other instances, the pet and human concerns that people alternate between are more like mirrors of one another. A woman at one institution launched into a lengthy castigation of people who mistreat animals—"They were made to be loved, not abused"—and then began to pepper her monologue with brief comments about how much she had been mistreated by the aunt and uncle who had raised her. A different woman, perplexed at how certain people can willingly acquire animals and then neglect them, began to interject criticisms of her own children for "abandoning" her in the home.

When people juxtapose their own experiences with those of pets, they often project parts of themselves onto these animals. In some of these projections, people also portray other members of their family. One elderly diabetic man, an amputee who had traveled a great deal during his life, once told a lengthy set of stories about the feral cats and dogs who lived near his former residence. He detailed his adventures with one particular cat whom he managed to partially tame, but who remained "very wild, a real scrapper, a womanizer." The man then went on to talk about his second marriage and his "hell-raising father-in-law," a widower who "would not settle down." He described this man in some of the same terms and in much the same spirit of admiration and envy that he used for the cat. The two tales of wildness were intertwined both narratively and thematically: they spoke of individuals who shared a great deal of freedom, enjoying life on the fringes of the domestic world. When he finished talking, the man looked down at his wheelchair and the empty space where one of his legs had once been. He said he had "seen the last of his travels." The cat and his father-in-law had capabilities that were "no longer an option" for him.

Pet visitations confirm that elderly people, when given the opportunity, can talk at great length and with great interest about all phases of their lives. The animals facilitate this by providing a medium through which residents can establish social relationships and begin conversations with volunteers. The latter become witnesses to what people have lived through. As one 95-year-old woman explained: "I have many happy memories, but I now have few friends who are old enough to remember me." Another resident noted that because institutional life has fewer responsibilities, but little freedom, reminiscing helps "to anchor the goings on." Pets do more than foster this process, however. They symbolize the animals who were once part of people's households and, thus, provide associations through which residents can recall, evaluate, integrate, and project the content of their family experience.

Pet Loss and Human Loss as Interrelated Experiences

The death of their pets is a topic that is frequently and spontaneously raised by many residents, and the circumstances of such losses are often described by them in considerable detail. The richness and emotiveness with which they communicate these sometimes distant events is particularly striking in the case of individuals who commonly exhibit poor short-term memory. People often interpolate comments about deceased family members who were connected to the animals being discussed.

The associations that residents make between pet and human loss, however, are often more subtle than simple connections between specific people and animals who have died. Deceased pets are also a subject that engenders thoughtfulness about broader issues of human mortality and morality. Some residents emphasize the longevity of animals that they have had, showing a special pride in the exceptional lifespans these pets achieved. Implicitly or explicitly, people take some of the credit for successfully sustaining their lives for so long. Among elderly people in frail health, surrounded by the death and decline of others, speaking about pets in this way provides an indirect opportunity for addressing some of their own concerns and hopes about life expectancy.

The lives and losses of the animals remembered also have intrinsic meanings of their own. Pets are recalled and mourned not only because they are a connecting thread to memorable experiences and deceased persons. Many residents also speak of their animals as sources of moral value: they are praised for giving and eliciting love, for demonstrating loyalty and trust, for teaching people how to care and be kind, and for offering opportunities to engage in life in a positive way. The death of a creature who embodies such memories and values thus constitutes the loss of a "significant other" for many individuals.

The perception of pets as members of the family also allows people to project onto their deaths a range of personal and domestic meanings. A small number of people told tales of the death of cherished animals whom they have never replaced because, as one man expressed it, he "just couldn't take the thought of losing another one like that." One devoted married couple who are avid, lifelong cat lovers, speak of not being able to imagine life without one another. In discussing their marriage and their former home, they describe the antics of their two favorite cats, a brother-sister team, whom they kept for 19 years. They invariably end their stories by noting that "when the brother died, the sister was so sad that she passed away within a week." The pets thus prefigure the kind of terrible grief they anticipate for themselves.

An elderly woman who had experienced the death of a sibling and two roommates within a five-month period was quite open about how depressed and lonely she had felt. She later received a roommate with whom she developed a very close and mutually sustaining friendship, and she would reflect on how empty her life had been before this person had come to join her. When a goldfish they had been keeping in their room died, this woman analyzed its death in the following words: "I think it died because it was all alone. It was lonely, swimming there by itself in that big globe." The fish thus became a way for her to speak about her prior loneliness as a near fatal experience.

Another example illustrates how one man drew an even more subtle connection between animal death and human loss. This individual is fairly mobile, and he has taken to leaving out food each day for some of the wild animals living in the wooded area surrounding his nursing home. He has recently begun to worry about whether these creatures were becoming dependent on him, and one day expressed his concern that they would die if he forgot to feed them or if he passed away himself. With only a brief pause, he went on to relate that he had gone to visit a friend of his on another floor of the institution that morning, and was told that this man had died. It was only then that he remembered that he had known this fact for several

days, but had somehow forgotten it. His embarrassment was mixed
with the sharp anxiety that he was losing his own memory. Within
one narrative event, then, he had connected the potential demise of
animals, the real death of a friend, his tenuous hold on responsibility, and the possible loss of his own capabilities.[2]

People's past experiences with pet loss can also color their response to current opportunities for animal companionship. Most individuals reached by the program show no long-term effects from
earlier pet deaths. They welcome a chance to renew animal contacts, and some indicate they would enjoy having a pet again, if it
were possible, in the home. But for others, past losses are an impediment to new relationships. One man who declined an offer to be
visited explained: "That's very kind, but I'd rather you didn't. Animals are too sad for me. I mean they remind me too much of the
ones I had. It's painful. I'd rather not if you please."[3]

Most volunteers have also been through the death of a pet, and so
they bring to their work their own interpretations of this experience.
They readily commiserate with residents on their losses, but tend to
emphasize to them the positive value of creating new ties with other
animals. In promoting pet companionship, some volunteers reverse
the emphasis by stressing the benefits that such ties have for the animals as compared to the humans. By means of this reversal, they try
to show residents that they can offer something of value to other
creatures—a self-affirming opportunity that is often lacking in their
daily lives. One woman exemplified this for a group of patients by
telling them the story of how severely depressed and withdrawn her
dog George had become "after the death of his sister" in an auto-
mobile accident. A few months later, when she began to bring him
to the pet program, the sociable interaction with people and animals
had helped to "draw him out again." The moral that the woman
drew from her story had a familial theme: people are not alone in
suffering loss, for animals experience the same devastation when, as
she put it, "their kin die." In her view, the re-engagement offered
by pet sessions can be as therapeutic for the animals as for the people they visit.

The Decline of Domesticity That People Go Through as a Result of Being Institutionalized

An administrator at one of the nursing homes graphically characterized the experience of institutionalization as one of "stripping":
people lose their homes, most of their familiar belongings, much of

their privacy, a good deal of their freedom, many of their friendships, their regular contacts with family, and, in some cases, their pets. Given this reality, it is significant that almost all of the residents who participate in the CCAP program speak positively of the particular facilities they live in. Except for critical comments about the food, their most generally voiced complaints center on the fact that they have been institutionalized rather than on the quality of the institutions themselves. As good as a facility may be, in some people's view, "it will never be like home."

Residents try to cope with this loss of domesticity in several ways. One of their most visible adaptations consists of efforts to domesticate their immediate environment. They render rooms more homelike with family photographs, Bibles, posters, knicknacks, flowers, and plants. The ubiquity of people's interest in animals is reflected in the large number of stuffed pets, plastic beasts, and animal photographs with which they decorate their walls, bureaus, and beds. Just as some individuals tell of having tried to tame wild animals in the past, most residents attempt to tame the institutional spaces they inhabit by populating them with pet images and other props.

Pet sessions also reveal attempts by residents to promote familial types of intimacy with people who had once been strangers. Their desire for contact with volunteers often exceeds their interest in pet companionship. Some residents at Lakeside Nursing Home, noting that certain volunteers come to visit them more regularly than members of their own family, have begun to refer to these volunteers as their "second family" or, with a touch of hyperbole, their "real family." Volunteers at this home are sometimes surprised by the strong expectations that residents have for ongoing, personalized contacts, and some have needed to reconceptualize their role as that of human companions, not just as transporters of animals. At Ithacare and the Reconstruction Home, where visits follow a group format, the presence of a regular core of volunteers, residents, and pets each week creates what some participants specifically identify as a "family atmosphere."

A particularly striking sign of people's desire for human company is their tactile response to volunteers. Not only do residents from the homes love to caress and hold the animals, but some of them also "pet" the volunteers by stroking their arms, holding their hands, and feeling their faces. Volunteers and pets are sometimes treated as if they have a single, undifferentiated body that can be touched and fondled without regard for boundaries.

As the CCAP program has evolved, many of its volunteers have come to accept and reciprocate the "familial" definition of their role. They have recruited such "significant others" as their spouses, children, parents, boyfriends, girlfriends, and roommates to accompany them on visits, transforming sessions into a shared experience. Such visits take on an added dimension for residents, too, who find themselves the focus of "family attention." Young children who are brought to sessions evoke particularly strong responses of interest and delight from elderly residents, who enjoy watching them interact with the pets and play among themselves. Children and animals also provide one measure of how sessions promote a degree of reality orientation among people: certain residents save up candy and treats from their own snacks during the week to give to youngsters and pets during visits.

The way volunteers handle their "presentation of self" (Goffman, 1959) offers further evidence of their desire to be perceived as "family" to the residents. The CCAP program once considered having its members wear name tags during visits so that residents could more easily identify them. But many volunteers strongly objected to the proposal, arguing that it would make them appear like staff and therefore cloud their identity rather than clarify it. At the meeting where the idea was being debated, one volunteer expressed the majority's feelings about their special status:

> We are more like friends and family to the people there, and it is important that they feel free to treat us that way. Some people are shy or reticent when staff are around, and we would not want that to happen with us.

Volunteers not only want to be seen as family, they also tend to identify the elderly with their own kin. Since many of the volunteers are college students, geographically separated from their families, residents serve *in loco familias* by becoming parental and grandparental figures for them. This convergence in how volunteers and residents perceive their relationship yields a shared defintiion of the situation. These two age groups, many of whom are deprived of large, extended families—one set because of old age and institutionalization in a home, the other because of youth and the institutionalization of higher learning—thus help to reproduce a family experience for one another.

Bringing animals into the presence of the elderly, then, does more than just revive memories. It momentarily helps to re-create an element of past domesticity that people can actively participate in. For many residents, the animals answer a need that photographs and flowers cannot satisfy, a desire, as one woman expressed it, for "something living that I can name."

Residents' Ties to Pets They had to Give Up When Moving into the Home, and Their Relationships with Those Family Members Who Are Currently Caring for Them

Residents who have had to give up pets when entering a nursing home have, in many cases, left them in the care of other members of their family. Companion animal visits usually stimulate people to talk about these pets, which, in turn, leads to conversation about the individuals with whom they are currently living. Residents often expand these discussions by commenting on, or telling anecdotes about, other family members, sometimes including stories about the animals that these people own. An experience that many student volunteers have in common with residents is that they, too, have been separated from pets who are being cared for by family members "back at home." This gives the two age groups a shared set of feelings and domestic ties that they can relate to one another about.

When residents talk about the current members of their family, their conversations run a full gamut of emotions and topics. Frequently, expressions of regret and longing over having had to give up a pet are mixed with gratitude for the person who has taken responsibility for it. Some people emphasize that these animals are "on loan" to the relative and that they ultimately expect to be reunited with them. The pets are thus a way for such individuals to voice their perception of nursing home life as a temporary situation. Furthermore, residents are usually able to report on the current health or recent adventures of their pets, indicating that their condition is a standard topic of conversation between the past and present owners, and that the animals provide one stimulus for contact between such persons.

In discussions of pets, care-givers, and other family members, people often choose to bring up the subject of how they themselves came to live in a nursing home. Despite stereotypes about the anger and resentment of residents living in such situations, we have encountered many individuals who feel that a nursing facility is the best place for them to be. Some compare the increasing helplessness they had been experiencing before entering the home to the dependency of domestic animals. "While not bed-ridden," said one man, "I could no more take care of myself than I could my dog." Staff members point out that a number of the more able-bodied residents, who can still get out into the community, perceive and use the homes as they would a hotel. There are, however, many people who feel that they have been placed in an institution against their will, and some claim that they have essentially been forgotten or abandoned by their families since moving into the facility. A number of residents argue that their kin were not incapable of caring for them, just unwilling to do so. This sometimes revives the themes of kindness, cruelty, and neglect in their discourse, but now the focus is on them rather than on animals. One woman, who had earlier praised her son and daughter-in-law for taking on her pet beagle, wryly observed that "they kept the dog and got rid of me."

The Occasional Visits of People's Kin While Pet Sessions Are in Progress

On occasion, residents receive visits from family members while pet sessions are being held. The reactions of these kin reveal feelings they have about their institutionalized relatives, about the latter's ties to animals, and about the nature of institutional life itself.

Family members display a range of delight and surprise when they encounter a pet session. Many of them have been unaware that such a program was being conducted in the home, and acknowledge its special relevance for relatives who have been separated from their animals. Some visitors, sensitive to how attached their kinsperson was to a pet, are emphatically relieved and grateful that there is an opportunity for residents to renew such contacts. The daughter of one elderly patient once took a volunteer into the corner of her mother's room and confided:

> My mother loves, absolutely loves, cats. She left me her two Siamese to take care of. I know she misses them. I have to tell you that one of them died—but I haven't told her. I just don't have the heart. Thank goodness she gets to see the animals that you bring here. I hope you visit her when you can. I know it will mean a great deal to her . . . and to me too.

Pets affect the dynamics of family visits by providing a focus and a topic for talk at a time that can be tense, awkward, or full of silence. Conversations during these visits frequently and easily become centered not only on the animals present in the room, but on those who are living at home. At Lakeside, which has a permissive attitude about animals being in the building, some families have been spurred by the model of the CCAP sessions to bring along pets on their own visits. Institutional staff, when taking the families of prospective residents on a tour of a home, often emphasize the special quality of the animal sessions as a selling point about the facility's recreational program. While the coincidence of family visits and pet sessions is not high, these occasions do highlight the ongoing role of animals in people's lives, and the attitudes and reactions that pets are capable of evoking.

COMPARISONS AND CONCLUSIONS

Domestic animals are a nearly universal feature of human societies. Many cultures retain animals as pets, but few have elaborated pet-keeping to the extent that contemporary Western peoples have (Savishinsky, 1983). Companion animal programs are a therapeutic expression of this pattern which scholars have recently begun to study and evaluate. The focus on the family relationships of institutionalized elderly people in this essay reflects only one of several emphases in the programs being analyzed, and it is important to recognize that these domestic data arise in the midst of pet encounters that are designed to be primarily tactile, social, recreational, and therapeutic in nature. The main findings described here can be summarized as follows:

1. Pet visits evoke memories from childhood and other life stages that contribute to the integrative process of reminiscing for the elderly.
2. People draw connections between human loss and pet loss, through which they confront issues of mortality and morality.
3. Animal visits help to counteract the decline of domesticity inherent in institutional life: pets are symbolic and literal embodiments of the more complete domestic experiences that residents once had, and companion animal volunteers help contribute to a family definition of the situation.
4. Visiting pets are associated with animals that residents have

had to give up, as well as with the family members currently caring for them. Sessions thus provide opportunities for people to praise, criticize, and explore these other domestic ties.

5. When residents' kin visit during pet sessions, animals help to ease the process of interaction between them and their institutionalized relatives.

A number of the assessments on animal companionship done by other scientists have also centered on the relationship between pets and the elderly, and this work can therefore be compared with the results of the research reported on here.

Several studies indicate that animal contacts provide a range of benefits for the aged that parallel those we found in the three nursing homes. Bustad (1980), Bustad and Hines (1982), McCulloch (1982, 1984), and Brickel (1980–1981) have summarized much of this research and the therapeutic effects identified in it. The humor, acceptance, relaxation, ease of conversation, sensory stimulation, opportunity to nurture, and tactile pleasure that they cite in other authors' writings have all been evidenced in our work. The animals' role in the creation of social ties and the renewal of memories, emphasized by various investigators, has also been observed by us.

It should be noted, however, that a number of other studies on animals and the aged have been done on facilities where pets are either part of controlled experiments or they live permanently within an institution, and so the animals' contacts with inhabitants can be much more frequent and intense than in the cases we examined. Brickel (1979), for example, found that resident cats were social facilitators for both patients and staff in a geriatric ward treating people with chronic brain syndrome. Yurdick et al. (1980) indicate that pets are an asset in nursing situations because they help the elderly feel needed, to develop a positive self-image, and to contribute to a variety of sensory experiences. Corson and his collaborators have introduced resident animals to both psychiatric and geriatric institutions and have found that they are a catalyst for interactions among and between the residents and the staff; that they improve morale and a sense of community within the facility; that they help severely withdrawn patients to expand their ties to other people; that they enhance self-reliance and reduce infantile behavior; and that they constitute a form of reality therapy by encouraging individuals to act responsibly, nurturantly, and appropriately in terms of their immediate social environment (Corson, Corson, and Gwynne, 1975; Corson and Corson, 1980, 1981). In a clinical study using a nonresident dog, Brickel (1984) has shown that pet-facilitated therapy can help counteract depression and improve self-perception in the institution-alized elderly. Animals have been found to contribute to short-term, transient improvements in behavior and sociability among the chronically-ill elderly by Hendy (1984) and Jendro, Watson, and Quigley (1984). Our own work, and some of the results that Bustad (1980), Brickel (1980–1981), and McCulloch (1984) cite, indicate that similar, if more modest benefits, accrue to nursing-home resi-dents who are the focus of visiting pet programs.

Aged people living in noninstitutional settings have also been studied with varied results. Mugford and M'Comiskey's (1975) ear-ly experiment in introducing caged birds to the isolated elderly in a British city showed positive effects of both a social and psychologi-cal nature. Recent surveys by Lago and his associates (Connell and Lago, 1983; Lago, Knight, and Connell, 1983), and Ory and Goldberg (1983), focusing on the satisfactions of pet ownership among older rural Americans residing in their own communities, demonstrate that companion animals are more beneficial for some elderly individuals than for others: people's sex, economic situa-tion, marital status, and degree of attachment to their pets are significant variables affecting how important animals will be as in-dicators of physical and emotional well-being. Some populations of female, married, and low-income pet owners, for example, exhibit lower health and morale. An Australian survey shows that divorced, separated, widowed, and childless people—that is, individuals lack-ing a normal family network—have more of their needs satisfied by pet dogs than is the case with dog owners at other stages of the fami-ly life cycle (Salmon and Salmon, 1983). Kidd and Feldman (1981) found that elderly pet owners have better self-images and more con-fidence in themselves than nonowners.

Levinson (1972), a clinical psychologist, was one of the first to note the comprehensive contributions that pets can make to the emo-tional well-being of the elderly by the way they increase security, reduce loneliness, improve self-acceptance, and stimulate activity. Subsequent studies have examined the impact of animals on the physical health of the elderly. Some writers suggest that indepen-dent aged people who keep pets may live longer and healthier lives than those without animals (Bustad and Hines, 1982; Messent, 1983), although contradictory and inconclusive findings have also been reported on this issue (Robb and Stegman, 1983; Lago,

Knight, and Connell, 1983). The ownership of companion animals has been positively correlated with better health status among people receiving medical treatment (Katcher and Friedmann, 1980; Robb, 1983), and has been related to enhanced survival rates among former patients of coronary care units (Friedmann et al., 1980). As suggestive as some of these data are, several of the studies from which they derive have been critized on methodological and interpretive grounds (Beck and Katcher, 1984). Furthermore, it should also be recognized that poets and novelists have long been aware of what behavioral and medical scientists have only recently discovered about pets. Writers such as Virginia Woolf (1933) and May Sarton (1973, 1981) have dealt movingly with the special meanings that companion animals can have for the seriously ill and elderly.

Pet research casts a special light on two issues that have drawn the attention of many people in gerontology, viz, reminiscing and disengagement. In the psychology of aging, reminiscence is no longer perceived of as a harmless, pointless acitivity. Rather, it is a healthy and productive process through which the elderly integrate the threads of their existence and come to an appreciation of what has been meaningful in their lives. Reminiscing is thus a developmental task that marks an older person's continued growth and present adjustment (Bulter, 1968; Myerhoff, 1978). Several observers have noted that pets facilitate this activity by triggering memories from childhood and other life stages, thereby contributing to the fulfillment of a significant endeavor (Levinson, 1972; Bustad, 1980; Brickel, 1984). A number of factors appear to underly this connection. First, animals are directly associated with real events in the personal histories of people who are lifelong pet owners. Second, pets encourage individuals to engage in regressive forms of play that characterized earlier stages of their development (Corson and Corson, 1980). Third, childhood experiences with pets have been shown to shape the adult patterns and relationships that people later establish with animals (Messent, 1983). Fourth, as Jung (1933) recognized over half a century ago, the elderly resemble children in that these two age groups are most readily in touch with the unconscious, a side of ourselves that animals symbolize. As tokens, totems, and symbols, pets may therefore foster communication with this part of the human psyche.[4]

Disengagement is another process that has been linked with the elderly (Cumming and Henry, 1961). It explains their status as the result of a mutual withdrawal by the aged and those who once associated with them. Critics point out that many older people do not want to dissociate themselves from social and cultural life, but are cut off from once satisfying experiences by the geographic mobility of other family members, the death of spouses and contemporaries, the institutionalization that they and significant others undergo, their poverty or reduced financial resources, the limitations imposed by their declining health and vigor, and cultural attitudes which stereotype and stigmatize elderly people in negative ways (Watson and Maxwell, 1977).

To the extent that disengagement comes about because of social, economic, and medical barriers, and because of the unilateral withdrawal of other people from the elderly, organizations such as CCAP counteract these forces and the attendant feelings of anger and abandonment they engender. Other recreational and volunteer efforts in nursing homes undoubtedly have a similar effect in combating ageism, segregation, and isolation (Corson and Corson, 1981). We also found, however, that although many of the people to whom the pet program is available accept its opportunities, its rejection by others may express the desire of certain persons to remain detached from social relationship. However, the readiness with which most participants welcome the chance to create new human and animal bonds suggests that, for them, the visits are a type of re-engagement.

Finally, our study indicates several gaps in the companion animal research that has been done to date. First, many studies mention, but do not explore, the family connections and symbolism that pets embody for the elderly. Since the loss of domesticity is one of the major deficits of aging, and this loss is aggravated by the conditions of life in "total institutions" (Goffman, 1961), the family meanings that animals possess for the aged are worthy of deeper analysis. Second, the focus of most pet therapy research on clinical applications, experimental situations, and survey data, has meant a relative neglect of the work done by voluntary organizations. In particular, the role of the volunteers, the effect on them of their experiences, and the significance of the human companionship that they intentionally or inadvertently provide, all deserve greater consideration (Savishinsky, 1984). It is tempting to overestimate the role of animals in such programs and miss the impact of the people standing beside or behind them (Hendy, 1984). Since most students of pet-facilitated therapy emphasize its adjunctive role in helping disadvantaged populations, it is important to explore the human context within which these encounters occur. Such attention would yield two dividends. It would allow for a better appreciation of volunteerism as an ethic in American society, and it would enrich our understanding of current attempts to treat animals humanely and the aged humanly.

END NOTES

1. Ruby (1983) has made similar observations on the significance of pet photographs in family imagery.

2. Levinson (1972) argues that the interest of the elderly in the preservation of wild animals may help to sublimate their fear of immediate death. Also, for the aged to perceive connections between human and pet loss is particularly important in view of the fact that researchers differ among themselves as to whether these two forms of death affect people in similar or different ways. Stewart (1983) feels that these losses lead to distinct types of behavior and bereavement, while Quackenbush and Glickman (1983) have found significant parallels in the human responses they evoke. In their experiences counseling individuals who have recently been through the loss of a companion animal, Quackenbush and Glickman (1983) note that older pet owners tend to experience more intense bereavement than younger persons. They feel that this may reflect the crucial importance of pets among aged people with reduced human contacts.

3. The potential for animals to mirror or evoke human pain is also reflected in a remark made by Carobeth Laird (1979), an elderly anthropologist who wrote her own "memoir of life in a nursing home by a survivor." Laird once declined to go on an outgoing to a zoo planned for the residents in her nursing home: "I felt too much like a caged animal myself to enjoy looking at other caged animals" (1979, p. 112).

4. It should be noted that these arguments about resemblances between children and the aged are not referring to senility or the way that institutionalization sometimes infantilizes the elderly. Rather, they draw attention to the childhood associations of the aged as a potentially positive aspect of their thinking and imagery.

REFERENCES

Anderson, R. K., Hart, B. L., & Hart, L. A. (Eds.). *The pet connection*. Minneapolis, Minn.: CENSHARE, University of Minnesota, 1984.

Anderson, R. S. (Ed.). *Pet animals and society*. London: Bailliere Tindall, 1975.

Beck, A. M., & Katcher, A. H. A new look at pet-facilitated therapy. *Journal of the American Veterinary Medicine Association*, 1984, *4*, 414–421.

Brickel, C. M. The therapeutic role of cat mascots with a hospital-based geriatric population. *The Gerontologist*, 1979, *19*, 368–372.

Brickel, C. M. A review of the roles of pet animals in psychotherapy and with the elderly. *International Journal of Aging and Human Development*, 1980–1981, *12*, 119–128

Brickel, C. M. Depression in the nursing home: A pilot study using pet-facilitated therapy. In R. K. Anderson, B. L. Hart, & L. A. Hart (Eds.). *The pet connection*. Minneapolis, Minn.: CENSHARE, University of Minnesota, 1984.

Bustad, L. K. *Animals, aging and the aged*. Minneapolis, Minn.: University of Minnesota Press, 1980.

Bustad, L. K., & Hines, L. Placement of animals with the elderly: Benefits and strategies. *California Veterinarian*, 1982, 36, 37–44, 50.

Butler, R. N. The life review: An interpretation of reminiscence in the aged. In B. L. Neugarten (Ed.), *Middle age and aging*. Chicago, Ill.: University of Chicago Press, 1968.

Connell, C. M., & Lago, D. J. A report on research on the effects of pets on the well-being of the elderly. *The Latham Letter*, 1983, *4*, 14–16.

Corson, S. A., & Corson, E. O. Pet animals as non-verbal communication mediators in psychotherapy in institutional settings. In S. A. Corson & E. O. Corson (Eds.), *Ethology and non-verbal communication in mental health.* New York: Pergamon Press, 1980.

Corson, S. A., & Corson, E. O. Companion animals as bonding catalysts in geriatric institutions. In B. Fogle (Ed.), *Interrelations between people and pets.* Springfield, Ill.: Charles C. Thomas, 1981.

Corson, S. A., Corson, E. O., & Gwynne, P. H. Pet-facilitated psychotherapy. In R. S. Anderson (Ed.), *Pet animals and society.* London: Balliere Tindall, 1975.

Cumming, E., & Henry, W. *Growing old.* New York: Basic Books, 1961.

Fogle, B. (Ed.). *Interrelations between people and pets.* Springfield, Ill.: Charles C. Thomas, 1981.

Fox, M. W. Relationships between the human and non-human animals. In B. Fogle (Ed.), *Interrelations between people and pets.* Springfield, Ill.: Charles C. Thomas, 1981.

Friedmann, E., Katcher, A. H., Lynch, J. J., & Thomas, S. A. Animal companions and one-year survival of patients after discharge from a coronary care unit. *Public Health Report*, 1980, *95*, 307–312.

Goffman, E. *The presentation of self in everyday life.* Garden City, N.Y.: Doubleday, 1959.

Goffman, E. *Asylums: Essays on the social situation of mental patients and other inmates.* Garden City, N.Y.: Doubleday, 1961.

Hendy, H. H. Effects of pets on the sociability and health activities of nursing home residents. In R. K. Anderson, B. L. Hart, & L. A. Hart (Eds.), *The pet connection.* Minneapolis, Minn.: CENSHARE, University of Minnesota, 1984.

Jendro, C., Watson, C., & Quigley, J. The effects of pets on the chronically-ill elderly. In R. K. Anderson, B. L. Hart, & L. A. Hart (Eds.), *The pet connection.* Minneapolis, Minn.: CENSHARE, University of Minnesota, 1984.

Jung, C. G. *Modern man in search of a soul* (W. S. Dell & C. F. Baynes, trans.). New York: Harcourt, Brace and World, 1933.

Katcher, A. H., & Beck, A. M. (Eds.). *New perspectives on our lives with companion animals.* Philadelphia: University of Pennsylvania Press, 1983.

Katcher, A. H., & Friedmann, E. Potential health value of pet ownership. *The Compendium on Continuing Education for the Practicing Veterinarian*, 1980, *2*, 117–122.

Kidd, A. H., & Feldmann, B. M. Pet ownership and self-perceptions of older people. *Psychological Reports*, 1981, *48*, 867–875.

Lago, D. J., Knight, B., & Connell, C. Relationships with companion animals among the rural elderly. In A. H. Katcher & A. M. Beck (Eds.), *New perspectives on our lives with companion animals.* Philadelphia: University of Pennsylvania Press, 1983.

Laird, C. *Limbo: A memoir about life in a nursing home by a survivor.* Novato, Calif.: Chandler and Sharp, 1979.

Levinson, B. M. *Pets and human development.* Springfield, Ill.: Charles C. Thomas, 1972.

McCulloch, M. J. Animal facilitated therapy: Overview and future direction. *California Veterinarian*, 1982, *36*, 13–24.

McCulloch, M. J. Pets in therapeutic programs for the aged. In R. K. Anderson, B. L. Hart, & L. A. Hart (Eds.), *The pet connection.* Minneapolis, Minn.: CENSHARE, University of Minnesota, 1984.

Messent, P. R. A review of recent developments in human-companion animal studies. *California Veterinarian*, 1983, *37*, 26–31.

Mugford, R. A., & M'Comiskey, J. G. Some recent work on the psychotherapeutic value of cage birds with old people. In R. S. Anderson (Ed.), *Pet animals and society.* London: Bailliere Tindall, 1975.

Myerhoff, B. *Number our days.* New York: Simon and Schuster, 1978.

Ory, M. G., & Goldberg, E. L. Pet possession and life satisfaction in elderly women. In A. H. Katcher & A. M. Beck (Eds.), *New perspectives on our lives with companion animals.* Philadelphia: University of Pennsylvania Press, 1983.

134   PETS AND THE FAMILY

Pet Food Institute. *Pet Food Institute Fact Sheet 1983.* Washington, D.C.: Author, 1983.
Quackenbush, J. A., & Glickman, L. Social work services for bereaved pet owners: A retrospective case study in a veterinary teaching hospital. In A. H. Katcher & A. M. Beck (Eds.), *New perspectives on our lives with companion animals.* Philadelphia: University of Pennsylvania Press, 1983.
Robb, S. S. Health status correlates of pet-human association in a health-impaired population. In A. H. Katcher & A. M. Beck (Eds.), *New perspectives on our lives with companion animals.* Philadelphia: University of Pennsylvania Press, 1983.
Robb, S. S., & Stegman, C. E. Companion animals and elderly people: A challenge for evaluators of social support. *The Gerontologist,* 1983, *23,* 277–282.
Ruby, J. Images of the family: The symbolic implications of animal photography. In A. H. Katcher & A. M. Beck (Eds.), *New perspectives on our lives with companion animals.* Philadelphia: University of Pennsylvania Press, 1983.
Salmon, P. W., & Salmon, I. M. Who owns who?: Psychological research into the human-pet bond in Australia. In A. H. Katcher & A. M. Beck (Eds.), *New perspectives on our lives with companion animals.* Philadelphia: University of Pennsylvania Press, 1983.
San Francisco Society for the Prevention of Cruelty to Animals. *Pets and older people: Senior services program.* San Francisco: Author, 1982.
Sarton, M. *As we are now.* New York: W. W. Norton, 1973.
Sarton, M. *A reckoning.* New York: W. W. Norton, 1981.
Savishinsky, J. S. Pet ideas: The domestication of animals, human behavior, and human emotions. In A. H. Katcher & A. M. Beck (Eds.), *New perspectives on our lives with companion animals.* Philadelphia: University of Pennsylvania Press, 1983.
Savishinsky, J. S. In the company of animals: An anthropological study of pets and people in three nursing homes. *The Lathan Letter,* 1983–84, *5,* 1, 9, 10, 21, 22.
Savishinsky, J. S. Volunteer experience in pets visits to three nursing homes. *People-Animals-Environment,* 1984, *2.*
Savishinsky, J. S., Lathan, R., Kobayakawa, M., & Nevins, A. *The life of the hour: A study of people and pets in three nursing homes.* Ithaca, N.Y.: Ithaca College, 1983.
Stewart, M. Loss of a pet—loss of a person: A comparative study of bereavement. In A. H. Katcher & A. M. Beck (Eds.), *New perspectives on our lives with companion animals.* Philadelphia: University of Pennsylvania Press, 1983.
Watson, W. H., & Maxwell, R. J. *Human aging and dying: A study in sociocultural gerontology.* New York: St. Martin's Press, 1977.
Woolf, V. *Flush: A biography.* New York: Harcourt, Brace, Jovanovich, 1933.
Yurick, A. G., Robb, S. S., Spier, B. E., & Ebert, N. J. (Eds.), *The aged person and the nursing process.* New York: Appleton-Century-Crofts, 1980.

The Death of a Pet:
Human Responses to the Breaking
of the Bond

Kathleen V. Cowles

ABSTRACT. The loss of a pet, whether due to the death of the animal or any other cause of separation, can be the impetus for acute grief responses in individuals of all ages. In 1981, the author completed an in-depth study that explored and reported descriptions offered by pet owners of the deaths of their pets and their perceived associated responses. This paper will examine the thinking and research in the area of human responses to pet death using the results of the author's study to highlight the major concepts.

HUMAN-ANIMAL ATTACHMENT

Non-scientific literature has long attested to the importance and value placed upon domestic animals by humans. Collections of short stories and poetry abound in tributes to animals who served their human companions and received words and gestures of love in return (Bourjaily, 1979; Byron, 1890; Eliot, 1971; Kipling, 1936; O'Neill, 1979; Yates, 1979). However, although animals have played an important role in the lives of many humans throughout recorded time (Arkow, 1977; Levinson, 1972), it was not until recently that the emotional bond that can exist between a human and a pet was recognized within the scientific literature.

Today, the emotional bond between human and pet has become the focus for researchers and authors from many disciplines. The pet has, for much of the scientific community, become legitimized as a significant attachment figure. Rhodes (1980), in discussing a need for greater human awareness among his veterinary students, emphatically stated that "a number of people are waking up to the

Kathleen V. Cowles, RN, MS, is on the faculty of the School of Nursing, The University of Wisconsin-Milwaukee, PO Box 413, Milwaukee, WI 53201.

fact that the Human/Animal bond is a very important aspect of human mental health'' (p. 2).

While both Keddie (1977) and Rynearson (1978) discussed the potential for complicated grief related to heightened attachment to or dependence on a pet, both also commented on the contributions domestic animals may make to the lives of their human companions. Rynearson (1978) stated, ''This paper suggests that the human and pet are significant attachment figures for one another. Under normal circumstances they share complimentary attachment because of mutual need and response'' (p. 553). Nieburg (1980) also noted that in the field of clinical psychology ''. . . we have become aware of their (pets) inherrent emotional value to human beings . . . as non-competitive, non-judgemental companions'' (p. 3).

Although pets are often viewed as companions, they are also considered by many owners as family members (Harris, 1984; Katcher & Rosenberg, 1979) or ''surrogate relatives'' (Keddie, 1977, p. 22). In this author's study, all of the subjects described the pet as a part of the family and/or as a child figure. One in particular commented that she gave her dog the status of ''a sibling with my children.'' However the bond is perceived, the human attachment to the pet is significant in many instances.

The study I undertook in 1981 involved 9 adult subjects, each of whom were interviewed in depth for their perceptions of the deaths of their pets and the associated grief responses. The subjects were recruited through several veterinarians and by word of mouth. They ranged in age from 21 to 65, had owned their deceased pets for between 2 and 19 years, and each had also owned pets at an earlier time. All subjects were of middle class background, employed, and lived in single family dwellings. With the exception of one middle aged woman, each of the subjects lived with a significant other whom they considered a support person.

THE BREAKING OF THE BOND

As with any attachment bond, the bond between human and pet can be and often is broken. The life span of most species of pets is relatively short, making separation by death a more frequent occurrence than is usually experienced in the human/human bond. Pets also run away or become lost. In addition, some individuals are forced to give up their pets for many reasons, including a move to housing where pets are not allowed or a previously undetected allergy of a family member. Whatever the cause of the separation, the loss of a pet is perceived as a loved being can be a profoundly disturbing experience.

The death of a pet may represent many different things to different persons, including an initial separation experience, a lessening of reality contact, or the loss of an otherwise unobtainable recipient of care and unconditional companionship (Levinson, 1972; Nieburg, 1979a). For children, the death of a pet may be their first encounter with a permanent separation. Because the young child often thinks of the family pet as similar to him/herself (Levinson, 1972), the death of the animal can be confusing and frightening. It can be interpreted by the child as a punishment, and if so, the child may ask why the pet was punished and if a similar punishment might ever occur to her/himself. Since most young children think that death is reversible (Nagy, 1948; Swain, 1979), they may at times wish the pet dead, thinking that they can resurrect it. Then when the animal does die and the finality of death becomes a reality, the child may experience extreme feelings of guilt and even nightmares in which the pet appears as a threatening, ferocious animal (Levinson, 1972).

Consistent contact with reality can be enhanced for many individuals by pet ownership. In an early study, Mugford (cited in Holden, 1981) assessed the personalities and social adjustment of 48 elderly persons who lived alone and were given to their care either a plant or a parakeet. At the end of three years it was found that the parakeet owners were distinctly better off emotionally and socially than were the plant owners. Mugford reported that "they had more friends, more visitors, and generally more links with their communities" (p. 418).

For those who are retired, time takes on a new, often less important meaning. The absence of a rigid daily schedule can lead to disorganization and occasionally, disorientation. According to Katcher and Friedmann (1980), "The presence of an animal, especially an animal that makes demands on the owner, provides a stimulus for maintaining a daily routine" (p. 119). With the loss of the pet, reality may become clouded as social contacts lessen and days become seemingly endless. In a study of pet bereavement in older owners, Quackenbush (1984) noted that "97% of them reported experiencing some disruption in their daily living routines; most often eating and sleeping schedules became erratic. . . . Socialization diminished for 82% of the elderly bereaved owners and 61% of the non-elderly bereaved'' (p. 295). In addition, Quackenbush noted a significant difference between the elderly owners and the non-elderly owners in terms of job-related problems following the death of a pet. He stated "One hundred percent of the working elderly bereaved experienced job-related difficulties after their pet's death while 55% of the working non-elderly bereaved experienced similar difficulties'' (p. 295). Even in younger owners the absence of the pet may cause momentary lapses in orientation. One subject in the author's study commented that she would periodically think "Oh, I have to take the dog out'' and then would realize that the dog was dead. These episodes would always end with the subject crying.

As a recipient of care and unconditional companionship, pets can play a major role in the lives of both young and old. Children and adults may accept an animal as a confidant and a source of emotional support, as well as a source of continuity at times of family stress (MacDonald, 1979). To the older child and adolescent, the pet may represent an accepting, noncritical friend, sometimes a rare commodity in adolescence (Nieburg, 1979b, Nieburg & Fischer, 1982). Women in their middle years may experience a sense of uselessness if they have devoted their earlier adult years to the care of children. A pet may easily serve as a surrogate for those children who have grown and left home. For the growing population of single adults who live alone, pets can play an integral role in providing companionship. And finally, for people of all ages, but especially for older adults, the pet may also meet the very basic human need of being needed. As a consequence of growing old in today's society one may lose both the opportunity and the means of care for others (Katcher & Friedmann, 1980). A pet, and especially an interactive pet, can help to reduce feelings of uselessness and the consequent feelings of lowered self esteem. The pet's role as companion and recipient of care is indeed an important one, and it is the loss of this animal that can arouse the most intense grief responses in the owner.

AFFECTIVE RESPONSES TO PET DEATH

Denial of impending death or the death in itself is often one of the first responses observed in bereaved pet owners. Denial is itself a cognitive response, but it serves as a mechanism to delay painful affective responses until the grieving person is able to cope effectively with them. Short term denial is normal and should not be cause for alarm in those who provide support to grieving persons. While questions of "Are you sure he's dead?" may be cause for frustration following a careful explanation of the demise of the pet, Hopkins (1984) suggested that allowing time for owners to work through denial is the best approach. He also noted, "Attacking denial more aggressively will only intensify the client's defense mechanism and leave you in a position from which you can help neither the client nor the patient" (p. 279). When denial can no longer be used to shield the person from the painful reality, it is replaced by numerous and varied affective responses.

Feelings of emptiness, sadness, and pain were those most frequently mentioned by subjects in the author's study. While feelings of guilt related to the pets' deaths were not reported by subjects in this study, they were documented by a number of other authors (Harris, 1984; Hopkins, 1984; Keddie, 1977; Levinson, 1972). Guilt is generally defined as anger turned inward. Harris particularly noted that when euthanasia is an issue, the guilt experienced by the owner may be overwhelming. Despite the cognitive awareness that the animal may be suffering, the affective response to actively terminating a life to relieve suffering is often one of guilt. Owners may question their own motives, knowing that they, rather than the pet, have the sole power to choose life or death. They may also question the adequacy of their previous care of the pet. That is, did they do all that could be done to avoid the illness or accident that brought them to the point of having to choose for or against euthanasia? Although euthanasia is not an accepted choice in human death situations, the guilt feelings of persons grieving a human loss are not unlike those expressed by pet owners. Therefore, while euthanasia may stimulate feelings of guilt in some individuals, it is not the only causative factor.

There are several possible explanations for the almost total absence of expressed guilt feelings in the author's study in which almost all of the pets had been euthanized. These possibilities are important in that they may provide some clues to effective intervention with grieving pet owners. While the majority of interviews were done within six weeks of the pets' deaths, this time interval may have been sufficient for the subjects to completely work through their guilt feelings. However, there was no indication that guilt had been experienced even immediately before or after the deaths. In fact, very little anger of any kind was detected in the subjects' reports. There appeared instead to be a sense of satisfaction on the part of the subjects that they had made appropriate choices and that their choices had been pet-oriented, rather than self-oriented. Most suggested that a choice against euthanasia would have been a selfish attempt to keep the animal alive for the owner's sake. Two subjects openly expressed feelings of relief in knowing that the animal would no longer suffer. What is most important is that all of these individuals commented on the support they had received from family members and from their veterinarians on the choice for euthanasia. None reported feeling forced to make a choice by any other person. This support may have significantly reduced the amount of self-doubt and helped to affirm the appropriateness of each individual's choice.

Anger that is directed toward others is another frequently experienced affective response to the loss of a significant other. Its occurrence in bereaved pet owners is reported extensively in the literature. While the anger of grieving persons may appear irrational to observers, it is very real for the bereaved and may serve to temporarily lessen the pain of grief. Often the anger is directed at the most available person; many times this is the veterinarian. As Harris (1984) noted, "They're angry at the death, the death that's taken away this loving creature that they cherish. But they can't deal with that because death is this nebulous thing. But they sure can deal with the veterinarian because he was there" (p. 263). In families with young children, anger may be directed by the children at the adult family member who has either made a decision for euthanasia or is perceived to not have "protected" the pet adequately and is therefore thought to be responsible for the death.

All of the literature that provides guidelines to veterinarians for supporting grieving clients urges an understanding of the anger as a defense mechanism as a means of coping calmly with a client's anger (Harris, 1984; Hopkins, 1984; Katcher & Rosenberg, 1979). Regardless of who is providing supportive services for bereaved pet owners, it is of utmost importance that anger not be responded to with anger.

The discomfort of many pet owners in expressing feelings related to the deaths of their pets has been repeatedly reported in the literature. Both Katcher and Rosenberg (1979) and Rynearson (1978) specifically noted that pet owners might be especially vulnerable because of a reluctance to express their feelings due to perceived negative societal attitudes toward human/pet attachment. Katcher and Rosenberg (1979) stated, "Owners interviewed after losing an animal commonly say that they have not talked with anyone outside the family about their feelings. . . . The lack of universal social mechanisms for dealing with grief for an animal probably impairs the resolution of grief and isolates the grieving owner'' (p. 890). One subject in the author's study bitterly reported that when she appeared upset at work the day following her dog's death, her boss responded by saying, ''Well, it's just a dumb dog.'' She then added that she made an additional effort to control her expression of feelings at work and noted, ''If people haven't had a pet, they don't understand.''

Professional awareness of the need of pet owners to express their grief is, however, becoming more evident. At least two grief counselors now work full time in large animal medical centers to provide support to pet owners (Cohen, 1983; Quackenbush, 1984). In addition, the veterinary literature is also providing information on the dynamics of grief and how to facilitate the grieving process to those who may be the first to encounter the pet owner's grief (Bernbaum, 1982; Holzworth, 1981; Katcher & Rosenberg, 1979; Nieburg, 1979a, 1979b; Thomas; 1982).

COGNITIVE RESPONSES TO PET DEATH

Memories of the pet, usually stimulated by particular daily activities associated with the animal, were reported by all subjects in the author's study. Two subjects also noted memories stimulated by what they described as searching behaviors of their other pets who had lived in the home at the same time as the deceased animal. While memories may at first be painful (Katcher & Rosenberg, 1979; Thomas, 1982), most owners will eventually derive comfort from recalling the pet and particular ''special'' times spent with the pet. Nieburg (1979b) suggested that owners should be encouraged to verbalize and share memories of experiences with the pet. It is through repetitive sharing of memories that energy bound to the pet can be released so that owners may invest in new objects and attachments according to Nieburg.

If the pet has died as a result of an accident, a cognitive reliving of the event may be evidenced in the owner. Rumination, or a frequent recall of the same event or thought, is necessary for some bereaved persons as it helps in establishing the reality of a shocking event. During the single 90 minute interviews conducted by the author, two subjects spontaneously repeated, almost verbatim, their entire detailed reports of the events occurring immediately before their pets' death.

Thoughts of previous loss experiences were also stimulated by the death of the pet in over half of the author's subjects. One subject described an increased frequency of thoughts related to the deaths of her husband and son, and to the death of a previously owned dog. She was uncertain as to how long the increased frequency of related thoughts had lasted, but estimated it to be "several weeks."

The death of a loved one almost always serves as a reminder of our own mortality (Harris, 1984; Katcher & Rosenberg, 1979; Levinson, 1972). For some, this reminder stimulates fear and this fear can be projected onto the animal. Some owners will dwell on thoughts of the fear the animal "must have felt," while others, whose pets are approaching death, will focus on the present fear of the pet. Katcher and Rosenberg (1979) suggested that some comfort can be offered to these owners by an explanation that the human anxiety related to the fear of dying is not shared by other animals.

A fear of approaching insanity during acute grief, especially in those whose life experiences have not included previous major loss, is not uncommon and is extremely frightening (Lindemann, 1944; Parkes, 1972). The fear usually stems from the overwhelming intense emotional response to the loss and the belief that no one has ever experienced these same feelings before. Grieving pet owners can and do experience this fear. Without support persons who understand and are willing to share in the grief for a lost animal, they may feel very alone and question their own psychological stability. One subject in the author's study stated rather disgustedly, "I feel ridiculous crying over a dog." Another admitted even more openly to her fear when she said, "I couldn't think. I couldn't concentrate. I thought I was going crazy." Reassurance by a trusted person that the intense emotional responses are, in fact, "normal" and appropriate for the situation is usually all that is necessary to alleviate this fear.

The need to make choices in response to both impending and actual pet death is an area that, in many instances, is unique to the human/animal bond. The subjects in the author's study described many different choices they made both before and after the pet died, and how they made them.

Usually the first choice that faces the owner of a very ill pet is whether or not to have the pet euthanized. The need to make this choice gives rise to strong ambivalent feelings for most owners and it is usually helpful if these feelings can be discussed with a knowledgeable support person prior to the time the choice is made. According to DeGroot (1984), "Such decisions call for the ultimate in unconditional love and caring on the part of the owners. They must care enough for their pets to do what is humanely correct . . ., disregarding personal emotional needs, guilt at playing God in the choice of death for the pets, and fear of death itself" (p. 283). Hopkins (1984) stated, "Ideally, there should be no chance of the client second guessing himself following euthanasia" (p. 281). The best way to prevent "second guessing" is to allow enough time for discussions of feelings and to allow each owner to make a personal choice based on adequate knowledge. As noted previously, subjects in the author's study evidenced minimal anger or guilt following euthanasia of their pets, and each had felt supported in the process of making their choices.

It is important to recognize that for some owners who firmly consider euthanasia to be morally wrong, there is no choice. For these individuals, assistance can be provided through teaching them how to care for the ill pet at home. One subject in the author's study who chose to keep his aging dog at home to die, noted that when taking a previously owned pet to be euthanized, he was haunted by thoughts of "betraying" the animal. He, like the other subjects in the study, gave evidence of satisfaction with his choice, stating that this dog died "peacefully" in its own home.

Other pre-death choices that may face owners are, who will take the pet to be euthanized and will the owner stay with the pet during the procedure. The large majority of recent literature on pet death suggests that owners who wish to remain with their pets during euthanasia be allowed to do so following some descriptive preparation for what will occur during the procedure (Bernbaum, 1982; DeGroot, 1984; Harris, 1984; Hopkins, 1984; Thomas, 1982). For those who do not wish to be present, an offer should be made to allow them to view the body after euthanasia. Viewing the body can, in many instances, promote a resolution and closure of grief. In discussing this procedure, Hopkins (1984) stated, "I even leave them alone for as long as they like. Judging from the letters I've received, this indulgence is greatly appreciated by clients" (p. 282).

Regardless of who is to bring the animal in for euthanasia or who will or will not remain with the pet, the recent literature also encourages that in order to afford some privacy to owners, the appointments for euthanasia be made at a time of day, usually during the end of office hours, when there will be the least number of people in the waiting area. Any necessary paper work and the bill for the procedure should be taken care of prior to the procedure so that the owner or other responsible person will not be bothered with these details after the death.

The post-death choices of bereaved pet owners usually relate to the disposition of the body and replacement of the pet. While some of these cognitive processes may take place prior to the death, the final choices often occur after the pet dies.

Disposition of a pet's body can range from mass cremation to individual burial in a pet cemetary. Whatever choice is made by the owner, it is often important for those who have loved the animal to experience some form of leave-taking ritual (Harris, 1984; Levinson, 1972). The ritual may be formal, such as an actual, prearranged funeral, or it may consist of family members simply sharing together photographs and memories of the pet. When children are part of the family, a ritual may be especially helpful as the children will begin to learn through adult example how they can cope with grief. According to Levinson (1972), "Children may participate in mock funerals and reenact the death of their pets in an attempt to master their fear and to understand their emotions" (p. 123). In addition, it is not uncommon for children to attempt to disinter the body of a pet. This activity may be related to the younger child's lack of comprehension of the finality of death or it may simply be to satisfy curiosity about what happens to buried bodies.

The choice of whether or not to replace a pet, like the other choices, should be an individual decision. Many well meaning persons will encourage the grieving pet owner to immediately acquire a new pet. However, this may not be an appropriate course of action for several reasons. Grieving is a painful, but necessary, human response to loss. If acquisition of a new pet occurs in an attempt to avoid grieving the lost animal, grief may be repressed or it may be channeled into other negative responses. Repressed grief will, at some future time, resurface and may be more painful than it would have been if the process had been interrupted initially. Unresolved grief can be a contributing factor in severe depression at a much later time.

Some owners who attempt to replace a pet too quickly will find themselves resenting the new animal. They will compare the new animal with the old, only to find that the new animal cannot totally replace the lost pet (Harris, 1984; Levinson, 1972). One subject in the author's study described how for several days she had completely ignored a new dog brought home by her husband even though her other dog had died two months earlier.

With healthy grief resolution will usually come a readiness and desire to reinvest emotionally in a new pet. At this time the deceased pet can be thought of with warm affection and the new pet can be loved for its own attributes. The majority of bereaved pet owners will know when the time for replacement of their lost pet is right for them. They need only to be supported in their decisions.

As with affective responses, pet owners may be hesitant to share their cognitive responses to the deaths of their pets. Bernbaum (1982) discussed one of the significant differences in grief for humans and pets as the lack of available support systems for the bereaved. She stated, "With the death of a close friend orrelative, it is expected that the bereaved will not be able to carry on with normal activities for a time. . . . With the death of a pet, the owner may not find sympathy from friends and family, but in fact may encounter impatience and ridicule . . ." (p. 2). Again, there is implication that professional support persons may play a key role in helping bereaved pet owners toward grief resolution.

PSYCHOMOTOR RESPONSES TO PET DEATH

With the exception of crying, psychomotor responses to the death of a pet are reported with less frequency in the veterinary literature. Perhaps this is because most veterinarians interact with the owners primarily at the time of death and do not have access to reports of behaviors related to the deaths that occur at a later time, usually in the owner's home. The subjects in the author's study described a variety of such responses, most of them occurring during the first two weeks following the death.

Crying is the one psychomotor response that is reported almost universally in the literature, and many authors suggest that it should be encouraged in those who seem reluctant to express their feelings. Harris (1984) discussed an approach to owners who apologize for crying. He stated, "What you do is say, 'It's okay to cry. It's okay to be sad.' You make it as comfortable for them as possible" (p. 270). Almost all of the author's subjects cried at the time of their pets' deaths. Intermittent crying, sometimes without an apparent stimulus, for several weeks following the death was also reported by most of the subjects.

Another response that seemed to puzzle subjects was the occasional unconscious attempt to locate the pet or what has been described as searching behavior. At times, however, it was difficult to distinguish between searching behavior and habituation. Most of the owners noted that they frequently looked in particular places in the house where the pet could often have been found. In addition, some noticed that they were careful where they walked so as not to step on the animal. One individual described periodically waiting for the pet to walk into the room. She said, "Sometimes you think you see a shadow and it's him. You have that feeling they're going to come in."

Collars, dog tags, food dishes, blankets, and favorable toys were some of the items reported to have been kept by the subjects. It is interesting to note that the retention of remembrances is not commonly reported in the literature on human grief. The behavior may be considered so "common" by those who grieve the loss of a human that it is just not thought of as a response to the loss. However, each of the subjects who discussed this behavior made a particular point of explaining why they had kept the items.

Appetite disturbances, sleeping more, sleeping less, and/or being awakened by dreams of the pet were responses also reported by over half of the subjects. All recalled that these behaviors subsided between two days and two weeks after the death.

Finally, the majority of subjects reported having actively sought out someone with whom to talk after the death. In situations of human death, survivors are often intially surrounded by others who are also grieving or who make themselves available for supportive purposes. This is not always the case in instances of pet death, and therefore, there may be a heightened effort by the pet owners to seek out support. Before anyone, friend, veterinarian, or professional counselor, can provide this much needed support, he or she must be acutely aware of the significance of the loss to the owner.

"For many complex reasons, the emotional attachment which many humans develop for their pets not only equals but indeed frequently transcends the emotional attachments which they form with humans" (DeGroot, 1984, p. 283). When this bond is broken, the grief responses experienced by owners can be profound. While the grief process through which pet owners pass is similar to that experienced with human death, there are some unique aspects as well. In addition, each individual experiences grief in a very personal way. Professionals from many disciplines can be in a position to offer support and therapeutic intervention for bereaved pet owners. They must, however, understand the grief process, acknowledge the need for all individuals to experience grief in their own unique ways, and be acutely aware of the significance of the loss of the pet to the owner.

REFERENCES

Arkow, P. (1977). Pet Therapy: A study of the use of companion animals in selected therapies. *American Humane*, June, 1–42.

Bernbaum, M. (1982). The veterinarian's role in grief and bereavement at pet loss. *Cornell Feline Health Center News, 7,* 1–3, 6–7.

Bourjaily, M. (1979). A pretty good teacher, for a cat. *Animals Can Be Almost Human.* Pleasantville, New York: Reader's Digest Association.

Byron, L. (1936). Epitaph to a dog, 1890. *The Best Loved Poems of the American People.* Garden City, New York: Garden City Books.

Cohen, S.P. (1983). Words of comfort. *People—Animals—Environment, 1*(1), 16–17.

DeGroot, A. (1984). Preparing the veterinarian for dealing with the emotions of pet loss. In R.K. Anderson, B.L. Hart, & L.A. Hart (Eds.), *The pet connection; Its influence on our health and quality of life. Proceedings of the Minnesota-California Conferences on the Human-Animal Bond,* (pp. 283–290). Minneapolis: University of Minnesota.

Eliot, T.S. (1971). *The complete poems and plays: 1909–1950.* New York: Harcourt, Brace & World.

Harris, J.M. (1984). Understanding animal death: Bereavement, grief, and euthanasia. In R.K. Anderson, B.L. Hart, & L.A. Hart (Eds.), *The pet connection; Its influence on our health and quality of life. Proceedings of the Minnesota-California Conferences on the Human-Animal Bond,* (pp. 261–275). Minneapolis: University of Minnesota.

Holden, C. (1981). Veterinarians, psychologists, and others believe time is ripe for a new interdisciplinary field. *Science, 214,* 418–420.

Holzworth, J. (1981). Easing grief over loss of a pet: Some practical suggestions. *The Latham Letter, 1*(4), 6.

Hopkins, A.F. (1984). Pet death: Effects on the client and the veterinarian. In R.K. Anderson, B.L. Hart, & L.A. Hart (Eds.), *The pet connection; Its influence on our health and quality of life. Proceedings of the Minnesota-California Conferences on the Human-Animal Bond,* (pp. 276–282). Minneapolis: University of Minnesota.

Katcher, A.H. & Friedmann, E. (1980). Potential health value of pet ownership. *Compendium on Continuing Education, 2*(2), 117–122.

Katcher, A.H. & Rosenberg, M.A. (1979). Euthanasia and the management of the client's grief. *Compendium on Continuing Education, 1*(12), 887–890.

Keddie, K.M.G. (1977). Pathological mourning after the death of a domestic pet. *British Journal of Psychiatry, 131,* 21–25.

Kipling, R. (1936). The power of the dog. *The Best Loved Poems of the American People.* Garden City, New York: Garden City Books.

Levinson, B.M. (1972). *Pets and human development.* Springfield, Illinois: Charles C. Thomas.

Lindemann, E. (1944). Symtomatology and the management of acute grief. *American Journal of Psychiatry, 104*(2), 141–149.

MacDonald, A.J. (1979). Review: Children and companion animals. *Child: Care, Health, and Development, 5,* 347–358.

Nagy, M. (1948). The child's theories concerning death. *Journal of General Psychology, 73,* 3–27.

Nieburg, H.A. (1979a). Psychological grief in response to loss of domestic pets. *D.V.M.*, February.

Nieburg, H.A. (1979b). Pet loss: Helping owners cope. *D.V.M.*, March.

Nieburg, H.A. (1980). Pet loss may be child's first (most crucial) death experience. *Thanatology Today, 1*(4), 2–3.

Nieburg, H.A. & Fischer, A. (1982). *Pet loss: A thoughtful guide for adults and children.* New York: Harper and Row.

O'Neill, E. (1979). The last will and testament of an extremely distinguished dog. *Animals Can be Almost Human.* Pleasantville, New York: Reader's Digest Association.

Parkes, C.M. (1972). *Bereavement: Studies of grief in adult life.* New York: International Universities Press.

Quackenbush, J.E. (1984). Pet bereavement in older owners. In R.K. Anderson, B.L. Hart, & L.A. Hart, (Eds.), *The pet connection: Its influence on our health and quality of life. Proceedings of the Minnesota-California Conferences on the Human-Animal Bond* (pp. 292–299). Minneapolis: University of Minnesota.

Rhodes, J. (1980). The human/animal bond's role in human mental health. *Thanatology Today, 1*(14), 2.

Rynearson, E.K. (1978). Humans and pets and attachment. *British Journal of Psychiatry, 133,* 550–555.

Swain, H.L. (1979). Childhood views of death. *Death Education, 2*(4), 341–358.

Thomas, P. (1982). When a pet dies. *Modern Veterinary Practice*, April, 273–277.

Yates, E. (1979). Skeezer, the dog who healed. *Animals Can be Almost Human.* Pleasantville, New York: Reader's Digest Association.

The Effects on Family Members and Functioning After the Death of a Pet

Betty J. Carmack

ABSTRACT. A pet's death can precipitate a grief as intense as that precipitated after the loss of a human. Because the pet is considered a family member, its death disrupts the lives of family members and family functioning. This article describes the family disruption that results from feelings of loss in four specific areas. It also discusses how a pet's death can lead to disorganization of family functioning. The nature and extent of family members' grief responses to pet death are described. Because of these losses, and the disruption and nature of the grief response, the need for counseling is established.

INTRODUCTION

I knew I'd miss him, but I never dreamed just how much. I don't care about anything else right now, not my job, not my family, nothing. Nothing else matters. I just want Rocky back. There is this big hole, empty place, in me and in my life and nothing has any appeal. My parents sent me $100 to do something special to try to ease the pain, to do something that might make me feel better. There is nothing that I can think of to spend it on other than as a memorial to Rocky, in his memory. Nothing, not opera, not tickets to anything, not a nice dinner, not a weekend away, nothing that I can think of will ease my pain. I wish I could think of something that could take it away, but nothing can.

This quotation illustrates the depth of grief a pet owner can feel after the loss of a much-loved companion animal.

Betty J. Carmack is Associate Professor at the University of San Francisco School of Nursing. She has a private practice in which she provides counseling to bereaved pet owners in addition to consultation to interdisciplinary health professionals.

149

The purpose of this article is not to examine the processes of grief, loss, and bereavement. These processes are well described in the literature, as are the appropriate interventions to use with grieving clients (Benton, 1978; Carlson & Blackwell, 1978; Kubler-Ross, 1969; Longo & Williams, 1978). Rather, this article demonstrates how grief is related to the death of a pet. Because the pet is considered a family member, this article examines the ways in which its death disrupts the lives of family members.

Specifically, I will show that family disruption results from feelings of loss and how pet death can lead to disorganization of family functioning. As a consequence of these losses and disorganization the family members' grief responses to pet death are described. And finally, based on the depth of these responses and the usual lack of societal supports the need for counseling is established.

For the past two years I have worked with grieving pet owners, both in individual and group counseling sessions. Over 90 people have come for counseling because of their grief related to the deaths of their pets. This article is based not only on this clinical experience but also on the work of others in the human/companion animal bond field.

LOSSES FOLLOWING PET DEATH

A Family Member

> Someone living with a pet is living with a family. The person is greeted at the door when he returns at night; he has someone to sit on the couch with and share the television. There is someone he must shop for, feed, care for and thus give to his own life the paced, circular rhythm of family life. (Beck & Katcher, 1983, p. 59)

Many pet owners in the United States see their pets as members of the family. Katcher and Rosenberg (1979) found that 93% of their subjects shared this point of view. In other studies (Beck & Katcher, 1983) the figure has ranged from 70 to 87%.

The role that the pet plays is usually that of a child (Beck & Katcher, 1983; Katcher & Rosenberg, 1979; Thomas, 1982). Like a child, the pet is cared for. Pets are given food, water, shelter, cuddled, loved, and talked to like small children. Beck and Katcher write that pets are treated like children because they provide "continual access to the kind of uncomplicated affection that parents exchange with young children'' (p. 61).

To illustrate this feeling of a pet as family with the accompanying affection, one of my clients said:

> Tiny, my cat was my love. She was the center of my life, my job, she's the reason I came home at night. My marriage is in trouble, and there are many times I wouldn't have come home if it hadn't been for Tiny being there.

To further illustrate this point, Prince was considered a family member. His illness and euthanasia had effects on his ''parents,'' a young married couple. Richard contacted me because of concern about his wife, Susan, who considered ''Prince as her real life baby.''

That Prince was a significant member of this family was readily apparent. Susan had had Prince for 10 years, long before she met Richard. She referred to Prince as ''my child who knows when we're fighting . . . Prince has had his attacks when we'd be fighting. He even gets jealous when we kiss and comes between us.''

She made continuous reference to Prince as ''my baby, my baby, I can't put my baby to sleep.'' She acknowledged that Prince's life was her highest priority and that she'd do whatever it took to keep him alive. Not working, Susan stayed home each day with Prince. Susan would spend hours handfeeding him even though he was physically able to eat alone.

Special Qualities of Pets

Loss is also experienced by owners who see their pets as special. This quality of specialness is frequently described by grieving pet owners with whom I've worked. ''He was such a special dog, he really was unusual. I've had dogs before, but this one was different.'' And again, ''I can't really expect anyone to understand just how special our relationship was. It really was.'' And, ''He really was an unusual cat. You'd have had to know him to understand just what I mean. I've never been able to have what we had with another cat, and certainly not with any other person.''

These quotations illustrate what pet owners regularly tell me. It's the perceived special qualities of the pet, as well as the perceived special qualities of the relationship with the pet that they miss.

When the owner has come to depend on these special qualities, the sense of loss can be profound. For example, a young husband said,

> We had a special relationship for seven years. She was as close as an animal could be to being human. We had a very special relationship. I don't expect people to understand. I've had many pets but this one was definitely special. She used to sleep in our bed under the covers with her head on the pillow. She was a child, but she was also a best friend, she was also like a lover.

Another unmarried man, said, "We had a very special relationship; he wasn't just a dog."

This feeling of specialness which pet owners describe can be compared to the "nonconventional human companion animal bond" described by Harris (1982). He describes such a bond as overdependence on the pet or an insistence on a special relationship with a companion animal where the pet is seen as a substitute for a human relationship. Harris writes that 35 to 40% of the clients in his private veterinary practice have such bonds.

The depth of grief that accompanies the death or loss of a pet is not only intensified but also occurs more frequently in owners who have these "nonconventional bonds" with their pets. Such owners are at a greater risk at the time of loss. "In cases where such overdependence on a pet does exist, there is likely to be a sharp reaction on the part of the owner when the pet dies or has to be put to sleep" (Keddie, 1977, p. 22).

Intimacy with Pets

Grief is also intensified in owners who have lost the intimacy they previously shared with their pets. This intimacy which grieving owners describe has support in the literature. Beck and Katcher (1983) studied the responses, both physiological and emotional, that pet owners exhibited when they interacted with their pets. They found that facial expressions become more relaxed and comfortable as if the owner were engaged in an intimate dialogue. They suggest that petting and talking to a pet feels good because it is a means of reducing tension (p. 125).

One of my clients, a single, middle-aged woman, never married, put it this way:

It felt so good to sleep with her. When we went to bed at night, she just settled down, right next to my back, snuggling in. Then I moved a little to snuggle in just a little bit more. It really felt wonderful. Then during the night when I woke up, I always felt her right there. It was so reassuring. I loved going back to sleep knowing she was right there beside me. When I woke up in the morning I felt for her, and she was right there curled up next to me. I liked to spend a few minutes touching and stroking her and petting her and telling her how much I loved her. That was really a nice way to start the day. I liked it. I'd imagine this was how it'd be if there was a person in my life, if I were involved with someone, but since I wasn't, she very much took that place, and I really didn't feel like I was missing out on anything. I felt so loved and so safe and so warm and cuddling when we were snuggling in bed like that.

Pet owners regularly tell me how much they miss talking with their pets. They feel the loss of ''conversations'' they had come to depend on. Again, Beck and Katcher provide support for this finding. Over 80% of their subjects believed their dogs were sensitive to their feelings, especially to their feelings of depression and anger. Intimacy develops when we are able to say what we want, the way we want to say it, and know that we will be understood. Being able to talk in this way to their pets gives pet owners the feeling that they have an intimate confidante (pp. 125–126).

Beck and Katcher found that pet owners derive a sense of closeness from the mere fact that the pet is there. The pet's greeting at the door ''is such a contrast to the meanness of the day that the animal is picked up and held and hugged like a talisman of safety and sanity'' (p. 127). The authors go on to describe the conversation that follows complete with dialogue, eye contact, body language, and bodily contact.

The intimate conversations that take place between pet owners and their pets do not depend on the use of language. By relating to our pets, we learn that a loving dialogue can be conducted without words. Pet owners interact and talk with their animals even though their animals cannot talk to them. ''They enjoy a state of relaxation which is fulfilling and restorative, without the assault of words'' (Beck & Katcher, 1983, p. 133).

Touch is another essential component of intimacy. In their study on the relationship between pet owners and their pets, Beck and Katcher write about the intimacy of touching: ''We touch animals with freedom and indulgence because animals have the capacity to call forth an immediate, childlike response which is usually not constrained by the rules of our culture'' (p.118).

One of my clients explained the intimacy he shared with his dog by saying, ''Punnkin gave us so much love and affection. She was just full of love and kisses. She'd lick me, she'd wash us with kisses. She'd put her arms around my neck and gave me love.''

Being Needed

A fourth loss—having been needed—can also cause disruption in family members' lives. A single woman said it this way:

> The loneliness now is just incredible. I miss her companionship miserably. I've got four other cats, but they don't need me. They aren't the companions that Candy was to me. Candy needed me, and I like being needed. I can remember when I was a little girl and my cat got an abcess, I really loved taking care of it because I was needed.

This sense of having been needed by the pet is also expressed by owners who have families. One woman—married and with a child—confided, ''My dog was always there for me, even when my husband and child weren't. Snooks was always there. She always needed me, and it feels so good to be needed.''

The nature of the relationship with the deceased person, including both the strength of the attachment and the dependency bonds affects the intensity and depth of the grief response (Benton, 1978; Carlson & Blackwell, 1978; Stuart & Sundeen, 1983). In my own practice I've consistently seen how important this factor is in contributing to the sense of being needed. Of the owners I have worked with, at least 51% had pets that had been ill for a long time and required extensive and intensive veterinary and daily nursing care. The dependency had been intense and prolonged. As a result, this dependency and attachment had intensified the grief experienced by the owner after the pet's death.

Mrs. Cook's situation illustrates this relationship between depth of attachment and awareness of being needed. Mrs. Cook sought counseling three weeks after her dog, Pudgie, whom she had had for 16 years, was finally euthanized. Pudgie had had numerous serious medical problems, and although Mrs. Cook had provided both veterinary and nursing care for him, his condition was obviously worsening. Both her husband and her adult children wanted Mrs. Cook to have Pudgie euthanized. She didn't want to; she couldn't bear the thought of being without Pudgie, but in the end it seemed to be the humane thing to do. Mrs. Cook's grief had been—and remained—profound.

Shortly after Pudgie died, Mrs. Cook's behavior changed. She became more disorganized and less functional and spent a lot of time crying. Since her husband and children didn't need her anymore, she became aware of not feeling needed. Because Pudgie was so dependent on her, he needed her. Since that was now gone, being needed was missing from her life. Mrs. Cook was able to recognize her desire to get another dog who would depend on her and need her. She put it this way, "they're like children who never grow up and leave you."

DISORGANIZATION OF FAMILY FUNCTIONING

In addition to family members experiencing these four areas of loss, a pet's death can cause disorganization in a family's usual way of functioning. Quackenbush (1982) looks at the loss of a pet within the context of the social system of the owner. Using a general systems model, he attempts to show that the death of a pet disrupts the owner's established social system. He suggests that the grief behavior seen in pet owners is due primarily to those disruptions. Owners no longer have the interactions with their pets that they have come to rely on. They struggle to make up for these missing interactions. During this period of readjustment, their interactions with humans also become disrupted.

Ninety-three percent of the subjects in Quackenbush's sample reported experiencing a certain degree of disruption in their daily routines, such as sleeping, eating, and social activities. Forty-five percent had job-related difficulties, such as missing 2 to 3 days of work or being distressed by their colleagues' insensitivity to their feelings. Quackenbush and Glickman (1981) suggest that the impact of a pet's death on its owner's daily life is related to the breaking of the bond that the owner had formed with the pet.

My own results support these findings. Repeatedly, pet owners who come for counseling report that they have difficulty sleeping, eating, and functioning on the job. They feel immobilized—unable to move out of their bereavement and get on with their life. They, too, agonize over the insensitivity of their family and friends. Their agony is mixed with anger. They have lost someone with whom they were intimate, and they find it intolerable that others do not acknowledge the loss.

In fact, the death of a pet may severely impair the communication system within the family. Often my clients will tell me that they cannot share their grief within the family circle. They need to hide it. They report that the spouse, usually the husband, just doesn't understand. As a result the grieving spouse stops trying to share her feelings; she expresses them either when she is alone or in the presence of the counseling group.

Sometimes the family never discusses the pet's death at all. In the course of working with one of the spouses I will ask how the other spouse is handling the death. Frequently the response will be, "I don't know. He won't say. He's a very private person. I wish I could tell you, but I really don't know. We don't ever talk about it."

The following case history shows how the death of a pet can disrupt a family's functioning:

Mrs. Miller is 62 years old and lives with her 37 year-old son. They have four cats. Nine months ago, Mrs. Miller's favorite cat, Baby, died after having been ill for over a year. They had taken Baby in for regular treatment. However, Mrs. Miller is convinced that the veterinarian misdiagnosed the cat's condition, and she holds him responsible for Baby's death. She verbally hints at her anger at this veterinarian, yet she refuses to confront him with her concerns. In addition, she refuses to explore her feelings of anger within the counseling sessions. As a result, her anger is being repressed, and she is stuck in her grief.

The disruption in Mrs. Miller's daily life has been significant. She has not slept in her bed since Baby's death, because she still remembers how Baby jumped up on the bed and slept with her. The thought of being in the bed alone is just too much for her. For 9 months now she has slept on the sofa in the living room with pictures of Baby close to her heart. She tucks one picture in her nightgown; the other she places on top of her robe next to her chest. Every Sunday afternoon Mrs. Miller insists that her son take her to the pet cemetery to visit Baby. She insists on keeping all of Baby's things just the way they were when Baby last used them. For instance, the litter box is just the way Baby left it, with the same scratches and marks in it. The scratching post is still in front of the chair where

Baby liked to sleep. No one is allowed to sit in this chair, and no cat is allowed to jump up on it.

Baby died on the seventh day of the month. As a result, Mrs. Miller doesn't like the number 7. Her son recently surprised her with tickets to a show. The performer is one of her favorites but the tickets were for April 7. When Mrs. Miller complained, saying that she couldn't enjoy the show, her son switched the tickets to the following night.

Mrs. Miller cries during the day while her son is at work, but when her son comes home, she refuses to discuss Baby's death. The son has told her he is tired of all of this, so Mrs. Miller feels she has no one to talk with. She continues to attend the monthly counseling sessions; she doesn't discuss her situation. When she tries to talk, she just cries for her Baby. She has refused to take the suggestions of anyone in the group, including mine.

In the case of Mrs. Miller there appear to be two factors at work. The first is the family disruption. The second is that Mrs. Miller is not undergoing any readjustment.

Although Mrs. Miller is an extreme example in the pathological grief she is experiencing, almost all pet owners have their lives disrupted to some extent. An unmarried woman puts it this way:

> We'd go out to the beach each day, just her and me. That's the time I'd get some exercise. I'd get mine because I knew she needed hers. I loved to see her run and have so much fun. Then when she looked for me and came running back to me, she even looked like she had a smile on her face. All kinds of things could be bothering me at work or in other areas of my life, but when I saw her running on the beach and having such fun, for those few minutes each day, the world seemed really o.k. I'm sure it had to do with her being there with me.

NEED FOR COUNSELING

The degree of disruption frequently requires professional assistance. Of those pet owners I've worked with, 80% were female and 20% were male. Bereaved pet owners were likely to live alone or to live with one or two other persons. Eighteen percent of my clients had only their animals as a live-in companion. These figures suggest why my clients depended so heavily on their pets for companionship and why they were so vulnerable when their pets died.

Because pet owners have such intense relationships with their pets—and indeed often perceive their pets as children—their grief for a pet can be as deep as grief for a human child.

Pet owners often grieve more deeply for their pets than they do for their own relatives. They usually acknowledge this in a tone of voice suggesting surprise. They were relieved to have their feelings understood and accepted; often they have suspected that they were abnormal. In fact, such feelings of grief are quite understandable. As we've seen, pet owners share a degree of intimacy with their pets that they rarely, if ever, shared with parents, siblings, or spouses. Veterinarians have told me of clinical cases in which pet owners openly state that they would rather lose their wife or husband than their pet.

Bereaved pet owners experience all of the usual characteristics of grief—painful regret, crying, shock and numbness, deep sorrow, despair, mental suffering, and loneliness. They also verbalize fears of losing control; the intensity of their feelings scares them. These feelings consist of guilt, anger, and helplessness. They felt helpless to save their pets, and now they feel helpless in living without them. Several have described wanting to die. Grieving pet owners often demonstrate varying degrees of pathological grief (Keddie, 1977). Sometimes this grief can be severe enough to precipitate suicide (Katcher & Rosenberg, 1979).

Professional assistance can help minimize the likelihood of subsequent illness. People who have lost a family member are especially vulnerable to illness in the first two years following the loss (Lynch, 1977). Bereaved pet owners are likewise susceptible to illness (Katcher & Rosenberg, 1979).

In addition, several clients have described an illusory phenomenon in which they actually seem to hear the dead pet or feel its presence. They describe hearing their pets' breath, or tails thumping against furniture, or feeling them rub against their legs. They need reassurance that this phenomenon can, and does, occur after the death of a loved one.

Writers agree that the wound of grief heals slowly. Peretz (1970) writes that grief lasts from 6 months to a year, and that the acute phase is over in 1 to 2 months. Katcher and Rosenberg (1979) say that grief related to pet loss lasts an average of 10 months.

My experience consistently shows that because of the nature and extent of the grief response, many grieving pet owners need regular ongoing counseling and support. Depending on the particular factors in the situation, certain pet owners may need support for as long as one year. Pet owners occasionally come to the group sessions saying that they need to work on their grief, even though their pet has been dead for over a year. One woman's dog had died 7 years ago; she came for counseling when the death of her best friend's dog reawakened her own feelings of unresolved loss.

One theme emerges regularly and contributes to the need for counseling. Most of these pet owners never thought their pets would die. Somehow they assumed their pets would live forever. This denial and unrealistic thinking made them that much more vulnerable when the death occurred. They were not prepared for the depth of loss and pain they experienced because they had never planned for— or even considered—life without the pet.

People who have lost a human significant other receive sympathy and support in our society. Yet even though many pet owners consider their pets to be members of the family, they receive little or no support when the pet dies.

Pet owners express concern about the way in which others respond to their grief. "If anyone else heard this, they'd think I was crazy" (Cowles, 1980, pp. 374–375). Outside the counseling setting they are usually reluctant to express their deep feelings. Often they refuse to discuss their feelings at all. Grieving pet owners need to be reassured that their sorrow is normal.

Their concern about others' responses is amply supported in the literature. "In our culture there really is no acceptable way of mourning a pet" (Neiberg & Fischer, 1982, p. xiii). Many people are unable or unwilling to acknowledge that a pet can be a legitimate attachment figure (Cowles, 1980; Katcher & Rosenberg, 1979). As a result they cannot recognize the significance of a pet's death. Grief for a pet is considered inapppropriate, since pets can be "replaced." This is an easy solution for those who have ever known attachment to a pet. But telling a bereaved pet owner to "just get another one" only adds to the person's feelings of isolation and despair (Cowles, 1980). "The lack of universal social mechanisms for dealing with grief for an animal probably impairs the resolution of grief and isolates the grieving owner" (Katcher & Rosenber, p. 890).

This lack of societal support does impair the resolution of the grief. Some pet owners hide coming for counseling from their spouses. One woman said, "If my husband knew I was here, he'd think I was crazy." Another asked me never to write or call her at home because her husband would be angry if he found out.

Pet owners immensely appreciate having a place where they can come and talk about their feelings. Repeatedly they tell me how grateful they are that they no longer have to hide their grief and loss. They appreciate having a place where it is safe to express feelings; aren't laughed at; the subject isn't changed; they are not offered a new kitten or puppy to replace the lost pet; and someone listens. Over and over again my clients tell me, "It's so good to be able to come here and talk about this with other pet owners who understand. I didn't have any place to go before."

CONCLUSION

The death of a companion animal family member can precipitate a grief that is as intense as that precipitated after the loss of a human family member. This intense grief disrupts the lives of individual family members as well as disorganizes the usual family functioning. There is a growing realization that grief following the death of a pet can be sufficiently severe to require professional support. The nature and extent of the family's grief responses can require assistance at both the time of anticipatory grief, such as deciding about euthanasia, as well as at the actual time of death or even later. Counseling may be needed up to one year due to the specific facts involved in a particular situation. Grieving family members are vulnerable both mentally and physically. Counseling provides bereaved families with the necessary support—a support that society in general does not provide.

REFERENCES

Beck, A., & Katcher A. *Between Pets and People.* New York: G.P. Putnam's Sons, 1983.

Benton, R.G. *Death and Dying Principles and Practices in Patient Care.* New York: D. Van Nostrand Co., 1978.

Carlson, C.E., & Blackwell, B. *Behavioral Concepts and Nursing Intervention.* Philadelphia: J.B. Lippincott Co., 1978.

Cowles, K.V. Loss of a Pet: Significance to the Owner, Implications for the Nurse. *Nursing Forum,* 1980, *19*, 372–377.

Harris, J.H. A Study of Client Grief Responses to Death of Loss in a Companion Animal Veterinary Practice. *California Veterinarian,* 1982, *36*, 17–19.

Katcher, A.H., & Rosenberg, M.A. Euthanasia and the Management of the Client's Grief. *Compendium on Continuing Education,* 1979, *1*, 887–891.

Keddie, K. Pathological Mourning After the Death of a Domestic Pet. *British Journal of Psychiatry,* 1977, *131*, 21–25.

Kubler-Ross, E. *On Death and Dying.* New York: The Macmillan Co., 1969.

Levinson, B. *Pets and Human Development*. Springfield: Charles C. Thomas, 1972.

Lynch, J.J. *The Broken Heart: The Medical Consequences of Loneliness*. New York: Basic Books, 1977.

Nieburg, H., & Fischer, A. *Pet Loss: A Thoughtful Guide for Adults and Children*. New York: Harper & Row, 1982.

Peretz, D. Reaction to Loss in Schoenberg, B. and others (ed.) *Loss and Grief; Psychological Management in Medical Practice*. New York: Columbia University Press, 1970.

Quackenbush, J. Social Work in a Veterinary Hospital: A Response to Owner Grief Reactions. Paper presented at the Symposium of the Thanatology Foundation, March, 1981.

Quackenbush, J. The Social Context of Pet Loss. *The Animal Health Technician*, 1982, *3*, 333–336.

Quackenbush, J., & Glickman, L. A Study of Social Work Services for Bereaved Pet Owners in a University-Affiliated Veterinary Hospital. Paper presented at the International Conference on the Human-Companion Animal Bond, Philadelphia, October, 1981.

Stuart, G.W., & Sundeen, S.J. *Principles and Practice of Psychiatric Nursing*. St. Louis: C.V. Mosby., 1983.

Switzer, D.K. *The Dynamics of Grief*. New York: Abingdon Press, 1970.

Thomas, C. Client Relations: Dealing with Grief. *New Methods*. 1982, 19–24.

Health, Aquariums,
and the Non-Institutionalized Elderly

Carol Cutler Riddick

ABSTRACT. The purpose of this study was to examine the effects of introducing a new hobby—fish aquariums—upon a sample of non-institutionalized elderly. When compared to two other groups, who did not receive this intervention, the aquarium group underwent significant positive changes in their diastolic blood pressure, overall leisure satisfaction, and relaxation states.

The effects of pets on humans is a phenomenon of recent origin. This is surprising since psychologists have a long-standing record of using animals for therapeutic purposes (Rice, Brown, & Caldwell, 1973). Most of the literature that does exist deals with anecdotal reports of psychological case histories (Brickel, 1980–81). A few research studies, however, have begun to provide us with some understanding of the ramifications of human-animal contact. Friedmann, Katcher, Lynch, and Thomas (1980) studied factors that affected the well-being of coronary patients. They found that the strongest predictor of survival was pet ownership—regardless if the pet was a dog, cat, fish, or iguana! Pet owners were more likely to be alive one year after hospital admission than non-pet owners.

The presence and observation of animals also has been documented as influencing blood pressure. Findings from a study conducted by Beck and Katcher (1981) revealed that staring at an aquarium was an effective way of handling stress and lowering blood pressure, especially for study participants suffering from high blood

---

Carol Cutler Riddick is Assistant Professor, Division of Human and Community Resources, University of Maryland, PERH Building, College Park, MD 20742.

This study was funded by a General Research Support Award by the Office of Graduate Studies and Research at the University of Maryland and supported by the University of Maryland's Computation Center. The assistance of Meg DeSchriver during various stages of the research is gratefully acknowledged. Thanks are also due to Dr. Jerrold Greenberg and Dr. Thomas Wolfle for their thoughtful comments on an earlier draft of this manuscript.

pressure. Friedmann, Katcher, Thomas, Lynch, and Messant (1983) have also reported that the presence of a dog resulted in lower blood pressures of children engaged in a stress related activity.

The handful of documented and semi-rigorous investigations dealing with the impact of animals on geriatric populations can be categorized as dealing either with institutionalized or community residents. Banziger and Roush (1983) studied 40 residents of a skilled-care nursing home who were randomly assigned to one of three groups: (1) those who received a wild bird feeder placed outside their window and a responsibility message; (2) those who did not receive a bird feeder but received a dependency message; and, (3) those who received neither a feeder nor a special message. The first group experienced greater happiness, life satisfaction, perceived control, and activity scores than the other two groups. Similarly, Corson and Corson (1979) concluded that introducing dogs to residents of a nursing home resulted in increased social interaction and activity as well as improved morale. Furthermore, when Brickel (1979) assessed the therapeutic role of cat mascots on a hospital-based geriatric population, mascots were observed as giving patients pleasure, stimulating patient responsiveness, and providing reality therapy.

The findings of systematic research efforts directed at measuring the impacts of pets on non-institutionalized elderly have been contradictory and inconclusive. Mugford and M'Comisky (1975) compared British pensioners who were given parakeets to others who had either received begonias or no intervention. The bird owners' health, as measured by changes in responses to physical symptoms and mood questions, improved compared with those who did not receive pets. Contrastingly, a number of investigators have reported that pet ownership had no significant bearing on the mental health of a nation-wide sample of community elderly (Lawton, Moss, & Moles, 1984), old-age veterans (Robb & Stegman, 1983) or the rural elderly (Lago, Knight, & Connell, 1982; Ory & Goldberg, 1982).

Beck and Katcher, (1984) in summarizing the research conducted on the health effects of animals and the efficacy of pet therapy programs, state that few systematic efforts have been directed at hypothesis testing. They point to a critical need for well designed studies that incorporate a comparison control group. The purpose of this quasi-experimental study is to ascertain if the introduction of animals—specifically goldfish—to non-institutionalized elderly resulted in subsequent health-related benefits. The hypothesis is that goldfish aquarium owners relative to non-owners would experience a greater positive change in their blood pressure, happiness, anxiety, loneliness, and leisure satisfaction.

METHODS

Subjects

The study was conducted in a low income public subsidized housing complex located in Montgomery County, Maryland. The apartment complex is 14 stories high and contains a combined total of 156 single and double occupancy units. A Senior Citizens Center, funded by the County Recreation Department, is located in the building. Additionally, a Congregate Meals Program operates in the building five times per week. In order to qualify for placement on the waiting list to live in the complex an individual must: be 62 years of age or be a handicapped adult; have an individual income of approximately $12,200 or a combined couple income of $13,800; and, be willing to pay 30% of their adjusted gross income towards rent.

Initially, in order to recruit study participants, a notice was hand-delivered to each apartment. The note explained the purpose of the study; described qualifications for study participation (i.e., an individual had to be 55 years of age or older, be willing to receive biweekly visits, and agree to participate in two interviews); and, contained an invitation to attend an orientation meeting about the project. At this meaning the principal investigator and her assistant were introduced along with members of the Advisory Committee for the project, a veterinarian, the County's Recreation Department Seniors Section Coordinator, and the Director of the Senior Center located at the facility. The purpose, rationale, and procedures for the study were then described in greater detail. Furthermore, an aquarium tank was also on display so meeting attendees could view it. The group was also told that for the first couple of months tank maintenance services would be provided with the understanding that tank recipients would take increasing responsibility, under supervision if needed, for this task over the course of the study.

Originally it had been planned that individuals would be randomly assigned to one of three groups: an aquarium group, a visitor group, or a control group. The rationale for establishing a visitor group was to hold constant any possible effects the tank maintenance visits might have on aquarium group members. At the orientation meeting, however, a number of persons expressed strong sentiments (e.g., "not having the time to care for an animal," or, ". . . really wanting an animal companion") about their willingness to be placed in a specific intervention group. Under the circumstances, it was deemed necessary to honor the 12 requests (evenly split between the aquarium and visitor groups) to join a specific intervention group. In total, seven individuals were in the aquarium group (five females and two males) and eight persons were in the visitor group (seven females and one male).

Participants in the control group were recruited from a list of names supplied by the resident manager of the apartment complex. The manager was asked to identify individuals who met the established age requirement and were likely to consent to the interviews. Initially, nine individuals were in the control group. Two persons eventually withdrew from the control group—one due to illness and the other simply refused to complete the posttest. Thus, five females and two males constituted the control group.

Of the apartment's 180 residents, 22 individuals ranging in ages from 57 to 94 years elected to participate in the study.

Intervention

The research project was a six month longitudinal study that began in February 1983 and ended in July 1983. Appointments were made with members of the aquarium group in order to install a 2-1/2 gallon tank. Fish, specifically goldfish, were chosen over other animals for two basic reasons. First, this species of animal was used because it can easily be cared for since it tolerates erratic feeding and maintenance schedules as well as extreme temperatures. Second, a regulation existed that prohibited occupants of the apartment complex from owning any other species of animal.

The subjects were encouraged to place their tanks in a location that was visible to them throughout the day. Each tank was equipped with a filter box and pump, natural color stones, a glass cover, a fluorescent light, and an aluminum foil backdrop. The cost (borne by a research grant) of the entire setup (including fish and food supplies) was approximately $20. After the tank was installed and filled with water, a three day waiting period took place so the water temperature and chemistry levels had time to stabilize. Subjects then chose two fish, from an available group, they wanted for their tank. Tank owners were also given information and literature on feeding and signs, symptoms, and treatment of fish diseases and illnesses. In case of an emergency (e.g., illness of a fish or leaky tank) subjects were instructed to contact the principal investigator. An answering machine was installed in the researcher's office, that allowed a caller to leave a message if no one was readily available to answer the phone. A remote beeper to the answering machine allowed 24 hour phone message monitoring capability.

During the six months intervention period, aquarium owners were visited 9 times and members of the visitors group received 10 visits. Members of this latter group received an additional visit in order to compensate for the time spent with the former group when installing their tanks and fish.

The researchers followed the same basic schedule each time they visited members of either intervention group. In order to reduce the likelihood that the personality of one of the researchers would bias the results, for each visit the names of the visitors were randomly placed in one of two groups. Generally, the researchers flipped a coin to decide the group they would be responsible for visiting.

During the biweekly visits with subjects who had fish aquariums, the researchers spent 15–20 minutes cleaning or assisting with tank maintenance duties. During the remaining 10–15 minutes of the visit, the researcher and the elderly subject watched and typically talked about their fish.

The subjects who received only the biweekly visits were given the opportunity to choose what they wanted to do during the 30–40 minute visit. Most preferred to sit and socialize in their apartment, a few wanted their visitor to join them in watching a television program (usually a soap opera).

Instrumentation

Six instruments were used for this study. Blood pressure was recorded using the arithmatic average of two or three resting blood pressure readings (a third reading was used if the first two readings were markedly different from each other). The protocol established by the American Heart Association was used for measuring blood pressure (American Heart Association, 1981). Happiness was measured by a 20-item revised version of the Memorial University of Newfoundland Scale of Happiness (MUNSH). The original scale has had a reported predictive validity of .58, a Cronbach Alpha of .86, and a test-retest reliability of .70 (Kozma & Stones, 1980). Applying the original MUNSH items for this sample, the Cronbach Alpha was .13. By dropping four items (numbers 3, 4, 10 and 23), the computation of Cronbach Alpha for participants in this study emerged as .50. Thus, this 20-item version of MUNSH was used for the remaining analyses reported for this study. Anxiety was measured by the 20-item A-Trait Scale of the State-Trait Anxiety Inventory. Regarding the A-Trait Scale, previous validity coefficients have ranged from .51 to .85, whereas Cronbach Alphas have been cited as between .86 and .92, and test-retest reliabilities as .73 to .86 (Spielberger, Gorsuch, & Lushene, 1970). The A-Trait Scale's Cronbach Alpha, for the elderly sampled in this investigation, was .89. Loneliness was recorded by the 20-item revised UCLA Loneliness Scale. Earlier works have reported validity coefficients of this scale as somewhere between .28 and .71 and the Cronbach Alpha as .93 (Russell, Peplau, & Cutrona, 1980). The present sample's Cronbach Alpha for the UCLA Loneliness Scale was .89. Leisure satisfaction was gauged by the 20-item Leisure Satisfaction Scale (LSS). Among other things the LSS examines the psychological, educational, social, relaxational, and physical effects of leisure satisfaction. This scale was established through the content validity approach and has a tested Cronbach Alpha of .88 (Beard & Ragheb, 1980). For the elderly group involved in this project, the LSS items had an internal consistency of .93. The sixth instrument used in this study measured demographic characteristics of the sample. Face validity was used in developing questions relating to background information about the individual.

The administration of the instruments was done in an interview format. With the exception of the demographic questionnaire, questions were posed twice—as a pretest and then as a posttest. Each administration took approximately one hour.

Analyses

Hypotheses testing proceeded along one of two lines. In instances where equivalency checks disclosed that the three groups were not distinctly different from each other at the beginning of the study, hypotheses testing was conducted using analysis of variance for gain scores. Otherwise, paired t test was used for examining a hypothesis.

In order to test the significant level of the stated hypotheses the .30 probability level was adopted. Winer (1962) has stated that the .30 and .20 levels of significance may be more appropriate than the .05 and .01 levels when the power of the tests is likely to be low. Labovitz (1968) further suggested that the power of a test varies directly with sample size. With a large sample size a small difference is likely to be statistically significant, while with a small sample size even large differences may not reach the predetermined level. In other words, smaller probability levels (i.e., $\leq .05$) should be used when one's sample size is large, and large probability levels (i.e., $\geq .10$ to $\leq .30$) should be used when the sample size is small. Several social scientists (Skipper, Guenther, & Nass, 1967; Winer, 1962; Labovitz, 1968) have suggested that the frequent use of the .05 and .01 levels of significance is a matter of convention and that "blind adherence" to such low levels can be a serious impediment to the interpretation of social science data.

RESULTS

Means and standard deviations are summarized in Table 1. Preintervention equivalency checks revealed that the three groups did not significantly differ from each other in terms of systolic blood pressure, $F(2,21) = 1.13$, $p = .34$; happiness, $F(2,21) = 1.26$, $p = .31$; anxiety, $F(2,21) = .33$, $p = .72$; loneliness, $F(2,21) = 8.87$, $p = .43$; or leisure satisfaction, $F(2,21) = .12$, $p = .89$. All this suggests that the three groups initially were equally matched on these characteristics. On the other hand, there was a significant pretest difference among the three groups in terms of diastolic blood pressure, $F(2,21) = 2.54$, $p = .11$. Post hoc Scheffe mean comparisons revealed that the aquarium group had a significantly, $p \leq .30$, higher initial diastolic blood pressure than the visitor group.

T test analysis indicated that a significant, $t(7) = 2.60$, $p = .04$, decrease occurred in diastolic blood pressure from the pretest to posttest measurement for the aquarium group. No significant pretest-posttest diastolic blood pressure differences, however, were found for either the visitor group, $t(8) = .96$, $p = .37$, or the control group, $t(7) = .46$, $p = .66$. Furthermore, the aquarium group experienced a significant positive change in their leisure satisfaction, $F(2,21) = 1.35$, $p = .28$, relative to the other two groups. Examination of what aspect(s) of leisure satisfaction changed the

Table 1

Summary of Pretest and Postest Comparisons for Three Groups

	Aquarium group (n = 7)		Visitor group (n = 8)		Control group (n = 7)	
	Pretest M(SD)	Posttest	Pretest M(SD)	Posttest	Pretest M(SD)	Posttest
Systolic blood pressure	135.71(11.51)	128.00(15.36)	127.50(16.41)	120.25(18.68)	137.43(12.37)	136.00(21.66)
Diastolic blood pressure	82.00(6.83)	74.57(5.26)	72.25(7.82)	69.50(8.67)	78.86(10.76)	76.00(8.41)
Happiness	-8.14(4.88)	-7.86(5.93)	-2.00(9.12)	-4.38(7.96)	-5.14(5.70)	-5.86(6.28)
Anxiety	36.71(12.90)	42.43(5.38)	42.13(14.36)	47.75(11.41)	39.43(10.91)	47.43(7.50)
Loneliness	36.14(12.14)	40.00(9.75)	45.38(13.86)	38.25(18.97)	42.00(14.63)	42.29(14.02)
Leisure satisfaction	63.57(19.99)	74.00(11.93)	68.50(16.74)	74.50(21.02)	67.00(22.46)	65.29(24.36)

most revealed that the aquarium group, more so than the other two groups, underwent a significant improvement in their relaxation, $F(2,21) = 3.17$, $p = .06$. Still another significant change took place for the visitor group. That is, the visitor group's overall reduction in their loneliness was significant, $F(2,21) = 2.86$, $p = .08$, compared to what the other two groups experienced. No significant gain changes in systolic blood pressure, $F(2,21) = .31$, $p = .74$, happiness, $F(2,21) = .94$, $p = .41$, or anxiety, $F(2,21) = .09$, $p = .92$, were registered for any group.

DISCUSSION

The results of the study support in part what has been suggested elsewhere (Brickel, 1979; Friedmann, Katcher, Thomas, Lynch, & Messent, 1983; Mugford & M'Comisky, 1975). That is, contact with animals was noted as decreasing blood pressure, improving overall satisfaction with one's leisure, and having a relaxational effect on non-institutionalized elderly persons. During the course of the study, numerous anecdotes were recounted to the investigator. Individuals in the aquarium group, for instance, reported that fish:

> Gave me a reason to get up in the morning. They depend on me to feed them. Their antics made me laugh. We watched television together. They make the apartment feel less empty, added happiness to my life, and were a way to meet or get to know other people.

Unlike what others have reported (Banziger & Roush, 1983; Corson & Corson, 1979), no substantial changes occurred in aquarium owners' happiness, anxiety, or loneliness. Indeed, members of the visitor group relative to the other two groups experienced a significant decrease in their loneliness. One explanation for this particular finding may be that the visits to the experimental group focused on the fish; whereas, the visits to the visitors group focused instead on the visitors. Other explanations as to why the present study's findings were inconsistent to what others have reported could center on methodological differences in terms of sample selection, instrumentation, and analysis. Different results may have been noted, for example, if anxiety had been measured using state (versus trait) anxiety, or if a different measure for happiness had been utilized.

Nevertheless, one persuasive finding accumulating on the topic is that animal-human interaction has positive ramifications for the well-being of older individuals. The fish aquarium, a unique, relatively inexpensive intervention, is apparently still another way to improve the physiological, and social-psychological health of some of our community elderly.

In conclusion, this exploratory project provides impetus for further studies addressing the effects of animal interaction on the elderly. Questions that remain unanswered and warrant further research include determining to what extent the findings are generalizable to other groups of older individuals; and, what are the circumstances that enhance the impact of pet ownership on the elderly's quality of life.

REFERENCES

American Heart Association. (1981). *Blood pressure: Its control and measurement.* Annapolis: American Heart Association, Maryland Affiliate.

Banziger, G., & Roush, S. (1983). Nursing homes for the birds: A control-relevant intervention with bird feeders. *The Gerontologist, 23,* 527–531.

Beard, J., & Ragheb, M. (1980). Measuring leisure satisfaction. *Journal of Leisure Research, 12,* 20–33.

Beck, A., & Katcher, A. (1981). Age of aquarium. *Psychology Today, 15,* 14.

Beck, A., & Katcher, A. (1984). A new look at pet-facilitated therapy. *Journal of the American Veterinary Medical Association, 184,* 414–421.

Brickel, C. (1979). Therapeutic roles of cat mascots with a hospital-based geriatric population: A staff survey. *The Gerontologist, 19,* 368–372.

Brickel, C. (1980–81). A review of the roles of pet animals in psychotherapy with the elderly. *International Journal of Aging and Human Development, 12,* 119–128.

Corson, S., & Corson, E. (1979). Pet animals as nonverbal communication mediators in psychotherapy in institutional settings. In S. Corson (Ed.), *Ethology and non-verbal communication in mental health.* London: Pergamon Press.

Friedmann, E., Katcher, A., Lynch, J., & Thomas, S. (1980). Animal companions and one-year survival of patients after discharge from a coronary care unit. *Public Health Reports, 95,* 307–312.

Friedmann, E., Katcher, A., Thomas, S., Lynch, J., & Messent, P. (1983). Social interaction and blood pressure; influence of animal companions. *The Journal of Nervous and Mental Disease, 171,* 461–465.

Kozma, A., & Stones, M. (1980). The measurement of happiness: Development of the Memorial University of Newfoundland Scale of Happiness (MUNSH). *Journal of Gerontology, 35,* 906–912.

Labovitz, S. (1968). Criteria for selecting a significance level: A note on the sacredness of .05. *The American Sociologist, 3,* 220–222.

Lago, D., Knight, B., & Connell, C. (1982). Rural elderly relationships with companion animals: Feasibility study of a placement program. In A. Katcher & A. Beck (Eds.), *New perspectives of our life with companion animals.* Philadelphia: University of Pennsylvania Press.

Lawton, P., Moss, M., & Moles, E. (1984). Pet ownership: A research note. *The Gerontologist, 24,* 208–210.

Mugford, R., & M'Comisky, J. (1975). Some recent work on the psychotherapeutic value of cage birds with old people. In R. Anderson (Ed.), *Pet animals and society*. London: Bailliere Tindall.

Ory, M., & Goldberg, E. (1982). Pet ownership and life satisfaction in elderly women. In A. Katcher & A. Beck (Eds.), *New perspectives on our life with companion animals*. Philadelphia: University of Pennsylvania Press.

Rice, S., Brown, L., & Caldwell, H. (1973). Animals and psychotherapy: A survey. *Journal of Community Psychology, 1*, 323-326.

Robb, S., & Stegman, C. (1983). Companion animals and elderly people: A challenge for evaluators of social support. *The Gerontologist, 23*, 277-282.

Russell, D., Peplau, L., & Cutrona, C. (1980). The revised UCLA Loneliness Scale: Concurrent and discriminant validity evidence. *Journal of Personality and Social Psychology, 39*, 481-495.

Skipper, J., Guenther, A., & Nass, G. (1967). The sacredness of .05: A note concerning the uses of statistical levels of significance in social science. *The American Sociologist, 1*, 16-18.

Spielberger, C., Gorsuch, R., & Lushene, R. (1970). *STAI Manual*. Palo Alto: Consulting Psychologists Press, Inc.

Winer, B. (1962). *Statistical principles in experimental design*. New York: McGraw-Hill.

Life in the Treehouse:
Pet Therapy as Family Metaphor
and Self-Dialogue

Eugene Rochberg-Halton

INTRODUCTION

Imagine the following therapeutic situations: you sit there, pouring out your emotions to an indifferent partner. Sometimes it seems as though you are talking to the wall, and you cannot be sure that the other has not succumbed to sleep. At other times he or she can be extremely warm—a ''selfobject'' in the terminology of psychoanalyst Heinz Kohut—mirroring your feelings back to you, empathically understanding everything (or so it seems) you say or feel or think. It seems as though he or she has solved the riddle of the Sphinx, and knows the answer to every question you could ask. Yet again, indifferent, mysterious, it would appear as though he or she were the very Sphinx itself, inscrutable, saying with Ralph Waldo Emerson's Sphinx, ''Of thine eye I am Eyebeam,'' or less poetically, I am the very structure of your ego, and you cannot truly know me because I am your own apparatus for seeing the world.

Imagine further that not only does your therapeutic partner partake of the role of therapist, but also that of patient, needing at times maternal nurturance, at other times testing your limits by fighting with others, refusing to listen to you, or even more primitively, by biting you. One poet described our therapeutic partner as follows:

His amiable eyes
Are very friendly, very wise;
Like Buddha, grave and fat,
He sits, regardless of applause,
And thinking, as he kneads his paws,
What fun to be a cat!—Christopher Morley

Eugene Rochberg-Halton is Professor in the Department of Sociology, University of Notre Dame, Notre Dame, IN 46556.

175

The therapeutic situations just described, as the reader was no doubt aware, were a parody of the Freudian and Kohutian psychoanalytic traditions. Though the idea of a pet taking on the different qualities of the therapist may seem somewhat outlandish, what in fact does occur in therapy according to Freudians, is that the therapist becomes a kind of chameleon, taking on at different points in the therapy the qualities of mother, father, child, friend, and even the self of the patient. In his or her silence or in reflecting back the patient's own problems, the therapist acts as a kind of externalization of the patient's psyche, enabling inner problems to assume the form of a therapeutic dialogue. And at the heart of the psyche in the Freudian model is the Oedipal family, that inner symbol which represents the state of one's balance between unconscious impulses and outer reality.

Whether one accepts Freud's *fin-de-siècle* version of the psyche or not, the significance of the "psychic family" in Freudian theory does illustrate how the family need not be seen only in the literal sense, but of how the *family metaphor* is a powerful social fact as well. Clearly many gender role stereotypes and social institutions are based on a family metaphor, such as in medicine, where the role of nurse is maternal, that of doctor is instrumental and unemotional, and that of the patient is to be the child. What I hope to show, as will become clearer, is how pets, specifically cats, can become significant partners in a therapeutic family metaphor by providing an externalized means for a self-dialogue through the affective relationships they make possible.

The theoretical framework I am adopting, however, is not the Freudian model, but one drawn from the American social-psychological tradition of Charles Horton Cooley, James Mark Baldwin, George Herbert Mead, Erving Goffman, and others. Despite its sensitivity to the dialogical nature of therapy, the Freudian model ultimately remains committed to an overly inner view of social life (Rochberg-Halton, 1984).

Although I will retain the idea of therapy as a dialogue emphasized by the psychoanalytic tradition, the insights of the social psychological tradition seem better suited to describe the concrete, social praxis therapy I will later describe. In this view, the essence of the self consists in its communicative relationship with its inner and outer environment, a relationship that includes real external social objects as well as their representation in mind.

In a study of the meaning of household possessions involving three-generation families in Chicago, (Rochberg-Halton, 1979a, b; 1984; Csikszentmihalyi and Rochberg-Halton, 1981) it became clear that the things people select out of the domestic environment and endow with special value act as external signs of the self. They communicate a sense of self through the personal experiences, memories, as well as age, sex, and the class attachments they signify. From this perspective the domestic environment, like all social environments, is a communicative medium of signs. Its special communicative purpose, however, is to convey what a person or family is about, both to the inhabitants and, in different ways, to visitors. In doing so it acts as a socializing sign-complex through the "dialogues" it makes possible between persons and their valued possessions. A stuffed animal toy or a living pet can act as play-mates, or as outlets for emotional expression, as can be seen in the following illustration from a twelve year old girl who described her cat:

> Whenever I have a problem, sometimes I go up to him and I hold him real tight and he gives me a little meow. He feels so good, he's so fluffy, and when I hold him, I love to talk to him. I love cats. He's real special. . . . If I didn't have my cat, then I wouldn't have something to hold when I had a problem, and I like to be alone, but then I'd really be alone. If I didn't have him then I'd be empty. There'd be a spot in me that was empty.

Obviously there is metaphoric intent in that girl's statement that without her cat "there'd be a spot in me that was empty." Yet she is also literally correct if we interpret the "me" in Mead's sense as the embodiment of "the generalized other," the internalized norms of the community. Through a "conversation of gestures" as well as the "significant symbol" of the cat itself, the girl carries on a social-izing dialogue with her self. The self grows through a progressive internalization of empathic, gestural, and verbal dialogues it has with its surroundings, and for this reason the foundation of the self should be seen as a social self-dialogue, rather than, as the Freudian view holds, an asocial reactor core of libido. As Cooley wrote at the turn of the century:

> The imaginary dialogue passes beyond the thinking aloud of little children into something more elaborate, reticent, and so-phisticated; but it never ceases. Grown people, like children,

> are usually unconscious of these dialogues; as we get older we
> cease, for the most part, to carry them on out loud. . . . But,
> speaking broadly it is true of adults as it is of children, that the
> mind lives in perpetual conversation. (Cooley, 1964: 89)

I shall discuss just such self-dialogues, in giving an account of a
pet therapy program begun in 1981 at Michael Reese Hospital in
Chicago. As part of the adjunctive therapy program an arrangement
was made to bring some adolescent in-patients to the "Treehouse
Animal Foundation" once a week as volunteers. Treehouse is a
shelter devoted to the care of neglected, injured, or abused cats, not
normally taken in by city and other animal shelters. Treehouse is a
particularly apt term in this context since it signifies a metaphoric
home, nearby the real one, but outside of it and with its own set of
rules. A treehouse is a place where for a time at least the children as-
cend into their own world and play at being adults. Both in-patients
and staff became Treehouse volunteers, spending the first hour each
week playing with and grooming cats, and the second hour handling
some clerical chores.

It was hoped that the Treehouse program would provide a unique
therapeutic environment, a sense of a home away from the "home"
of the hospital in which patients could engage in a self-dialogue of
emotions through play activities with cats. The working hypothesis
was that by assuming the role of caretakers instead of patients, and
by taking on the identity and responsibilities of volunteers in the
community instead of in-patients removed from community participation, the Treehouse milieu could act as a significant experience to
improve patients' sense of self worth. What I hope to show is how
these adolescent psychiatric in-patients were enabled to construct a
"therapeutic family" in which they could, for a brief time, "take
the role of the other," and through caring for these cats, establish a
therapeutic self-dialogue.

THE CULTURE OF PETS

Pets are a noticeable exception to the rather restricted channels of
emotional expression in American culture and the typical American
family. It is acceptable, for example, to hug, fondle, pet, talk baby
talk, and even kiss one's dog or cat, whereas signs of affection toward friends and family are often much more limited. There is a

cemetery near Hollywood memorialized in the documentary, *Gates of Heaven*, that caters specifically to pets, and individuals from the most sophisticated society in the world give large sums of money to have their pets memorialized there. This fetishism of "soulless" non-human animals illustrates how not only the human social status system continues after death in the choice of the financial level of burial, but how the pet, as symbolic family member, should retain the family hierarchical position of status, even in death, by being buried in an elite property that symbolizes its family wealth. Some other cultures find our personification and general treatment of what they consider to be food, strange and even perverse, just as we have trouble understanding why beef, i.e., the cow, is held to be sacred in many parts of India.

The domestication of animals to become house pets originally may have been associated with beliefs about their sacred powers, or with their role as hunters' assistants, but clearly one of the central reasons for keeping pets is companionship. Pets enjoy receiving affection—that is why we call them pets in the first place—and they return affection to us. They provide a means for gestural and verbal communication, and in doing this, enable us to carry on a self-dialogue of emotions. They are not only mere outlets for emotional expression, but also genuine channels that enable us to cultivate our emotions in a dialogue freed from the frictions that beset normal human interactions. And cats in particular possess the qualities of softness and warmth in their own inherent character, and in this way are perhaps the emotional "objects" of the domestic sphere *par excellence*. As gerontologists and other researchers and therapists who have introduced a dog or cat into a ward have begun to discover, the pet becomes a vehicle for communication between patients, as well as a personified companion who "listens" to what the individual patient says or communicates (Katcher, 1979; Bustad, 1980; Mugford, 1979a, 1979b). After discussing the adolescents' socialization into the Treehouse community, I shall return to case studies of self-dialogue.

SOCIALIZATION INTO TREEHOUSE

The Treehouse cat shelter is a two-story, bright yellow house located in a neighborhood in Uptown, and only noticeable because of a small sign next to the front door. On the first trip I went with Bob

Glaser, director of the adjunctive therapy program for adolescents, and two adolescents, both about 17 years old, who had been hospitalized for close to a year.

The first thing one notices on entering is a large number of small brass name plates in the shape of a tree on the wall of the front office area. These were the sponsors and patrons of Treehouse. About 6 cats were scattered throughout the room, most of them sleeping, but they began to stir as we entered. One of the patients, whom I shall call Linda, said she had never seen so many cats in one room, and we all agreed with her as we began to pet some of them. We were then given a slide and cassette presentation that explained the organization and its specific purpose both as a shelter caring for animals not protected by other agencies, and as an adoption center.

After the slide show we went upstairs to a second floor teeming with cats. We walked into the front room where most were sleeping, and just absorbed the sight of approximately 50 cats lying on the floor, on top of the few cages against the wall, and in the carpeted "cat homes" scattered around the room. As Jennene Keating Colky, the Treehouse representative, explained more about the cats, we all tentatively began to interact with them, and immediately began to sense some of the different personalities. We heard how the cats in the large cages with separate beds, food, and kitty litter, were there either because they were ill and on medication, or because they could not relate well with the other cats. The director said the Treehouse staff officially called these cages, "playpens," because Treehouse claims to be a shelter where the animals roam freely. But smiles came over the faces of the two adolescents, which they communicated to the other staff member and myself, because they instantly recognized that "playpens" translated into what the hospital called "restraints." Indeed we later found out that the unofficial Treehouse terminology for the cages was "jail," and cats that were too violent would be put there so they would not hurt themselves or other cats, and yet remain in the social milieu of the other cats.

Although we had not planned on it, it soon became apparent that Treehouse was in many ways a microcosm of the hospital situation, and for this reason provided a therapeutic "mirroring" environment, where, for a time, the locus of problems was in the cats, not oneself. Here the staff-patient distinctions were not as prominent, because all were expected to assume the role of responsible caretakers for the cats. We made it clear to the adolescents who took part in the program that we were all there as volunteers, and not solely for entertainment. One of the central treatment goals was simply to develop in the patients a sense of active participation, in which others depended on them as responsible and autonomous persons. Thus, whereas the initial instructions were usually given by Jennene Keating Colky, the continuing socialization process consisted of both the activities themselves, and the shared conversations about the behavior of a particular cat or how a clerical task might best be accomplished. Linda and Frank, whom I shall describe shortly, clearly relished the task of making telephone calls concerning previously pledged donations to Treehouse. They would say, for example, "Hi, my name is Frank and I am a volunteer for Treehouse," to people who did not know they were stigmatized as mental patients. Instead of their negative social status as mental patients being prominent, they had a positive role as volunteers for an institution highly regarded both in the community and Chicago at large.

An equally important socializing factor was the way in which the Treehouse experience was brought "back home" to the hospital. All the adolescents who went up regularly were given Treehouse t-shirts and ID cards, tangible signs of their new roles. One girl, Linda, wore her t-shirt faithfully every Monday, even when she could not go because of a medical appointment, or when she did not want to go because of depression. She and another patient, Skip, clearly enjoyed this visible symbol of their identity as Treehouse volunteers. The shirts were, on the one hand, their "uniforms" while at Treehouse, identifying them as members of that "family" and on the other hand, "badges" that distinguished them in the eyes of their fellow patients at the hospital.

Photographs also emerged as one of the most valued trophies of Treehouse. A number of snapshots of the patients with the cats were taken, which immediately became prized possessions that they could bring back to the hospital as souvenirs and share with their friends.

PET THERAPY AS FAMILY METAPHOR
AND SELF-DIALOGUE

During the course of my observations at Treehouse, a total of 7 adolescents participated in the program. I shall turn now to four case studies in order to highlight some of the varieties of therapeutic situations that arose, and to illustrate the self-dialogue these situations provided.

Linda and Frank

The first two cases studies concern the two patients who went on the first trip to Treehouse, Linda and Frank. They were the two oldest and most mature patients at the time, and because we were setting up an experimental program, participation was initially limited to those who were less severely disturbed in social interactions.

On the very first trip, as we began to interact with the cats upstairs, one reddish cat would follow and sit nearby, but not always close enough to pet. The distance seemed to make it possible for him to run at any minute. Linda chose this cat as the one she really liked, and called him to come over to her. Both the adjunctive therapy director and I noted the approach-avoidance behavior of the cat, and how by choosing this particular one, she seemed to be selecting an appropriate reflection of herself. It later became apparent that she had selected a very disturbed cat, and that her devotion to it and the relationship she cultivated proved a positive therapeutic experience both for her and the cat.

Frank also gravitated toward a particular cat very quickly, a big burly cat that obviously reflected big burly Frank. The second week, Frank immediately sought out the cat, whose name was Oz, and found him sleeping atop one of the cages. He began to pet the cat, and was delighted to hear it purr. Later, as we all sat on the floor grooming the cats, he called to Oz, who came over to him, stayed for awhile, and then left—very friendly for the cat, but Frank didn't realize this. He responded by calling Oz to come back, saying, "Oh you're going over to them, you don't want to stay with me," and seemed to feel slighted. He was not aware that cat rules for interaction are different from canine or human rules, and we discussed how cats have a unique personality. I mentioned to him that it was unusually friendly for a cat to come over at all when his name was called, and how one has to give a cat its own say in the conversation, unlike a dog, who will move on command. This aspect of the therapy program proved to be crucial, as Frank and some of the other patients were to learn. The cats had at least one clear advantage over psychiatrists: sooner or later the patients had to realize they could not argue with the limits set on the interaction by the cats. One of the explicit signs of advance in the program occurred when the adolescent could recognize and tolerate the limits of the cat in play and grooming situations.

Linda also wanted to see the cat to whom she had become attached the previous week, but as we were being instructed how to groom the cats, it did not seem to be wandering around. We soon discovered that it was in one of the backroom "playpens," because it had undergone testing for leukemia, which is somewhat common in cats, and the results were not yet final. It seemed at the least ironic that Linda had chosen the cat that had to be isolated. But the shelter manager said that Linda could groom the cat in the doorway of the cage, which pleased her greatly.

The following week it was apparent on the ride up to Treehouse that Linda was severely depressed. She was under extreme pressure from her family to leave the hospital, and earlier in the day had to undergo a confrontation between the family and her doctors. Her own family desperately needed her back to submerge herself in the role of victim and scapegoat, needed her back so desperately that they were forceably trying to remove her from the hospital, even though the doctors, and Linda herself, agreed that she would die if she went home. The family had even had difficulty the previous year understanding why she was transferred into the psychiatric unit from the medical recovery area, after she almost died of a suicidal overdose of barbituates.

We arrived and went upstairs to play with and groom the cats, and Linda immediately sought out "her" cat, Rudy. It turned out that he was not sick, but merely had a bad temper. He had been moved into the front room, but was still in a "playpen." Linda, with Jennene's assistance, removed Rudy from the cage and began to groom him on the floor. Although restless, he soon enjoyed the grooming, until other cats moved too close, and then began hissing and lashing out with his claws. At one point Linda got a small nick on her wrist and Jennene decided the cat was too restless, and they put it back in the cage.

Later on in the hour a small dark cat followed us up from the kitchen and stayed nearby, but when petted with a brush would hiss and claw the brush. Linda tried to groom it softly, but when another cat came over, it began to hiss and swing at her brush. She later said more than once to Jennene, "Why don't your cats like me . . . they don't seem to like me today." I said to Linda, "Well, you seem to have picked out the more difficult ones to handle today, maybe that's why," and she agreed that she had been concentrating on the problem cats. It was clear that rejection, which was so concrete in her morning meeting with her parents, was being symbolically re-created in the Treehouse. The whole family of cats seemed to be re-

jecting her, just as her own family was rejecting her for not fulfilling the role of scapegoat. But here at Treehouse, Linda was setting up a possible rejecting situation by turning to these particular cats. It was not clear whether she was attempting to set up another situation that would just play out the rejection again, or simply trying to soothe and nurture these cats who were, like herself, the rejected, and thus undo what she experienced in the morning. The therapy milieu did enable her to bring to articulation her major problem, and provided an opportunity for the other staff member and myself to discuss the issue of rejection with her, through the symbolic mirror provided by the cats.

Linda was committed to her relationship with Rudy, and the following week the Treehouse director worked out a system whereby she and Linda would take Rudy into an unused room to groom him, where he would not be made violent by the other cats. This proved to be successful, and, as Linda said on emerging, "He only hissed at me once!" Soon Rudy was allowed to run freely, as his tolerance level of the other cats increased, and we all made it clear to Linda that her "one-to-one" work with him was the main reason for his improvement. Her confidence in herself also improved, and she seemed to enjoy the responsibility entrusted to her, both with the cats and with her clerical and telephone chores. About six weeks later Rudy was adopted, which caused Linda to say half-jokingly, "How can he be adopted, he's mine!" But we reminded her that he was only adopted because of her work with him, and that although it was sad that he was not there, we were trying to provide companionship for the cats to help them get adopted. She made a point of writing his name on the adoption blackboard later, to signify, perhaps, that *her* cat had been adopted.

In the following weeks the confrontation between her family and the hospital placed extreme pressures on her, but she continued in the program, and seemed to genuinely profit from the experience. Frank, too, gained a surer sense of his abilities as a volunteer, although he did not develop the individual relationship with a cat that Linda had. Within a month he lost all interest in Oz, in a way that resembled his lack of strong and enduring relationships with other people. His capacities for maintaining an ongoing self-dialogue of emotions with a particular cat were much more limited than were Linda's, but he did take pride in his increasing knowledge of grooming and clerical work, and understanding of cat behavior. When new patients would arrive at Treehouse, for example, he, as an "old timer," would help to initiate them into the world of the cats.

Linda's and Frank's choosing of a favorite cat within the first 15 minutes of interaction with the cats, despite the fact that Frank did not maintain the relationship, was in stark contrast to two other patients, who did not differentiate at all between the cats, and whose differentiation of people, too, was severely restricted. The case of Donna provides a good example.

Donna

Donna had only been an in-patient for a couple of weeks when the decision was made to allow her to participate in the program. I met her for the first time on the trip up to Treehouse. Donna, who was 15, seemed extremely narcissistic and regressed, and my immediate reaction was to feel as though I wanted to draw away from her. On the ride up to Treehouse she constantly tested the limits of another staff member, Barbara, who was her representative in the general adjunctive therapy program. She would ask questions about the staff member's family, about whether she could move in with her family, and when the staff member responded in the negative, she would say, "You don't like me." Linda tried valiantly to carry on a conversation with her, but it was difficult to keep it going, as Donna's associations were somewhat schizophrenic.

Once we were upstairs with the cats at Treehouse, it seemed to me, and to the other staff members, that Donna could not fully cope with the experience on her own, and that at least one of us should remain close to her. A large fat white cat, with some black markings on it lay down in front of Donna, and enjoyed being petted by her. We, staff as well as Linda and Frank gave her some tips on grooming, and she seemed to take delight in having the cats pay attention to her.

Later in the hour, Donna, the other staff member, and I were in the upstairs kitchen room, playing with the 4 kittens that had recently arrived. We were only supposed to have 2 of them out of the cage at a time, but Donna passively let the other 2 out by opening the cage slightly and then having trouble getting them all back in again. She set up a situation in which we had to go over and put them back.

Soon Donna put her head on the other staff member's knee, lying down. It suddenly became apparent that she was exchanging places with the cats, that she wished to be the one petted and groomed. Donna, who was regressed and interacted in some ways like a spoiled 6 year old, saw in the mirror of the cats a chance to merge with us as an infant. She did not have the psychic resources to maintain the level of caretaker and to carry on a self-dialogue mediated by the cats. Instead, she merged with the mediator and symbol of self, the cat, thus destroying the mediated self-dialogue. She could express a wish for immediate gratification by *becoming* the object of affection. It was clear that Donna was not functioning well enough to take on the responsibilities of Treehouse, and that the experience was merely over-stimulating rather than therapeutic, so she did not continue in the program. Despite the fact that the Treehouse milieu provided a wide range of challenges that included very simple tasks, her experience demonstrated that a higher level of functioning was necessary for the program to be therapeutic.

Skip

Skip represents almost the opposite experience of Donna. He is about 15 years old, black, and comes from a lower class family background in which there was extreme emotional deprivation. He spent his initial time in the hospital under the sheets of his bed almost constantly, and was fearful of the guinea pigs being kept in the adolescent lounge as pets. But after a couple of weeks in the hospital his functioning improved markedly, and he was asked if he would like to participate in the Treehouse program. He was enthusiastic about going, and later, when I asked him what he expected it would be like, he mentioned that he saw the photos that Frank and Linda had brought back, and it "looked hip." It appeared that the socializing image of Treehouse had been brought back to the hospital in these trophy-photos.

After arriving at Treehouse we all took turns explaining to Skip what the organization was about and what we were expected to do. He was shy of the cats at first, although he did try to pet them. I petted the cat next to him while we were all in the front room, mentioning how cats like to be petted in the same direction as their hair—front to back—and that if they put their claws on you they aren't trying to hurt you but are either just being friendly or attempting to balance themselves. Skip seemed to be catching on, and over the course of the time we were upstairs with the cats, he gradually began to loosen up and be more relaxed with them. He enjoyed playing with a ball of yarn, making the more frisky ones jump up in the air, and seemed genuinely to be enjoying the entire experience.

Afterward, at the fast food restaurant we usually stopped at on the way back to the hospital, and while the two other patients were getting food, the staff director for the adjunctive therapy program asked Skip what he thought of his experience at Treehouse. Skip gave a most sincere answer, which was surprising in its depth and expression of emotion. He said:

> Beautiful. It was beautiful. And it was more beautiful upstairs. The feeling. It was warm and friendly. I liked the cats and they were friendly. They like you, they just come on over to you. . . . (DID YOU HAVE A FAVORITE?) I liked those white ones downstairs. They were real nice. I would like to have one of them. And the black and white one upstairs that hugged Frank and came over and climbed up on me and hugged me (THE CAT PUT ITS PAWS ON HIS TWO SHOULDERS), that was my favorite.

Skip later gave his favorite cat, which had already been named by the Treehouse staff, his own name, "Toby." There was a little house in the back room with the name "Toby's House" printed on it, and this seemed to be the source for the name he devised. He continued calling the cat by this name, even though the Treehouse staff used a different one, and it was clear that the act of naming was a positive way of personalizing the relationship.

In a few weeks Skip seemed more sure of himself, but had begun to do some "acting-out," such as playing too wildly with the cats, or not closing the door of the kitten room. Given the severe emotional deprivation of his background, and the almost abusive discipline imposed by his father, some manifestations of his self-assertion were probably healthy, within limits. But the qualities of his interactions with the cats, as well as some of the other patients, had become too chaotic and amorphous, and it was decided that some portion of the time upstairs should be spent working with a particular cat. The increased structuring of the grooming and play activity seemed to work well for him and the others at this time. The most valuable aspect of the program for Skip was simply to experience unthreatening interactions, filled with positive emotions and warmth. For him the possibility that there could even be such interactions was a new experience, one that he had not experienced within his family. The metaphoric family of Treehouse provided him with a situation in which he could act as a responsible "sibling" with the cats, within the structure imposed by the staff. Where Linda and Frank could move into the caretaker and "parent" roles with a high degree of responsibility, and Donna was unable to move beyond a primitive level of functioning as an infant competing *against* the cats for attention, Skip moved into an immediate level in the therapeutic family hierarchy as a "sibling" to the cats, but also needing to slip into irresponsible, though supervised, play.

SUMMARY

In viewing these person-pet interactions as therapeutic self-dialogues, some themes emerge. The ability to develop a "favorite"; to single out, identify with, and maintain a relationship with a cat for some period of time may be both an indicator of a patient's capacity for social interaction, but more importantly, it perhaps should be viewed as one of the goals of the therapy itself. Those patients who did cultivate a relationship with a particular cat, along with group interactions, such as Linda, Frank, and Skip, seemed to manifest a better level of functioning than those who did not, such as Donna and another patient.

A program such as this illustrates the value of a concrete, social, praxis-oriented therapy, and how it might contribute to the wider treatment programs of patients. What could be more concrete than to play with pets? And yet we have seen how important personal issues come into play, and how they can be raised to the level of articulation through the self-dialogues these activities make possible.

Similarly we may see by analogy the importance of the pet as symbolic mediator within the home. For the average family the pet is more than another possession, it is usually regarded as another family member (Rochberg-Halton, 1979a, 1984; Csikszentmihalyi and Rochberg-Halton, 1981). Yet it is a peculiar family member: at different times it is the eternal child, lovable, playful, getting into trouble; at other times it provides maternal emotional warmth, "someone" to whom you can go and be sure to receive a warm emotional response, soothing negative feelings; the family dog also can take on the paternal role as watchdog for the family. Like any symbol, however, the family pet can take on a life of its own in a more negative way, by absorbing the genuine family emotions that should be directed toward the human family. When the emotional life of a family becomes too restricted, it can become too easy to rely on the non-threatening channel of the family pet to express one's feelings of affection, rather than doing the work of keeping the human channels of communication open. Just as a television can serve as a surrogate for personal communication, so too can a pet. And, as I have tried to show, a pet can further serve as a temporary therapeutic symbol through which to work out family problems that can then be redirected within the family context itself. Through the self-dialogues it makes possible, one can externalize one's emotions and thoughts about problems to reflect on and resolve them.

A treehouse is usually built by children as a place of communal privacy and autonomy, where one can play and converse with friends up in a tree, away from family and the wider world and its demands. The Treehouse I have described is similarly a social self-dialogue, built and cultivated by the adolescents themselves, a refuge away from the demands of family and hospital world, a place where they are accepted with warmth, and with no questions asked.

REFERENCES

Bustad, L.K. *Animals, Aging, and the Aged.* Minneapolis: University of Minnesota Press, 1980.

Cooley, C.H. *Human Nature and the Social Order.* Introduction by Phillip Rieff, Foreword by George Herbert Mead. New York: Schocken Books Inc. 1964 (1902).

Csikszentmihalyi, M. and Rochberg-Halton, E. *The Meaning of Things: Domestic Symbols and the Self.* Cambridge: Cambridge University Press, 1981.

Katcher, A. Support and Mental Health: Effects of Pet Ownership. *Proceedings of the Meeting of Group for the Study of Human/Companion Animal Bond.* Dundee, England, March, 1979.

Mugford, R. Basis of the Normal and Abnormal Pet/Owner Bond. *Proceedings of Meeting of Group for the Study of Human/Companion Bond.* Dundee, England, March, 1979a.

_____. The Social Significance of Pet Ownership. In S.A. Carson (ed.), *Ethology and Nonverbal Communication in Mental Health.* London, Pergamon Press, 1979b.

Rochberg-Halton, E. Cultural Signs and Urban Adaptation: The Meaning of Cherished Household Possessions. Unpublished PhD dissertation. University of Chicago, 1979a.

_____. The Meaning of Personal Art Objects. In J. Zuzanek (ed.), *Social Research and Cultural Policy.* Waterloo, Ontario: Otium Publications, 1979b.

_____. Object Relations, Role Models and Cultivation of the Self. *Environment and Behavior*, May, 1984 (in press).

Health Benefits of Pets
for Families

Erika Friedmann
Sue A. Thomas

ABSTRACT. During the last decade, the common belief that pets are good for their owners has gained concrete scientific support. In this paper we review the evidence for the health benefits of pets, discuss the importance of pets in the family system, and explore the implications of this information for therapists.

Pets play a variety of health promoting roles which are particularly important for individuals lacking support from family members or close friends. We present research evidence supporting the health benefits of pets ranging from the facilitation of social interaction while walking dogs to the physiological effects of the presence of animals on cardiovascular responses to mild stressors.

INTRODUCTION

The individual is the focus of most assessments of health care needs. Introduction of a total family system assessment in illness is a recent innovation which provides an increased understanding of complex interactions in symptom production and relief (Kerr, 1981). The roles of pets in families and in family health have not been investigated adequately (Cain, 1983). Our purposes are to review the research literature supporting the role of the pet in the family in relation to family health and to the health of individual family members. In this paper we present scientific evidence for the health benefits of pets, a discussion of the importance of pets in the family system, and implications and practical applications of family system therapists.

Erika Friedmann is Associate Professor of Health Science, Brooklyn College of City University of New York.

Sue A. Thomas is Associate Professor, School of Nursing, and Clinical Director, Psychophysiological Clinic, School of Medicine, University of Maryland.

The importance of pets in our society is demonstrated repeatedly through frequent accounts of pets in the popular press, movies, and books. Prior to the last decade there were few scientific studies of the benefits of interactions between people and pets.[1] The existing scientific literature emphasized the health problems caused by pets (Beck, 1975) rather than the importance of the companion animal in the family. In the psychiatric literature of the past 20 years there are number of case reports documenting the positive influence of pets (Bossard and Stoker, 1966; Speck, 1964). However, most information about the value of pets to their families was based upon anecdotal information without the support of systematic scientific investigation.

In the last ten years the common belief that "pets are good for you" has gained concrete scientific support. While most researchers have concentrated on examining the health effects of dogs, there is considerable evidence that other pets are equally beneficial. Researchers have suggested several ways that pets can help improve family members' health (Katcher and Friedmann, 1980). Pets decrease owners' loneliness and depression by providing a source of companionship, an impetus for nurturance, and a source of meaningful daily activities. They also decrease owners' anxiety and sympathetic nervous system arousal by providing a source of contact comfort, a relaxing focus for attention, and a feeling of safety. In addition a pet can help its owner improve or maintain physical fitness by providing an impetus for exercise. Evidence for these health benefits of pets for their families follows.

REVIEW OF LITERATURE

There is abundant evidence that loneliness causes increases in both morbidity and mortality (Cobb, 1976; Lynch, 1977). If a pet can cause decreases in loneliness, decreases in the pathological effects of lack of support from family members and close friends.

Pets act as companions for their owners. In several questionnaire surveys of pet owners (Cain, 1983; Friedmann, Katcher, Eaton, and Berger, 1984; Friedmann, Katcher, and Meislich, 1983a; Katcher, Friedmann, Goodman, and Goodman, 1983b), researchers found that over eighty percent of pet owners considered their pets to be family members. Furthermore over fifty percent of the pet owners questioned talked to their pets frequently, talked to their pets as if they were people, and thought their pets were sensitive to their moods.

Ory and Goldberg (1983) produced important evidence suggesting that the health benefits of a pet are dependent on the owner's attachment to the pet. In a study of life satisfaction in elderly women, they found that happiness was higher in pet owners who are attached to their pets than in non-pet owners or people who are not attached to their pets.

While there are no large scale studies of relative mortality of pet owners and non-pet owners, there is evidence that pet owners' health benefits from the companionship their animals provide. In the only direct study of the health benefits of pets, Mugford and M'Comisky (1975) gave birds or plants to a small number of elderly pensioners who were living alone. They compared changes in attitudes toward people and toward their own psychological health over the course of the study among six subjects given birds, six subjects given begonias, and six subjects given no intervention. Five month improvement in these health measures was seen in those who received birds but not in those who received plants or no intervention. However due to small sample size, non-randomness of assignment to groups and the statistical analysis of combined groups the generalizability of their findings is limited. Large scale longitudinal studies of health are necessary for further elucidation of the effect of pet ownership on mortality and morbidity.

In the course of a study of the social, psychological, and physiological factors affecting coronary heart disease patient survival pet ownership was related to one year survival. Only three of the fifty-three pet owners died within one year of admission to a large urban university hospital for coronary heart disease (severe angina pectoris or myocardial infarction), while eleven of the thirty-nine non-pet owners died in this same period. As was expected, the most important predictor of survival was the physiological status of the patient. The effect of pet ownership was independent of the physiological severity of the illness; the combination of pet ownership and physiological severity was better at predicting survival than was physiological severity alone. Furthermore, the beneficial effect of pet ownership was not limited to socially isolated individuals. These findings led to the conclusion that the effects of pets on health were distinct from the effects of other people (Friedmann, Katcher, Lynch, and Thomas, 1980).

Researchers hypothesized that the differences in outcome between pet owners and non-pet owners could be due to differences in the personalities of these groups rather than to the pets. In a survey of over 300 college students, researchers found no differences between pet ownership groups on the aforementioned scales and on profile of mood states (tension, depression, anger, vigor, fatigue, and confusion scales), cognitive-somatic anxiety, state-trait anxiety, coronary prone behavior, androgyny, and sensation seeking scales once residence type was controlled (Friedmann et al., 1984). On the basis of available information pet owners and non-pet owners do not differ in personality.

The previous research has pointed to direct health benefits from the companionship provided by animals. Pets can also lead to increased companionship by facilitating interactions with other people. In Messent's (1983) observations of people walking their dogs, people walking their dogs experienced more social contacts and conversations, and engaged in conversations of longer duration than lone walkers. Pets also can provide important links to friends and relatives in the outside world for hospitalized patients (Friedmann et al., 1983a). Over 80% of the 36 owners who were interviewed while hospitalized were receiving information about their pets, over 60% received this information at least once a day, and over 20% "talked to" their pets on the telephone daily. Thus the desire to find out how their pets were faring during their absence necessitated communication with the people who were caring for the pets.

Membership in a network of mutual responsibility is an important element of social support. Frequently people who live alone or lose reciprocity in their relationships with others become depressed, feel unneeded, and lose self-esteem. A lack of social support increases responses to stressors. Increased stress responses lead to diminution of the body's ability to fight infections and resist disease. Thus social support decreases the impact of stress on the body and lessens the likelihood of the development of new diseases or exacerbations of old ones (Cobb, 1976; Dubos, 1955).

Caring for a pet can also improve self-image and facilitate caring for one's self. Kidd and Feldman (1981) used questionnaires to compare the self-images of senior citizens who did and did not own pets. They found that pet owners felt significantly more self sufficient, dependable, helpful, self-confident, and optimistic than non-pet owners.

Elderly people in Edinburgh, Scotland, when given a pet bird by a social worker and instructed to maintain higher house temperature for their pets, did not experience hypothermia that winter. Since hypothermia is a major problem for the elderly in that city, the pets undoubtedly contributed to their owner's health.[2]

Pets also contribute to life styles associated with better survival among the healthy elderly. In a large scale longitudinal study of physiological, social, and behavioral predictors of ten year survival for healthy elderly men, only two variables, not smoking and having a complex and varied life style, are strong predictors of survival (Yaumans and Yarrow, 1971). Certainly pets can help make owners' lives more complex and varied.

Touching a pet, as well as being a means of expressing affection, affects owners' cardiovascular systems. Researchers have reported that interacting with (talking to and petting) a pet is less arousing to the owners' cardiovascular system than talking with people (Baun, Langston, Bergstron, and Thoma, 1984; Friedmann, Katcher, Meislick, and Goodman, 1979; Grossberg, 1984; Katcher, 1981). On the basis of previous investigations of the cardiovascular response to communication (Lynch, Thomas, Long, Malinow, Chicadonz and Katcher, 1980; Lynch, Long, Thomas, Malinow, and Katcher, 1981) they expected owners' blood pressures and heart rates to increase while talking to and petting their pets. The owners' cardiovascular levels did not increase when they talked to and petted (using engaged petting) their dogs. As was expected, pet owners' blood pressures and heart rates increased significantly when they communicated with other people or read aloud. The authors concluded that petting and talking to their pets was less arousing to the owners than communicating with other people (Friedmann et al., 1979; Katcher, 1981).

Baum and associates (1984) confirmed the effect of petting pets on their owners' cardiovascular levels. They also compared the effects of petting their own dogs and unfamiliar dogs. In this study, the beneficial effect of petting on blood pressure and heart rate occurred only with the owner's dogs. The dog owners studied were all members of a dog breed club, and the unfamiliar dogs used were of a dissimilar breed. From these data it is not clear whether dogs similar to their own dogs, or familiar dogs would have had different effects on the subjects. In contrast Grossberg,[3] in a complex study of college students interacting with unfamiliar but friendly dogs, confirmed the original findings (Friedmann et al., 1979; Katcher, 1981). Furthermore two very different dogs led to consistent results in Grossberg's population.

It is not clear what characteristics of the dogs or the people led to these disparate results. An indicator of participants perceptions of the unfamiliar dogs might be useful in clarifying these experimental discrepancies. Additional studies comparing the effects of familiar and unfamiliar dogs on people are needed.

Katcher and associates (Katcher, Friedmann, Beck, and Lynch, 1983a; Katcher, Segal, and Beck, 1984) found that BP decreased progressively while watching fish swimming in an aquarium. The decreases in blood pressure which occurred while looking at fish swimming were compared with those which occurred while looking at a poster or at identical tanks without fish. The decreases continued for a longer period when looking at fish than in the other situations. Similarly, the cardiovascular response to verbalization was diminished after watching the fish swimming compared with at the beginning of the session. The decreases in resting blood pressure and in the cardiovascular response to verbalization were most pronounced in those subjects whose initial blood pressures were highest. Watching the fish swimming in their tank prior to dental surgery was also an effective means of increasing patient compliance, and decreasing perceptions of pain and concomitant increases in blood pressure during the dental procedure (Katcher et al., 1984). In this study watching fish swimming in an aquarium was as effective as hypnosis at improving these measures. Furthermore the effect of watching the fish plus hypnosis was no greater than the effect of just watching the fish.

It is clear that looking at fish swimming in an aquarium can provide relaxation. Further research is needed on the relaxing effects of attending to other types of pets as well as the use of pets as a means of relaxing patients before medical appointments or procedures.

The presence of an unknown dog had psychologically and physiologically calming effects on both pet owners and non-pet owners. Pets are frequently included in pictures and advertisements to make settings appear more homelike, less threatening, and more friendly. Lockwood (1983) scientifically investigated the effect of the presence of animals on people's perceptions of scenes. He had students rate their perceptions of pictures from sets of identical scenes with and without animals. Subjects' ratings of the scenes showed that situations and the people in them are perceived as more friendly and less threatening when an animal is included, than when no animal is present.

Two different research groups showed that the presence of an unknown dog led to decreases in anxiety in mildly stressful situations. Sebkova[4] investigated the effect of the presence of her dog on other people's anxiety. She had 20 people complete psychological check-lists and observed their behavior in two environments. People indicated lower anxiety levels and behaved in less anxious manners when her dog accompanied her to the psychology laboratory than when she met them alone. Furthermore people paid more attention to her dog in the more anxious atmosphere of the laboratory compared to more familiar atmosphere of their own homes.

Researchers extended Sebkova's findings by investigating the physiological effects of the presence of a "friendly" dog. Friedmann et al. (1983b) studied the effects of the presence of an unfamiliar dog on resting cardiovascular levels and the cardiovascular response to verbalization. The blood pressures and heart rates of 38 children were measured over two four-minute periods. The experimenter was accompanied by a dog in one of the two periods for each child. The dog was present in the first period for half of the children and the second period for the others. In each period the child was asked to rest for two minutes and read aloud for two minutes. The presence of the dog resulted in lowered blood pressures both while the children were resting and while they were reading. The presence of the dog at the beginning of an experimental session was associated with lower blood pressures throughout the procedure, even once the dog had left the room. Thus the dog apparently made the setting seem less threatening and more friendly.

Pets who need exercise provide an impetus for the owner to exercise and companionship during the exercise period. Thus the dog cannot only encourage its owner to go out and get started, but also induce longer periods of exercise by reducing boredom and loneliness. Since improved physical fitness is associated with improvements in psychological status and health, physical fitness gained through walking pets can benefit the pet owner. Only one study has documented the effect of pets on their owners' exercise habits. Messent (1983) observed people on walks. He found that people who walked with pets spent longer on their walks than people who walked alone.

The health benefits of pets are only beginning to be documented; additional information is crucial for a more complete evaluation. Information about the health benefits of pets for the general population is lacking. Many of the studies reviewed in this paper have focused on select groups and/or have small sample sizes. Comparison groups were often inadequate or missing. Many large epidemiological studies of various populations are ongoing. Inclusion of a few questions in these large longitudinal studies could provide valuable information about pet owners and their health. Since the pet owning population is very large, random selection of subjects for studies should be possible. Certainly Dr. Smith's ideas (1983) of selecting subjects when they were shopping for pet food could provide a far more representative sample than using clients attending a veterinary clinic. Obviously health care institutions provide a large population, not selected for their pet ownership characteristics.

Many studies have documented the health benefits of pets indirectly. However, the few researchers who even attempt to experimentally document directly physiological or psychological effects of pets concentrate on the short term. It is critical that experimental studies document the direct health effects of pets on both the short and long term.

SUMMARY

Companionship is the most researched aspect of the health benefits of pets. The companionship provided by a pet often leads to decreased loneliness and improvements in psychological and physiological status. Additionally, the presence of a pet provides "social lubrication" which increases contacts with others that are particularly crucial to individuals lacking support from family or close friends.

All health professionals should include questions concerning pet ownership in their initial evaluations of patients. This is especially important for the hospitalized or institutionalized patient. Care for the pet when the owner is disabled is often a source of anxiety for the patient and should not be overlooked.

Pets can help people who have lost contact with others through bereavement or emotional dysfunction regain contact with the world. Once contact with an animal is established, it is easier to enter into relationship with other people. The special kinds of relationships people have with animals, the non-judgmental nature of the animals' response, and the inability of the animal to bargain for its love, make relationships with pets less threatening than contact with people.

Caring for a pet can promote health by giving people responsibility, providing time orientation, and promoting an interesting and a varied life style. Caring for a pet provides a sense of being needed and self-worth similar to that obtained from caring for other people. Taking responsibility for a pet can be especially important to patients whose activities are limited due to chronic diseases, handicaps, or social isolation. Caring for a pet often facilitates caring for one's self. The requirements of keeping a beloved pet healthy have been used as inducement for maintaining healthy living conditions for pet owners.

Any factor which decreases or prevents anxiety and depression is likely to have positive effects on health. These effects may be manifest as decreased incidence or slowed progression of a broad spectrum of chronic diseases including coronary heart disease, hypertension, and diabetes. Pets can decrease owners' depression, anxiety, and sympathetic nervous system arousal.

The introduction of aquarium in waiting rooms, treatment rooms, and community areas within institutions has great potential for decreasing anxiety and concomitant physiological arousal. This easily achieved addition is inexpensive, and requires very little maintenance. Certainly the health benefits far outweigh any inconvenience of this environmental manipulation.

Pets provide a crucial source of touch for individuals who would otherwise be without this sensory input. Touching an animal decreases individual's anxiety and physiological arousal and can have important health effects. Playing with pets by institutionalized and chronically ill patients can lead to improved attention to their environments and to increased socialization. In cases where there is not a definite contraindiction hospitalized persons should be allowed to have their pets visit. In any institution there are obstacles to pet visitation. However, the staff as well as the clients can benefit from the introduction of pets. The presence of pets can lead to significant improvement in staff morale, which can eventually improve staff-patient relations and care.

The health benefits of moderate exercise have been well established in every age group. Physical fitness improves psychological and physiological well-being. By providing a little extra push, pets help their owners maintain a regular exercise program. Getting out and exercising a pet often leads to contacts with other people. This is important for those people who are lonely, depressed or have decreased physiological functioning.

IMPLICATIONS FOR THERAPISTS

Pets are important to their family members' health. Discussions about the care of the pet while the owner is disabled or incapacitated must be taken seriously. These concerns are similar to those about dependent children. Worries about the care of their pets may lead to delays in seeking individual health care or to terminating hospitalization. Health professionals must evaluate disruption of the care of the pet in the same manner as they would for a dependent child. Intervention may involve eliciting the cooperation or assurances of other family members, the help of social agencies, or actually placing the pet in a temporary care situation. Patients should be encouraged to keep in touch with their pets so that their concerns will be decreased. Health professionals should be sensitive to the patient's reluctance to burden others concerning their pets and therefore should encourage the individual to discuss his concerns. This is important to the emotional and physiological health of the pet owner.

Death of a pet should be treated in an equally sensitive manner. Social disruptions have been shown to precipitate major illness. Though it has not been thoroughly researched, the death of a pet can certainly have catastrophic consequences. Grieving for one's pet is not always supported in our society. Whereas rituals governing family behavior provide support when people die, formalized grief rituals are not generally initiated when a canine, feline, or other type of family pet member dies. Therapists should encourage pet owning families to discuss the loss of their pet. Several researchers have documented parallels in the process of grieving for a pet to those for a person (Stewart, 1983). The resolution of grief may be a prolonged process. The special circumstances surrounding euthanasia often require intense support for the grieving family.

The sensitivity of the family therapist toward the special needs of pet owning families can improve communication as well as facilitate therapy. The issues surrounding pet ownership allow opportunity to foster closer dialogue between the therapist and family members and within the family itself.

NOTES

1. Okoniewski, L.A. The psychological aspects of man-animal relationships. Masters Thesis, Hahnemann Medical College, Philadelphia, 1978.

2. Walster, D. The role of pets in the mental health of the elderly. Paper presented at the

Meeting of the Group for the Study of the Human/Companion Animal Bond. University of Dundee, Dundee, Scotland, March 1979.

   3. Grossberger, S. San Diego State Univ., personal communication, Feb. 1984.

   4. Sebkova, J. Anxiety levels as affected by the presence of a dog. Unpublished senior thesis, University of Lancaster, 1977.

REFERENCES

Baun, M.M., Bergstrom, N., Langston, N., & Thoma, L., Physiological effects of petting dogs: Influences of attachment. In *The pet connection: Its influence on our health and quality of life*. R.K. Anderson, B.L. Hart, & L.A. Hart (Eds.), South St. Paul, Minn: Globe Publishing Co., 1984, Pp. 162–170.

Beck, A.M. The public health implications of urban dogs. *American Journal of Public Health*, 1975, *65*, 1315–1318.

Bossard, J.H.S. & Stoker, E. *The sociology of child development*. New York: Harper and Row, 1966.

Cain, A.O. A study of pets in the family system. In *New perspectives on our lives with animal companions*. A.H. Katcher & A.M. Beck (Eds.), Philadelphia: University of Pennsylvania Press, 1983, Pp. 72–86.

Carding, A.H. The growth of pet populations in Western Europe and the implications for dog control in Great Britain. In *Pet animals and society*. R.S. Anderson (Ed.), London: Bailliere Tindall, 1975, Pp. 66–68.

Casler, L. The effects of extratactile stimulation on a group of institutionalized infants. *Genet Psychological Monographs*, 1965, *71*, 137–175.

Cobb, S. Social support as a moderator of life stress. *Psychosomatic Medicine*, 1976, *38*, 300–314.

Dubos, R.J. Second thoughts on the germ theory. *Scientific American*, 1955, *192*, 31–35.

Friedmann, E., Katcher, A.H., Eaton, M., & Berger, B. Pet ownership and psychological status. In *The pet connection: Its influence on our health and quality of life*. R.K. Anderson, B.L. Hart, & L.A. Hart (Eds.), South St. Paul, Minn: Globe Publishing Co., 1984, Pp.300–308.

Friedmann, E., Katcher, A.H., Lynch, J.J., & Thomas, S.A. Animal companions and one year survival after discharge from a Coronary Care Unit. *Public Health Reports,* 1980, *95*, 307–312.

Friedmann, E., Katcher, A.H., & Meislich, D. When pet owners are hospitalized: Significance of companion animals during hospitalization. In *New perspectives on our lives with animal companions*. A.H. Katcher & A.M. Beck (Eds.), Philadelphia: University of Pennsylvania Press, 1983a, Pp. 346–350.

Friedmann, E., Katcher, A.H. Meislich, D., & Goodman, M. Physiological response of people to petting their pets. *American Zoologist*, 1979, *19*, 327.

Friedmann, E., Katcher, A.H., Thomas, S.A., Lynch, J.J., & Messent, P.R. Social interaction and blood pressure: Influence of animal companions. *Journal of Nervous and Mental Disease*, 1983b, *171*, 461–465.

Garfield, C.A. *Stress and survival: The emotional realities of life threatening illness*. St. Louis, C.V. Mosby, 1979.

Goffman, I. Gender advertisements. *Studies in Anthropology of Visual Communication*, 1976, *3*, 69–154.

Harlow, H.F. The nature of love. *American Psychologist*, 1958, *13*, 673–685.

Harlow, H.F. The development of affectional patterns in infant monkeys. In *Determinants of infant behavior*. B.M. Foss (Ed.), London: Methuen, 1961, 7, Pp. 75–97.

Johnson, B.S. The meaning of touch in nursing. *Nursing Outlook*, 1965, *13*, 60–61.

Katcher, A.H. Interactions between people and their pets: Form and function. In *Interrela-*

tions between people and pets. B. Fogle (Ed.), Springfield, Ill: Charles C. Thomas, 1981, Pp. 41–67.

Katcher, A.H., & Friedmann, E. Potential health value of pet ownership. *Compendium on Continuing Education for the Practicing Veterinarian*, 1980, *2*, 117–122.

Katcher, A.H., Friedmann, E., Beck, A.M., & Lynch, J.J. Talking, looking, and blood pressure: Physiological consequences of interaction with the living environment. In *New perspectives on our lives with animal companions*. A.H. Katcher & A.M. Beck (Eds.), Philadelphia: University of Pennsylvania Press, 1983a, Pp. 351–359.

Katcher, A.H., Friedmann, E., Goodman, M., & Goodman, L. Men, women, and dogs. *California Veterinarian*, 1983b, *37*, 14–17.

Katcher, A.H., Goodman, L., & Friedmann, E. Human-pet interactions. *American Zoologist*, 1979, *19*, 326.

Katcher, A.H., Segal, H., & Beck, A.M. Contemplation of an aquarium for the reduction of anxiety. In *The pet connection: Its influence on our health and quality of life*. R.K. Anderson, B.L. Hart, & L.A. Hart (Eds.), South St. Paul, Minn: Globe Publishing Co., 1984, Pp. 171–178.

Kerr, M.E. Family systems theory and therapy. In *The handbook of family therapy*. A.S. Gurman (Ed.), New York, Brunner/Mazel, 1981, Pp. 226–264.

Kidd, A.H., & Feldman, B.M. Pet ownership and self-perception in older people. *Psychological Reports*, 1981, *48*, 867–875.

Krieger, D. *Therapeutic touch: How to use your hands to help and heal*. Englewood, NJ: Prentice Hall, 1976.

Krieger, D. Therapeutic touch. *Nursing Times*, 1976, *April*, 572–574.

Lockwood, R. The influence of animals on social perception. In *New perspectives on our lives with animal companions*. A.H. Katcher & A.M. Beck (Eds.), Philadelphia: University of Pennsylvania Press, 1983, Pp. 64–71.

Lynch, J.J. *The broken heart: The medical consequences of loneliness*. New York: Basic Books, 1977.

Lynch, J.J., Long, J.M., Thomas, S.A., Malinow, K., & Katcher, A.H. The effects of talking on the blood pressures of hypertensive and normo-tensive individuals. *Psychosomatic Medicine*, 1981, *43*, 25–33.

Lynch, J.J., Thomas, S.A., Long, J.M., Malinow, K.L. Chicadonz, G., & Katcher, A.H. Human speech and blood pressure. *Journal of Nervous and Mental Disease*, 1980, *168*, 526–534.

McCoy, P. Further proof that touch speaks louder than words. *RN*, 1977, *Nov*, 43–46.

Messent, P.R. Facilitation of social interaction by companion animals. In *New perspectives on our lives with animal companions*. A.H. Katcher & A.M. Beck (Eds.), Philadelphia: University of Pennsylvania Press, 1983, Pp. 37–46.

Montagu, A. *Touching: The human significance of the skin*. New York: Columbia University Press, 1971.

Mugford, R.A., & M'Comisky, I.G. Some recent work on the psychotherapeutic value of cage birds with old people. In *Pet animals and society*. R.S. Anderson (Ed.), London: Bailliere Tindall, 1975, Pp 54–65.

Ory, M.G., and Goldberg, E.L. Pet ownership and life satisfaction. In *New perspectives on our lives with animal companions*. A.H. Katcher & A.M. Beck (Eds.), Philadelphia: University of Pennsylvania Press, 1983, Pp. 303–307.

Ory, M.G., and Goldberg, E.L. An epidemiological study of pet ownership in the community. In *The pet connection: Its influence on our health and quality of life*. R.K. Anderson, B.L. Hart, & L.A. Hart Pp. 320–330.

Robb, S.S. Health status correlates of pet ownership in a health-impaired population. In *New perspectives on our lives with animal companions*. A.H. Katcher & A.M. Beck (Eds.), Philadelphia: University of Pennsylvania Press, 1983, Pp. 318–327.

Smith, S. L. Interactions between pet dog and family members: An ethological study. In *New perspectives on our lives with animal companions*. A.H. Katcher & A.M. Beck (Eds.), Philadelphia: University of Pennsylvania Press, 1983, Pp. 29–36.

Speck, R.V. Mental health problems involving the family, the pet, and the veterinarian. *Journal of the American Veterinary Medical Association*, 1964, *145*, 150–154.

Spitz, R. Childhood development phenomenon: The influence of mother-child relationships and its disturbance. In *Mental health and infant development.* K. Soddy (Ed.), New York: Basic Books, 1956, Pp.

Stewart, M. Loss of a pet—Loss of a person: A comparative study of bereavement. In *New perspectives on our lives with animal companions.* A.H. Katcher & A.M. Beck (Eds.) Philadelphia: University of Pennsylvania Press, 1983, Pp. 390–404.

Whitcher, S.J., & Fisher, J.D. Multidimensional reaction to therapeutic touch in a hospital setting. *Journal of Personal and Social Psychology,* 1979, *37*, 87–96.

Youmans, E.G., and Yarrow, M. Aging and social adaptation: A longitudinal study of healthy elderly men. In *Human aging II: An eleven year follow-up biomedical and behavioral study.* S. Granik, & R.D. Patterson (Eds.), DHEW Publication #(HSM) 20-9037. Washington, D.C.: U.S. Government Printing Office, 1971, Pp. 95–104.

The Pet in the Military Family
at Transfer Time:
It Is No Small Matter

Lynn J. Anderson

ABSTRACT. One hundred eighty four military families were surveyed in person and their pet involvement at transfer time and shortly thereafter was ascertained. Comprising the 184 families were 3 stratified random samples made up of 93 junior enlisted families, 48 officer families, and 43 senior enlisted families. As a very early study in this specific subject a major portion of the study explored and identified by rank the frequencies relating to type of pet involvement, the species of pet involved, the reasons for pet ownership, the reasons for leaving behind, bringing, or acquiring a pet, and the effects noted from either leaving, bringing, or acquiring a pet. Finally, early hypothesis testing using chi square was used in establishing differences and/or similarities between the rank groupings in their pet involvement and effects derived therefrom. As a result, those concerned with military families at transfer time now have evidence that the pet as a factor is pertinent to a great many families and that its impact is no small matter to these families.

INTRODUCTION

Background, Problem and Purpose of Research

Disruption of friendship and associative bonds occurs every time a military transfer occurs. It was suspected that one constancy amidst

Lynn J. Anderson, is a 1978 graduate of Washington State University Veterinary School and has served since that time in the U.S. Army Veterinary Corps. He recently received his Master's Degree of Social Work (MSW-1984) from the University of Hawaii where he specialized in the Human-Animal Bond as it relates to the military family and community. He is currently involved in further research in this field while assigned to the U.S. Army Health Services Command at Fort Sam Houston, Texas. He is a member of the American Veterinary Medical Association, Delta Society, and the Society for Companion Animal Studies.

The author's address for reprints is Headquarters, U.S. Army Health Services Command, ATTN: HSVS-P, Fort Sam Houston, TX 78234-6000.

The opinions or assertions contained herein are the private views of the author and are not to be construed as official or as reflecting the views of the Department of the Army or the Department of Defense.

this otherwise changing and stressful situation could be the family pet. But what if these pet-owning military families decided to leave this "member of the family" behind at transfer time?

It was an assumption of this study that many families were faced with decisions about pets at transfer time and that many were actually forced to leave them behind due to factors such as expense, inconvenience, health of the animals, etc. It was also assumed that such disruption of bonds could further contribute to family problems at an already disruptive time. Conversely, it was suspected that when the pet goes with the family it could be beneficial to the family. Finally, it was suspected that the number and proportion of military families directly affected by pets during transfer time was not small.

The purpose of this research then was two-fold: (1) to determine whether the pet factor was pertinent for a substantial number of military families, and (2) if it was, to provide information that could inform families, human-services professionals, and also military policymakers of the impact of pet involvement in the lives of military families. Thus, families could better weigh their decisions regarding whether or not to take their pet knowing how similar decisions had affected others, human-services professionals could better consider the pet factor as it affects their client's and/or subject's mental health, and military policymakers could be better informed when making decisions concerning care and assistance allowable for these non-human "family members."

LITERATURE REVIEW

That man has had a long standing cooperative relationship with animals is a well documented fact (Bustad & Hines, 1984; Messent & Serpell, 1981). That this same relationship exists today is also well known. Statistical data on the numbers of pets in our modern society relies on limited information generated most often by member organizations of the Pet Food Institute. For example, General Foods Corporation (1981) reported that it is estimated that the total dog population of this country is 44 million owned by some 31 million households. Beck and Katcher (1983) reported that "Americans own more than 1.2 trillion pet creatures—dogs, cats, birds, horses, small mammals, reptiles and fish. They spend more than $4 billion a year to feed this menagerie and another $4 billion on accessories such as leashes, collars and cages." So, although these figures on pet ownership are far from definitive in numbers and details, it would appear that the pets in our society are extremely important ($8 billion per year) to at least some of their owners.

In spite of this apparently large normal segment of our society that is deeply committed at least monetarily to its pets, the major thrust of research in the human-animal bond field has been directed towards the intriguing idea that animals can be an effective treatment modality in working with humans with various physical and/or emotional disabilities. For example, one of the pioneer studies was conducted by Corson et al. (1975) wherein Pet Facilitated Psychotherapy (PFP) was used as a treatment modality in fifty cases that had been treated unsuccessfully by other means. Impressive positive results were obtained in the form of greatly improved psychosocial functioning in almost all cases.

As previously stated, it is much more difficult to find empirical research that deals with the pet animal's benefit to man in a non-pathological state such as to a normal functioning family. Levinson's 1972 and 1978 works are a mixture of empirical and anecdotal evidence pointing out the value of the pet animal in society. As a professor of psychology and a diplomate in clinical psychology, the late Dr. Levinson was well-versed and experienced in all stages of the human lifecycle. Additionally, as a noted authority and pioneer in the human-pet interaction, his works very ably take the reader through each of the human phases of life and relates each to the positive influences upon man that can be gained through involvement with pets.

Further, it has been documented that adults who grow up with pets of a specific kind will be strongly influenced to have a pet in later life and most likely of the same kind as possessed when a child (Kidd, 1981–82; Serpell, 1981). Perhaps it could be also demonstrated that where a pet was a ''family member'' when a subject was a child, a pet would be considered an integral part of the same person's family as an adult.

Only recently has a study looked specifically at the role of the pet in military families. Catanzaro (1983) surveyed 961 military pet owners as to their opinions concerning the role of their pets in their lives. Psychosocial factors relating to the human-pet interaction within military families were identified.

Missing from the literature are studies that address the implications of the pet to the military family's stability and emotional well-being at transfer time. Also missing are any studies relating to the magnitude of the phenomenon. It was this researcher's impression from his previous experience in practice as a military veterinarian that there were a great many families experiencing problems related to pets and transfers. This study has confirmed this impression. Hopefully then, it will be only the first of many studies by many researchers in this important field.

CONCEPTUAL FRAMEWORK AND HYPOTHESES

We see then a definite need to evaluate more fully the theory that the human-animal bond is often a substantial contributor to the social and emotional well-being of many people. That this theory relates to the military especially at transfer time had not yet been adequately explored. Thus, the primary purpose of this study was to explore the phenomenon and describe first its existence and then its magnitude. Once that was done, primarily through subjective surveys and frequency tables, the testing of several early hypotheses became possible and worthwhile.

This study tested several such hypotheses. First, it was hypothesized that the potential negative effects of periodic and recurrent transfers of military families can be significantly compounded for one or more members of some military families regardless of rank, when factors necessitate the disposition of the family pet prior to such a move. Such factors include financial expenditures, difficulties affecting the health of the pet, and inconveniences to the owners. Secondly, it was hypothesized that the rank of the service families does affect the relative distributions of whether they bring their pet, leave it behind, acquire one here or stay uninvolved with pets altogether. Thirdly, it was hypothesized that the rank of the service families does not affect the status given by the families to their pets. Finally, concerning the expense factor, it costs approximately $500 per pet to bring one from the mainland to Hawaii. Most of this cost is due to the four month quarantine requirement. It was therefore also hypothesized that the families that value their pet as a family member and yet still leave them behind will most frequently be those of the junior enlisted group.

METHODS

Sampling, Sample, and Instrumentation

The state of Hawaii is home for approximately 18,000 military families composed of Army, Navy, Air Force, Marine and Coast

Guard personnel. As a representative group of housing areas for which statistical breakdown by rank was readily available, Fort Shafter, Schofield Barracks and Aliamanu Military Reservation housing areas were chosen. Considered as a single group (N=6118) and broken down by rank, there are 4191 junior enlisted families of the ranks E4-E6, 776 senior enlisted families of the ranks E7-E9, and 1151 officer families of the ranks W1-06. Of this population, 3 stratified random samples were taken from Aliamanu Military Reservation's 2596 families. The first consisted of 210 families of the junior enlisted ranks. The second consisted of 87 families of the senior enlisted ranks. The third consisted of 89 families of the officer ranks. Of these families selected in the random sample, 93 of the 210 junior enlisted families were contacted (44.29%), 43 of the 87 senior enlisted families were contacted (49.43%), and 48 of 89 officer families were contacted (53.93%) for the final combined sample of n=184.*

During the month of March, 1984, the researcher personally interviewed the 184 families concerning their status at transfer time relating to pet involvement. Utilized was a contingency type questionnaire that divided the samples into 5 categories (see Table 1). Pet Status 1 (PS1) identified those families that brought their pet with them from their former duty station. Pet Status 2 (PS2) identified those families that left their pet behind and did not replace it. Pet Status 3 (PS3) identified those families that left their pet behind but did replace it. Pet Status 4 (PS4) identified those families that acquired a pet in Hawaii, not having had one at transfer time. Pet Status 5 (PS5) identified those families that had neither pet involvement at transfer time nor at the present time.

The interview also included other questions pertinent to this study as applicable to each particular pet status noted above. Generally, they were all asked what was the species of the involved pet, why they now owned or had owned a pet, why they left the pet behind when applicable, and what were the effects of bringing, leaving or acquiring their particular pet(s)? The answers were categorized by the researcher into the most applicable of the choices provided on the questionnaire.

---

*The slight difference in composition ratio (junior enlisted:senior enlisted:officers) between population and sample was taken into account by constructing weighted and speculative influential tables. The resulting statistics did not differ significantly from those reported in this paper so are not reported. Full details are available from the researcher upon request.

THE PET IN THE MILITARY FAMILY AT TRANSFER TIME

TABLE 1: PET STATUS* OF MILITARY FAMILIES AT TRANSFER TIME BY RANK GROUPING (n-184)

PET STATUS

FREQUENCY (ROW %)	PS1	PS2	PS3	PS4	PS5	
JR. ENLISTED	8 (8.60)	7 (7.53)	19 (20.43)	21 (22.58)	38 (40.86)	93
OFFICER	15 (31.25)	5 (10.42)	7 (14.58)	7 (14.58)	14 (29.17)	48
SR. ENLISTED	6 (13.95)	6 (13.95)	11 (25.58)	10 (23.26)	10 (23.26)	43
	29 (15.76)	18 (9.78)	37 (20.11)	38 (20.65)	62 (33.70)	184 (100.00)

RANK

*PET STATUS (PS) DEFINED

PS1 - BROUGHT PET WITH THEM FROM LAST ASSIGNMENT

PS2 - LEFT PET BEHIND, NOT REPLACED IN HAWAII YET

PS3 - LEFT PET BEHIND, REPLACED IN HAWAII

PS4 - NO PET AT TRANSFER, BUT ACQUIRED ONE IN HAWAII

PS5 - NO PET INVOLVEMENT

Design

This study was primarily descriptive in nature and employed the interview research design. Additionally, some early hypothesis testing was made possible by considering the different rank groupings (junior enlisted, senior enlisted, and officer) as independent random samples (RG) all receiving the same intervention (I) namely that of being transferred to Hawaii and the outcome (0) being the responses of the families interviewed.

RGI	I	0
RG2	I	0
RG3	I	0

With such a design, the construction of applicable contingency tables was possible which were analyzed for differences using the Chi Square test.

As evidenced by its absence in the human-animal bond literature, there is the need for much descriptive information concerning its application to the military family at transfer time. Until this study questions such as (1) how many families in the military have pets, (2) how many of them are involved with pets at transfer time, (3) what do they do with their pets at transfer time, and (4) how do these decisions affect their family, have been only a matter of conjecture. This study has provided some early statistics that provide a basis for early discussion and further research.

Finally, as mentioned, several hypothesis were tested in this study using the Chi Square test. First tested was the hypothesis that the effects of leaving a pet behind would be the same regardless of the rank group of the family. Second tested was the hypothesis that there was a difference in the way each rank grouping is distributed in relationship to whether or not they bring their pet, leave it behind, acquire one here, or don't have one at all. Third tested was the hypothesis that all rank groupings are similar in their positioning of pets in their family structure, i.e., part of the family or property only, etc. Fourth, the hypothesis that the junior enlisted group would more often choose expense as the reason for leaving their pet behind was tested.

RESULTS

Sample Results

The first portion of the results of this study are descriptive in nature and are in terms of frequencies. Although many have felt that the pet factor in military families at transfer time was most likely applicable to many, there has been no data to confirm such feelings. This is no longer the case as seen from the findings of this study.

Table 1 summarizes the basic composition of the sample (n = 184). It was found that 29 or 15.76% brought their pets with them (PS1), 18 or 9.78% left their pets behind and did not replace them (PS2), 37 or 20.11% left their pets behind but replaced them in Hawaii (PS3), 38 or 20.65% had no pet at transfer time but acquired one in Hawaii (PS4), and 62 or 33.70% had no pet involvement during or after their transfer to Hawaii (PS5).

Looking only at those families that had some pet involvement at transfer time or soon thereafter (PS1, PS2, PS3, PS4), we find that 122 or 66.30% of the sample are within this grouping. Eliminating those that acquired a pet only after arrival (PS4) and considering only those families that had actual involvement with pets at transfer time (PS1, PS2, PS3), we find that there are still 84 families or 45.65% of the total sample so involved. Finally, after eliminating those families that brought their pets with them (PS1), we find 55 families or 29.89% of the total sample that left their pets behind (PS2, PS3).

Of the 184 families, we find then that there were only 62 families or 33.70% that had no pet involvement at either transfer time or up until the time the sample was taken (PS5). Additionally, it was also found that 35.85% of those in the no pet involvement category planned to obtain a pet sometime in the future (see Table 2). Applying this to the total sample, it could then be said that 78.38% of the sample had had pet involvement at transfer time, shortly thereafter, or planned to do so in the future.

The species of pets in those families involved were also determined. The 104 (56.52%) families that owned pets at the time of the interview owned at least* 62 dogs, 33 cats, 13 birds, 2 fish, and 4 + miscellaneous species of pets. Another 18 families (9.78%) didn't

---

*The interview questions asked for "at least" 1 pet of a given category. Many of the families had multiple pets of a given species. Only one was counted.

THE PET IN THE MILITARY FAMILY AT TRANSFER TIME

TABLE 2: FOR THOSE WITH NO PET INVOLVEMENT AT TRANSFER TIME (PS5), BY RANK DO THEY PLAN TO ACQUIRE A PET IN THE FUTURE? (n-53*)

PLAN A PET IN THE FUTURE?

FREQUENCY (ROW %)	NO	YES	
JR. ENLISTED	19 (63.33)	11 (36.37)	30
OFFICERS	9 (64.29)	5 (35.71)	14
SR. ENLISTED	6 (66.67)	3 (33.33)	9
	34 (64.15)	19 (35.85)	53 (100.00)

RANK

*n FOR PS5=62, HOWEVER 9 FAMILIES DID NOT ANSWER THE QUESTION.

213

have pets at the time of the interview but had owned pets at their last duty station. These 18 families that didn't replace their pets (PS2) when combined with the 37 that did (PS3) left behind at least 33 dogs, 16 cats, 3 birds, 1 horse, and 2+ miscellaneous species of pets. These figures, when translated to the larger numbers in the population from which they were drawn, represent an substantial number of pets involved with all of the attending implications.

All families involved with pets at transfer time were asked what role their pet played in their family. Their responses were included in (1) part of the family, example: friend, companion, etc.; (2) family property , example: education, protection, breeding, etc.; or (3) other, please specify. It is particularly noteworthy that of the 84 families that had pet involvement at transfer time (PS1, PS2, PS3), 83 or 98.81% considered their pet a part of their family. For those that acquired their pet in Hawaii (PS4), their question had the same choices but the question related to why they had obtained the pet. In this case, 6 or 15.79% of the families had acquired their pet to become property (mainly security reasons) and 31 or 81.58% of the families had acquired their pet to become part of the family. The obvious question that comes from such results is did the percentage of those that consider their pet as part of the family increase after the initial acquisition? Based on the 98.81% figure for those that had owned their pets for a period of time, it is strongly suspected that those pets enjoying family status would increase following the initial procurement. Unfortunately, that question was not asked and will need to be explored in future studies.

If so many families consider their pet to be a part of their family, why did they leave them behind? Table 3 summarizes the results of that question. The choices possible were (1) expense, (2) pet too old, (3) quarantine too long (120 days rabies quarantine in Hawaii), (4) too much inconvenience, and (5) other, please explain. Forty-three or 78.18% of the total cases fell into the expense and quarantine categories. However, some differences in percentages are noted when comparing the rank groupings. The junior enlisted families listed expense as the primary reason for leaving pets behind (58.85%), whereas officer families listed it 41.67% of the time, and senior enlisted families listed it only 29.41% of the time. The senior enlisted families listed the quarantine length as the primary reason for leaving pets behind (58.82%), whereas officer families listed it 25.00% of the time, and junior enlisted families chose it 23.08% of the time. For the officer families, another important factor appears

THE PET IN THE MILITARY FAMILY AT TRANSFER TIME

TABLE 3: FOR ALL FAMILIES THAT LEFT THEIR PET(S) BEHIND AT THEIR LAST DUTY STATION (PS2, PS3) BY RANK, WHAT WAS THEIR MAIN REASON FOR DOING SO? (n-55)

REASONS

RANK	FREQUENCY (ROW %)	EXPENSE	PET TOO OLD	QUARANTINE TOO LONG	TOO MUCH INCONVENIENCE	OTHER	
	JR. ENLISTED	14 (53.85)	0 (0.00)	6 (23.08)	3 (11.54)	3 (11.54)	26
	OFFICER	5 (41.67)	3 (25.00)	3 (25.00)	0 (0.00)	1 (8.33)	12
	SR. ENLISTED	5 (29.41)	1 (5.88)	10 (58.82)	0 (0.00)	1 (5.88)	17
		24 (43.64)	4 (7.27)	19 (34.54)	3 (5.54)	5 (9.09)	55 (100.00)

to have been the old age of the animal which was chosen 25.00% of the time.

We see then that a substantial portion of military families leave their pets behind at transfer time even though the great majority of them consider their pets as a part of their family. What are the effects? Table 4 summarizes the responses given to the question by those of the applicable groups (PS2, PS3). The possible choices were (1) long-term saddening for at least one family member—more than 2 weeks, (2) temporary saddening for at least one family member—less than 2 weeks, (3) made happier, (4) no effects noticed, and (5) other, please explain. Every rank reported that at least 75% of their numbers had experienced or were still experiencing long-term saddening as a result of leaving their pet behind. Collectively, 96.36% of the families that left their pets behind are experiencing or have experienced either long-term or temporary sadness resulting from leaving their pet behind.

For those families that brought their pets with them (PS1) they were likewise asked to describe the effects of so doing. Their choices were (1) made family happier, (2) made family sadder, (3) no effects noticed, and (4) other, please explain. Twenty-eight of twenty-nine families (96.55%) responded that it had made their family happier. No families responded that bringing a pet made them sadder and only one family indicated a neutral response.

For those families that did not have a pet at transfer time but acquired one after arriving in Hawaii (PS4), the same choices were available as for PS1. Thirty-three or 89.19% responded that it had made their family happier, 8.11% or three families responded that there had been no effects noticed and the remaining 2.70% (one family) responded "other." No families responded that acquiring a pet made them sadder.

Chi Square and Binomial Results*

The second portion of the results of this study involved the use of the Chi Square Test and in one case the binomial distribution. The null hypotheses that were set up for testing were (1) that there was no difference in the effects noted by junior enlisted, officer, or senior enlisted families that resulted from leaving their pets behind,

---

*Full details (including tables) are available to interested parties upon request of the author.

THE PET IN THE MILITARY FAMILY AT TRANSFER TIME

TABLE 4: FOR ALL FAMILIES THAT LEFT THEIR PETS BEHIND (PS2, PS3) BY RANK, WHAT WERE THE EFFECTS ON AT LEAST ONE MEMBER OF THE FAMILY OF LEAVING THE PET AT THE LAST DUTY ASSIGNMENT? (n-55)

EFFECT

RANK / FREQUENCY (ROW %)	LONG SAD	TEMPORARY SAD	HAPPIER	NO EFFECT	
JR. ENLISTED	20 (76.92)	6 (23.08)	0 (0.00)	0 (0.00)	26
OFFICER	9 (75.00)	1 (8.33)	1 (8.33)	1 (8.33)	12
SR. ENLISTED	16 (94.12)	1 (5.88)	0 (0.00)	0 (0.00)	17
	45 (81.81)	8 (14.56)	1 (1.82)	1 (1.82)	55 (100.00)

217

(2) that there was no difference by rank in the distribution of those bringing their pets and those leaving their pets behind, (3) that there were no differences by rank in the status given their pets by families that owned pets at transfer time, and (4) that there were no differences by rank in the reasons that families left their pets behind.

The first null hypothesis tested was that there is no difference by rank in the effects noted by families that leave their pets behind. It was suspected that the null hypothesis would not be rejected at the 0.05 significant level. Using a two-tailed test (no direction was predicted), Chi Square is equal to 2.523 with 2 degrees of freedom yielding a probability of 0.2833. Therefore, as predicted, we failed to reject the null hypothesis at the level designated indicating that all groups experienced essentially the same saddening effects from leaving their pets behind.

The second null hypothesis tested was that there was no difference by rank in the distribution of those bringing their pets and those leaving their pets behind. It was suspected that the null hypothesis would be rejected at the 0.05 level, the alternate hypothesis being that there was a difference by rank and that the junior enlisted families would leave their pets behind a greater proportion of the time than would either the officer or the senior enlisted families possibly due to the lower income level of the former. Using a one-tailed test since direction is predicted, a chi square equal to 7.826 with 2 degrees of freedom yields a probability of 0.01. Therefore, we are able to reject the null hypothesis with a comfortable margin. Interestingly though, it was not just the junior enlisted but also the senior enlisted that left behind a majority of their pets, whereas the officers brought the majority of their pets with them. It would appear that income level alone is not totally predictive of whether a family will bring their pet with them or not. Table 3 as described above looked at reasons for leaving pets behind and gives insight into this finding. Effects on the animal vs. effects on the pocket book appear to be the major consideration for leaving a pet behind for the senior enlisted group.

The third null hypothesis tested was that there were no differences by rank in the status given to their pets at that time. It was suspected that we would fail to reject the null hypothesis. Chi Square turned out to be totally non-applicable in this case with such a scarcity of respondents in half of the cells. We in fact see that with only one exception, all subjects considered their pet as part of their family and the null hypothesis intuitively stood very little chance of rejection.

Looking at the data in another way, consider the probability of getting 83 out of 84 subjects choosing family member status for their pet as opposed to all other choices. Using the conservative approach the $p = 0.5$ and $q = 0.5$ the probability of such a binomial distribution occurring by chance is so small that it is not calculable on most calculators. Therefore, we have strong evidence that military families involved with pets at transfer time, in either bringing them or leaving them behind, do consider them part of the family regardless of their rank.

The final null hypothesis tested was that there was no difference by rank in the reasons that families left their pets behind. It was suspected that the null hypothesis would be rejected at the 0.05 level, the alternate hypothesis being that there were differences mainly related to a belief that junior enlisted families would most often choose expense as the reason for leaving a pet behind where officers and senior enlisted families would choose other reasons more often. As it turned out, the null hypothesis could not be rejected at the 0.05 level, however some trends are noted. The alternate hypothesis does have support at least in direction even if statistical significance is only at the 0.1419 level for a one-tailed test (direction predicted). The junior enlisted families listed expense as the reason for leaving their pets behind in greater than 50% of the cases where the trend is reversed for the officer and the senior enlisted families where other reasons comprise the majority of their responses.

DISCUSSION

Conclusions

A substantial number of military families are involved with pets at transfer time or shortly thereafter (66.3%) Further, it is concluded that a substantial number of military families do consider their pets as a part of their family (98.81% for those with pet involvement at transfer time and 81.53% for those that acquired a pet only after their arrival in Hawaii). Even so, many of these families left an alarming number of pets behind for various reasons that were often beyond their control. As a whole, those families leaving their pets behind constituted a substantial portion of the entire population with or without pets (29.9%). It was further found that of the total population a large proportion of families had experienced or were still experiencing a saddening effect directly related to leaving their pets behind (28.8%).

All rank groupings (junior enlisted, senior enlisted, and officer) were similar in effects noted from leaving the pets behind, and in the status given by the family to their pets. Also significant was the finding reached that junior enlisted families far more often than the other groups left their pets behind as a result of the expense factor. Senior enlisted also left a great many of their pets behind but for them it appeared that the effects on their animals were being considered more than the effects on their pocket books.

Finally then, for those concerned with military families at transfer time, this study presents significant evidence that the pet as a factor is pertinent to a great many families and that its impact is no small matter to these families.

Limitations

The conclusions of this study are directly generalizable only to the Fort Shafter, Schofield Barracks, Aliamanu Military population (N = 6118) from which the stratified random samples (junior enlisted = 93, officer = 48, senior enlisted = 43) were drawn. By determining the breakdown of the entire 18,000 military family population in Hawaii by rank groupings, it could be further generalized to that population. Generalizations to military populations outside of Hawaii must be made conservatively due to the four month rabies quarantine in Hawaii which was identified as a significant factor influencing the decision about whether or not to bring their pet with them. On the other hand, generalizations to military and civilian populations being transferred overseas and especially to locations having long expensive quarantines (Australia, Guam, and Great Britain) would most likely be more justified.

Finally, as noted, 100% of each stratified random sample was not obtained due to time and economy considerations. Although the times selected for conducting the interviews were varied, and multiple attempts were made to locate many families, those that were easiest to find home were those most often sampled thus resulting in a possible bias towards the inclusion of such families. It should also be noted however that many of those never found at home did have pets as evidenced by barking dogs, etc. They, of course, were not counted in the sample.

Future Research

Subjectively, it has been established in this study that saddening is a very real result of leaving a pet behind and that bringing one has the opposite effect to those families concerned. It follows now that these same findings need to be confirmed using objective measures that can measure the degree of family disruption caused or prevented through pet involvement. Further, intervening variables such as the coping abilities possessed by the families being compared should be considered in future research.

Further, we see indications that a great many pets are left behind by owners being transferred to Hawaii. What happens to those pets and to those acquired to adopt them or pick them up as strays? Also, it is assumed that fewer pets are left behind as a result of non-overseas transfers and to areas lacking quarantines. Is this assumption true? Either way, the effects of all transfers on owners and pets needs to be examined.

Other examples of future research in related areas are numerous. What are the effects of pets in the lives of civilian families that are moving to a new job? What is the role of a mascot in the lives of those in a military company having such an animal? What specific factors cause thousands of families every year to spend approximately $500 in quarantine related fees to enable them to bring their pet with them in Hawaii? What are the effects on a military-dog handler and on the dog when they are separated either by death or by transfer? The preceding are only a few of the questions yet to be explored.

Implications

In a military or civilian system, factors that can be shown to have a negative impact on the lives of service members' or employees' families are eliminated if possible. Conversely, positive factors are encouraged and/or created, also if possible.

This study concerned a phenomenon that affects the well-being of a great number of military families, namely the role of a pet in a family at transfer time. Hopefully it has given credibility to the argument in favor of assisting with the movement of this pet member of the family at transfer time. At the very least, it has hopefully made better known to the families themselves, to their commanders

and/or employers, to the policymakers that often determine the fate
of these pet members of these families, and to the human services
professionals that serve these families, one other significant factor
that may be seriously contributing to either family disruption or stability at the time of their transfer from one duty station to the other.
Truly, the pet in the military or other mobile family, especially at
transfer time, is no small matter.

REFERENCES

Beck, A. & Katcher, A. *Between Pets and People*. New York: G. P. Putnam's Sons, 1983.
Bustad, L. K. and Hines, L. Historical perspectives of the human-animal bond, in R. K. An-
    derson, B. L. Hart, & L. A. Hart (Eds.), *The Pet Connection*. Minneapolis, Minn: CEN-
    SHARE, University of Minnesota, 1984, pp. 15–29.
Catanzaro, T.E. The human-animal bond in military communities, in R. K. Anderson, B. L.
    Hart, & L. A. Hart (Eds.), *The Pet Connection*. Minneapolis, Minn: CENSHARE, Uni-
    versity of Minnesota, 1984, pp. 341–347.
Carson, S. A., Corson, E. O., Gwynne, P. H. and Arnold, L. E. Pet facilitated psycho-
    therapy in a hospital setting, in J. H. Masserman (ed.), *Current Psychiatric Therapies*,
    Vol. 15. New York: Grune & Stratton, 1975, pp. 277–286.
General Foods Corporation. *The Dog in Society*. White Plains, New York: Gaines Profes-
    sional Services, 1981.
Kidd, A. Exploring Aspects of the Human/Companion Animal Bond. *Latham Letter*,
    1981–82, *3*(1), 18–19.
Levinson, B. M. *Pets and Human Development*. Springfield, Ill: Charles C. Thomas, 1972.
Levinson, B. M. Pets and personality development. *Psychological Reports*, 1978, *42*,
    1031–38.
Messent, P. R. and Serpell, J. A. An historical and biological view of the pet-owner bond, in
    B. Fogle (ed.), *Interrelations Between People and Pets*. Springfield, Ill: Charles C.
    Thomas, 1981, pp. 5–22.
Serpell, J. Growing up with pets and its influence on adult attitude. *Group for the Study of the
    Human Companion Animal Bond Newsletter*, 1981, *2*(1), 17–20.

A Historical, Interdisciplinary Analysis of the Animal and Human Social Ecosystem

Kris Jeter

In 1935, A. G. Tansley provided a seminal definition of the ecosystem regardless of size or type:

> The more fundamental conception is . . . the whole system . . . including not only the organism-complex, but also the whole complex of physical factors forming what we call the environment. . . . We cannot separate them from their special environment with which they form one physical system. . . . It is the system so formed which . . . are the basic units of nature on the face of the earth.

In this analytic essay, I discuss and relate four classic books representing different disciplines which describe the animal and human ecosystem. A chronological order from prehistoric to more recent times is employed.

M. Esther Harding, Jungian psychologist, portrays the first societies in which deities were animals and people acted with empathy and knowledge in their relationships with animals. All were at one with nature's cycles.

Then, power over one's life and environment became a priority for humans. Animal domestication was born out of the unconscious social needs of both animals and humans and occurred in stages. Frederick E. Zeuner presents these animal domestication stages chronologically from the perspective of an archaeologist and paleontologist.

Anthropologist Marvin Harris analyzes two small scale farming families: the Hindu family with cow and human members and the

---

Kris Jeter, PhD, is Principal, Beacon Associates LTD, Inc., Newark, Delaware.

© 1985 by The Haworth Press, Inc. All rights reserved.

223

Maring family with pig and human members. These life styles are disrobed of guises and explained with scientific data, the relationship of family members and their domesticated animals within the ecosystem.

Boris M. Levinson seeks to reaffirm the present day family as a micro-ecosystem in the larger ecosystem of nature. As a psychotherapist, he bonds family members first with the inanimate, then with the animate nonhuman animal, and lastly with the animate human members of the immediate family and the family of nature referred to by Harding, Zeuner, and Harris.

In all four books and in this analytic essay the homeostasis or equilibrium of the animal and human social ecosystem is emphasized. What is the coterie of processes which act to govern a stable ecosystem? Does the acknowledgement by the human of the animal as a basic unit of nature in our contemporary post industrial family ecosystem assist each in returning to harmony with nature's cycle?

MYTHOLOGICAL APPROACH TO THE ECOSYSTEM

M. Esther Harding in her germinal volume, *Woman's Mysteries: Ancient and Modern*, first published in 1935, traces the history of lunar mythology relating it to Jungian psychology. The earliest animal human ecosystem was steeped in the feminine knowledge of the lunar system. This view was later replaced by the masculine perception of the sun.

In earliest times humans survived from recognizing and abiding by the varied life cycles. All humans experienced the day and night cycle. However, only women experienced the menstrual cycle so akin to the lunar cycle, ebbing and flowing in 28 day spans. Men respected the lunar cycle and the woman's connection with it.

> From the earliest human cultures, the mysterious magic of creation was thought to reside in the blood women gave forth in apparent harmony with the moon, and which was sometimes retained in the womb to "coagulate" into a baby. . . . [The man] regarded this blood with holy dread, as the life-essence, inexplicably shed without pain, wholly foreign to male experience. (Walker, p. 635)

This acknowledgement of the moon-female connection produced a lunar mythology, a story to explain a natural phenomenon, attendant beliefs, and practices. The mythology connected human to animal to nature. The stages that evolved as recognition of the moon which developed into worship of the moon deity are symbolized by the fish, mammal, spirit, Goddess, and human before the upsurge of sun worship. The moon deity changed in form as ecosystems increased in size from the family, kin, and tribe to the classical world empires.

Moon

In the majority of ecosystems representing most climates, especially those where daylight scorched life, the sun was thought to be the antagonist and the moon the protagonist to the vital spark of life. The moon alone was able to fertilize the inactive seeds to germinate, blossom, and reproduce.

Fish

The moon deity was first a fish signifying the willingness of women to adhere instinctively to nature. Being cold-blooded, the fish reproduces without love. Derketo in Babylon and Atargatis in Phrygia represented this original Moon Mother. This fish deity "was born from the sea foam. In one form she was even represented as half fish, a sort of mermaid or leviathan, inhabitant of the primal waters" (p. 162).

Mammal

Then, the moon deity became a mammal. Being warm blooded she demonstrated a passionate sexual drive, maternal nurturing skills, and the ability to protect offspring.

Lion

The lioness and panther in heat exhibit intense sexual craving which induces males of the species in the vicinity to abandon all activities to satisfy the female in heat. Cybele, Goddess of the Earth and the Moon revered in Phrygia before 900 B.C., was originally a lioness.

The mammal in heat was related to the menstruating woman. The menstrual taboo in which the woman physically isolates herself from the rest of the community, excluding herself from partaking of cooked food, laboring, and journeying, was the woman's acknowl-

edgement of the need for instinct to be governed. Indeed, cultural
survival required adult humans to focus thought and action on the
environment and needs of the ecosystem rather than to "evil" sexual instincts. The menstrual taboo is the ancestor of the Sabattu of
Babylon which means the "heart rest"; the day the full moon rests
because it is menstruating, neither expanding or reducing in round-
ness. On this day, each woman and man adopted the menstrual taboo
practices excluding the practices of eating cooked food, working,
and traveling. The observance of the Jewish Sabbath imitated the
Babylonian Sabattu, providing the human with an opportunity to rest
the heart at each quarter of the moon's phases.

Cow

The maternal and nurturing roles of the moon and the female are
protrayed by the cow. The horns of the bull, cow, or goat depict the
horned or crescent moon. In Egyptian mythology of 3000 B.C., Isis,
as the moon, lost her crown of light and so was either disfigured or
murdered before being reinstated to life as Hathor, the Horned
Crescent.

Bear

The bear depicts the ability to procreate the breath of life as well
as the ability to act scathingly harsh and to destroy the life force.
The cub is protected; the enemy is killed. Life is given; death is de-
voured. Artemis, the early Greek goddess of the crescent or waxing
moon and also a midwife, was a bear in later Roman mythology became Diana, Opener of the Womb.

Spirit

With time, the moon deities in the form of the animal, be it the
lion in heat, the maternal cow, or the protector bear, became the
deified spirit. For example, Apis, the Bull, worshipped in Egypt approximately 1000 B.C. was the spirit of Osiris first revered in 3000
B.C. The Apis spirit would appear whenever the powerful moon-
light illumined the cow in in estrous. "This was, perhaps, the most
sacred symbol of the Egyptians. A real bull, called the Apis, was
reared at Memphis as the image of the soul of Osiris. Its food and
care were under special ritual regulations" (p. 184).

Goddess with Animal Attendents

In the next stage, the moon goddess followed the rise of the feminine emotion from expressing animal instinct to human love. Yet, she at-oneness with nature is maintained through her affinity and proximity with the animal. Cybele, Phrygian Goddess of the Earth and the Moon, now rules from a lion throne and travels in a lion drawn chariot. She evolves into Atargatis, the Queen of Heaven, seated upon a lion. The moon goddess wears the cow horns as a crown and is attended by the lion, cow, and bear, as well as the dove and the serpent.

Dove

The bird, usually the dove, is able to wing from the illuminated moon to the earth. The dove, moon, and woman are sages with deep and profound lunar wisdom which can enlighten the earth.

Serpent

The serpent also personifies the moon and the female. All three possess the power of self-renewal and immortality periodically appearing to die, shedding the vital flame of blood or skin, and resurging revived. The cold-blooded snake, the night moon, and the instinctual woman are able to traverse the crevices of the earth to the dead of the underworld and return to the surface unscathed. The snake also represents the fertile phallus needed for conception.

Human as Animal

The animal attendent was supplanted by the human being who assumed the power and identity of the name of the animal. Fortified with the animal energy under the cloak of the animal mask and costume, the endowed human would dance as if she or he were the animal.

Sun

The worship of the moon was gradually replaced with the worship of the sun. Charlie Murphy writes and sings of the transition.

"In the cool of the evening they used to gather
'Neath the stars in the meadow circled
    near an old oak tree
At the times appointed by the seasons of
    the earth and the phases of the moon
In the center often stood a woman, equal with
    the others and respected for her worth . . .
the healers and teachers of the wisdom of the earth
The people grew through the knowledge she gave them . . .

There were those who came to power through domination . . .
They sought control of the common people by demanding
    allegiance . . .
it was war against the women whose powers they feared
In this holocaust against the nature people . . ."

Matriarchy was superseded by the patriarchy. Men valued and used personal physical force to overpower primary groups and nature and to amass land, people, and wealth. Martial despots commanded their subjects in such captured lands as Babylon and Egypt, to abandon the worship of the feminine moon goddess and in its stead to worship the masculine sun. The homeostasis of the animal and human social ecosystem became unbalanced.

AN ARCHAELOGICAL AND PALEONTOLOGICAL APPROACH TO THE ECOSYSTEM

In 1946, Frederick E. Zeuner, Professor of Environmental Archaelogy at the University of London drew together the scattered research on dating the past and coined the term for this infant scientific discipline, "geochronology," His volume, *Dating the Past*, became a standard textbook being republished at regular intervals until 1958. In the first preface, he writes: "The chief field of application of geochronology is in prehistoric archaeology and human paleontology. The evolution of [the hu] man, both from the anthropological and the cultural points of view, cannot be understood properly unless the time element is introduced."

During these years, Zeuner observed that only three texts, and these were not recent publications or written in English, which addressed the history of domesticated animals. Thus, in 1963, he published *A History of Domesticated Animals*, a landmark work applying geochronology to archaelogy and paleontology (historic biology).

Zeuner refutes early theories of the domestication process. For instance, Hahn in the late 1800s proposed that animals were domesticated to be used as religious sacrifices. Hilzheimer in the early 1900s determined that humans domesticated animals to procure meat for food and skins for clothing and shelter. Others hypothesized that totem animals were not killed because of their sacred powers and, thus, became tame.

Symbiosis

Zeuner dates animal domestication to early Neolithic times, 8000 years ago, in the Near East. Domestication ensued when humans altered the natural environment, transforming it through the development of agriculture and, thereby, creating a human-made environment.

Zeuner's thesis is that domestication was born out of conscious social needs of both animals and humans during hunting, and, later, farming. Animals and humans willingly entered a symbiotic relationship, one of benefit to both animals acting in the role of the guest and humans in the role of the host. Zeuner's step pyramid (Figure I) illustrates the range of roles intrinsic to the guest-host association.

The animal as the exploiting guest assumes any of three roles before entering a symbiotic relationship with the human. The scavenger, such as the pig, salvages food discarded by the human. The robber, for instance, the hyena, steals food from the human. The social parasite is dependent on the human for existence without reciprocity. For example, the reindeer whose only available water

Figure I

supply is melted snow, is dependent upon the human's urine as a salt lick.

The human as the exploiting host assumes one or more of three roles essential to the formation of a symbiotic relationship with the animal. The human could provide food to the animal; then make the animal docile and submissive; and, finally, adapt the animal to life in an intimate relationship with the human.

The Stages of the Process of Domesticating a Particular Breed

A wild animal would be captured by the human, penned, and bred over generations with attention to animal appearance and size and human needs. After this refinement, the original species would be considered devalued and exterminated. The five stages of the process of domesticating a particular breed follow.

1. First, the animal was unrestrained by the human and bred freely with the wild beasts.
2. Second, the human caged or penned the animal and only permitted interbreeding. In time, the captive animal tended to become smaller in size and of a varied color when compared to the original stock. The Neolithic human took residence in Europe with undersized, discrete breeds of cattle, pig, and sheep. Likewise, the Mesolithic human entered Europe with a domesticated dog.
3. During the third stage, the human, aware of the decreasing size of the captive breed, intentionally interbred the domesticated animal with a chosen breed or wild stock to develop particular characteristics. It is thought that the Neolithic and Bronze Age human purposely interbred cattle and that the Maglemose of Denmark bred an attack dog.
4. In the fourth stage, the human desired increased economic outputs (meat, milk, wool) and morphological appearances (color, shape). Breeding was a refined art. Before 3000 B.C., cattle, goat, and sheep breeds with specific markings were developed in the Middle East.
5. By the fifth stage, the domesticated animal varied so distinctively from the original stock, interbreeding would have reversed the labor of many generations of humans. The domesticated animal satisfied the needs of humans and the wild animal

was of use only for the sport of the hunt. Thus, the wild animal was exterminated. During the Middle Ages, the tarpan or wild horse and the wild cow were slaughtered by the Europeans to prevent undesired intermixing with the domesticated animal.

The Chronological Entrance of Varied Species into Domestication

As the human altered the environment through the introduction of agriculture and the development of increasingly sophisticated farming practices, animals became domesticated. Species entered domestication in an orderly progression, being displaced from homelands by the human and satisfying human needs.

1. During the pre-agricultural Mesolithic phase, the dog was attracted to the human for provision of food, sociability, and protection. In turn, the dog assisted the nomad human in corralling and domesticating the camel, goat, horse, reindeer, and sheep. Consequently, the food gatherer became the food producer.
2. In the early agricultural phase, the human, especially if located by a river, would destroy plant cover and displace large ruminative animals. The banteng, cattle (ox), gaur, Indian buffalo, yak, as well as the pig came to steal the harvest. The human domesticated the crop robber, feeding the captured animal farm waste products of fodder, leaves, and straw. The animal's product of meat and milk were used as human food.
3. As the human expanded the area of land in which vegetation was grown, and the population increased and centralized to cities, the mammal was needed to transport the produce and trade for goods. This mammal also labored, and, thus, for the first time in history, the human was relieved from doing many arduous tasks. In the tropical forests of approximately 2500 B.C., the Indian elephant was domesticated for transport and labor. In central Asia, the fast-pacing horse, and in central and western Asia, the water-holding camel were domesticated. In the semi-arid Nile Valley, the ass was bridled to be the beast of burden. This working animal was respected as a companion, helper, and social partner and was not eaten as food.
4. As the human learned to control crop production, within the bounds of weather, grain was stored to maintain a balanced

diet from one harvest to the next. With this further manipulation of the environment by the human, the rodent came to the storage bins as a crop-robber. In Egypt, the cat and the mongoose and, in the east, the ferret entered into a partnership with the human to destroy the rodent.

In each of Zeuner's stages of animal domestication, the human changes the environment, and an animal species responds and is specifically bred, requiring the services of another animal species who is then specifically bred. The social needs of both the animal and the human act as the initial bonding mechanism. The caliber of equilibrium of the animal and human ecosystem is set and reset as another animal species is domesticated and its original stock exterminated.

ANTHROPOLOGICAL APPROACH TO THE ECOSYSTEM

In 1974, anthropologist Marvin Harris wrote, in piquant style, *Cows, Pigs, Wars, and Witches: The Riddles of Culture.* Harris insists that customs and life styles of a particular people can be dissected using science and logic. He addresses two cultural life styles which pertain to the animal and human social ecosystem.

The Cow in the Hindu Family

Western agronomists and lay people have often questioned why India permits human starvation while protecting the cow sacred to the Hindu. The zebu cow scavenges and eats food not edible by the human: rice husks and straw plus wheat bran. A small-bodied survivor, the zebu cow is able to persevere throughout the cyclic Indian droughts and famines, using the energy hoarded in the back's hump. This cow's immune system defies the tropical diseases which beset other breeds.

The zebu cow is a member of a small-scale farming family. The local priest, friends, and neighbors rejoice when the cow bears a calf and pray for the ailing and dying cow. The cows are decorated with cloth and flower ornaments. The zebu cow has three important roles in the family. First, the cow births rugged male traction animals to plow the land for dry field farming and to pull the oxcart. Second, the cow provides milk to family members in a land where many exist on substandard diets. Third, the cow produces dung. Much dung is used for farm fertilizer in lieu of chemicals. Dung also provides fuel for slow cooking. Dung and water paste leveled on the dirt floor dries into a sturdy flat floor.

The zebu cow is also a protected member of the community. The Indian government supports homes for dry aged cows, and the board is free. Police corral wandering cows in fields neighboring the police station and tend to their health needs. There is no conflict between the cow and human. The cow is a symbol of the strife between the financially poor who label the stray scavenging cow as a "blameless saint asking for alms" and the rich farmer who calls the cow a "robbing crook."

> . . . cow love is an active element in a complex, finely articulated material and cultural order. Cow love mobilizes the latent capacity of human beings to persevere in a low-energy ecosystem in which there is little room for waste or indolence. Cow love contributes to the adaptive resilence of the human population by preserving temporarily dry or barren but still useful animals; by discouraging the growth of an energy-expensive beef industry; by protecting cattle that fatten in the public domain or at landlord's expense; and by preserving the recovery potential of the cattle population during droughts and famines. (p. 24)

The Pig in the Maring Family

Harris investigates the Maring, a horticultural tribe who live in villages located in the Bismarck Mountains of New Guinea. Family members are both pig and human.

The Maring man prepares gardening plots in the thick, tropical forest. Torrential rains detere nitrogen and other nutrients from the soil, making a plot viable for only two or three consecutive years. The man clears and burns a portion of land which as time goes on becomes more and more distant from the home and the village.

The Maring woman grows sweet potatoes, taro, and yams; prepares meals, constructs clothing and bags; and rears children. The infant human and infant pig are carried by the woman to the work sites and often during each task. Upon weaning, the pig is taught to follow the woman. The four- or five-month-old pig scavenges each day for food in the forest and then returns home when called and is fed low grade produce. The pig is embraced, petted, and spoken to by name with endearment. The pig sleeps and eats with the family, being given special privleges. The adult pig will weigh 135 to 150 pounds. The Maring family may have six pig members.

About once or twice a generation, the intensity of the intra-family and inter-family conflict escalates to an intolerable pitch. The pig population has multiplied to a number which threatens the food supply and health status of the human (and pig) population and disturbs the social ecosystem. Women grumble about the responsibility of caring for large families of pigs. They dislike carrying increased amounts of produce from plots cleared further and further in distance from home to feed the family. Pigs trespass on the neighbor's property; families quarrel over the territory encroachment. The clan mourns the loss of the security felt when all families lived and farmed in close proximity to each other. The men, in time, decide that the number of pigs is sufficient to hold a kaiko and so uproot the rumbin tree, symbol of peace, from its sacred ground.

The kaiko is a year long festival involving extensive preparation, ritualistic sacrifice, and slaughtering of the majority of pigs. The family attends to the departed ancestor's yearning for pig meat. Each family is to beat with a club a loved pig family member on the burial place of a human ancestor. The dead pig is then roasted in an oven constructed over the grave. The family patriarch feeds his brother-in-law cool saline stomach fat with the intention of obtaining devotion from the extended kin. "The climax of pig love is the incorporation of the pig as flesh into the flesh of the human host and of the pig as spirit into the spirit of the ancestors" (p. 39).

The clan through the kaiko can restore communal ties and insure triumph in war. Clan members, kin, and guests devote much time and energy into painting and wearing the appropriate image, which is then displayed during ceremonial dancing. Single men and women survey each other in search of a potential marital partner. Possible allies are persuaded to participate in a war. It is not unusual for each person to eat twelve pounds of pork in five days. Gluttony is the basis for reuniting the communal ties and preparing for conquest.

Within the three months of the final convening of the kaiko, the warriors, full of nutritious protein and fat and the spirit of the pig and human family members, conduct a war against a neighboring enemy. Land is either gained or lost in the struggle.

A ceremony is then held to proclaim the end of the war. Each adult male touches the sapling rumbim tree with his hands as it is planted on holy land. The war magician speaks to the ancestral and current clan of gratefulness for the safe return of the warriors and of the low number of surviving pigs. It is now the intention of the clan to increase the number of pig and human members of each family. War will not resume until sufficient pigs can be sacrificed to satisfy the yearning of the human ancestors for pig meat and spirit.

Pig love for the Maring insures the proper distribution of animals, humans, and vegetation in the Bismarck Mountains. When the number of pigs in the clan has increased to overencumber the women and threaten the production of crops, the kaiko occurs; "the role of the ancestors being to encourage a maximum effort at pig raising but at the same time to see to it that the pigs do not destroy the women and the gardens" (p. 47).

Such variables as health and population of the clan and neighboring enemy plus availability of space are acknowledged through the custom of periodic scarcity and sufficiency. The homeostasis of the animal and human social ecosystem of the Maring is maintained through a time-honored and tested custom.

PSYCHOTHERAPEUTIC APPROACH TO THE ECOSYSTEM

In 1969, Boris M. Levinson addressed the effects of separation from animal life and nature on the twentieth century Western human. Alienation, anxiety, despair, fear, insecurity, isolation, and tension have their roots in human mastery over nature. Levinson writes with eloquence his thesis that self love and self respect can only follow love and request for nature.

Levinson's proposition originated quite by a chance in the 1950s. A client diagnosed as "withdrawn" arrived several hours early for the first psychotherapy session. Levinson's dog, Jingles, greeted the client and mutual affection was expressed. Levinson believed that Jingles "broke the ice" and quickened the therapeutic process considerably. He has since utilized pets as co-therapists, facilitators of psychological assessment, and motivators for learning in individual and family therapy and in residential settings.

The theoretical roots in Levinson's thesis lie in developmental psychology. The infant resides in a state of omnipotence, feeling at one with the world. Through the use of the first developing sense, touch, the infant explores the world. Touch of the nurturing parent becomes associated with feelings of comfort, love, and security.

The child, aged four months to one year, resolves the issues of outer and inner worlds through the cuddling of a soft, warm "transitional object," such as a blanket, toy, or pet. The "transitional object" provides the encouragement to the child to move developmentally from the state of omnipotence to affiliate with the sensorially perceived objective reality.

Levinson recommends that a person desiring mental well-being should initially renew and restore connections with the inanimate, then with the animal, and finally with the human. The early developmental stages are repeated with intention. Touching the animal who accepts unconditionally the affection can assist the human to feel once again the comfort, love, and security of the infant with the parent. The pet can then also act in the role of the "transitional object" providing comfort as risks are taken crossing the span from the inanimate to the human.

Levinson contends that the mentally healthy human establishes a continuous relationship with nature. The "law of relatedness" governs psychological wellness. The human relates the inner self to the outer world, the recognized to the unrecognized while communicating with the greater, the similar, and the lesser. Levinson urges an achievement of ecosystem homeostasis which promotes symbiosis among all members.

CONCLUSION

Two themes which interplay consistently in the history of the animal human social ecosystem are adaptation and dominance. The human generally chooses optimal levels of stimulation, thus requiring adaptation. Adaptation is the process of creating and sustaining a comparatively constant mutual interchange between the system and the environment. The system and the environment modify their unique functions to create and sustain a lasting and enduring fit. A change in consciousness accompanies the adaptation. (See Figure 2.)

In the process of adaptation, the system and the environment vie to command and control the interchange. The theme of dominance is prevalent in the history of the animal and human social ecosystem. The four classic volumes discussed in this analytic essay each represents a different discipline's approach to viewing the animal and human social ecosystem, ordered to span time from earliest times to present. In a continuum from nature domination to nature and human harmony to human domination, it is evident that gradually in the adaptation process the human has mastered nature and animal life, sacrificing congruity with creation and the universe.

As society has become more complex, a shift in balance has taken place in the animal and human social ecosystem. Machines born out of the industrial revolution have been produced to conduct work activities and transport people and things, tasks once performed by animals. Chemicals have been isolated and combined to form cloth, fertilizer, floor coverings, and even food. This complex ecosystem spurns rapid discoveries and waste products and, thus, has become known as the "throw-away" society.

The study of ecology is slowly effecting this shift in the ecosystem balance. Paul Taylor reports recent laboratory research which indicates that the BTU (British Thermal Unit) value of both East Texas dung and lignite is equal, 4,200 BTU a pound. By 1987, two $80 million power plants will be operating in Texas, each of which will convert 16,000 tons of cow manure a day into electricity to meet the needs of 200,000 families. There is wisdom in the Hindu cow taboo.

Breeding of animals has become a finite science. Whole breeds of animals have been developed under laboratory conditions as part of the food supply. Other breeds of animals are now developed for pleasure and for therapy. What has developed over many years as a

Dominance	Ecosystem Described in Analytic Essay	Life Style
Nature dominates the Human		
Nature and Human Harmony	Lunar Mythology	Pre-agricultural, agricultural
	Animal Domestication	Pre-agricultural, agricultural
	Hindu Family with cow members	Small scale agricultural
	Maring Family with pig members	Small scale agricultural
The Human dominates Nature	Alienated Family members in psychotherapy	Industrial, post-industrial

Figure II

symbiotic relationship between the human and the pet animal still persists and is the bond that links together the two with joy, love, and respect. As Hildegard of Bingen, a Middle Ages abbess, musician, physician, scholar, and scientist who bridged the original matriarchy mythology with Christianity, wrote:

> "I have my home on high,
> I meet every creature of the world
>   with grace." (p. 96)

REFERENCES

Harding, M.E. *Woman's Mysteries: Ancient and Modern.* New York, New York: Harper Colophon Books, 1976.

Harris, M. *Cows, Pigs, Wars and Witches: The Riddles of Culture.* New York, New York: Vintage Books, 1974.

Murphy, C. "Burning Times." *Catch the Fire.* Seattle, Washington: Good Fairy Productions, 1981.

Levinson, B. M. *Pet-Oriented Child Psychotherapy.* Springfield, Illinois: Charles C. Thomas, 1969.

Tansley, A. G. "The Use and Abuse of Vegetational Concepts and Terms." *Ecology* 16 (1935): 284–307.

Taylor, P. "Holy Cow, It's Manure Power: A Feed-lot Byproduct will Light Up Austin." *The Washington Post National Weekly Edition* 2:10 (January 7, 1985):21.

Uhlein, G. *Meditations with Hildegard of Bingen.* Santa Fe, New Mexico: Bear and Company, Inc., 1983.

Walker, B. G. *The Woman's Encyclopedia of Myths and Secrets.* New York, New York: Harper and Row, Publishers, 1983.

Zeuner, F. E. *Dating the Past.* Fourth Edition. London, England: Methuen, 1958.

Zeuner, F. E. *A History of Domesticated Animals.* London, England: Hutchinson, 1963.